Indians,
Franciscans,
and Spanish Colonization

Indians,
Franciscans,
and Spanish Colonization

The Impact of the Mission System
on California Indians

Robert H. Jackson
Edward Castillo

UNIVERSITY OF NEW MEXICO PRESS / ALBUQUERQUE

Sections of Chapter 1 and Appendix 1 and 3 originally appeared as "The Changing Economic Structure of the Alta California Missions—A Reinterpretation," *Pacific Historical Review* 61:3 (1992), 387–415. This material is reproduced by permission.

Sections of Chapter 5 originally appeared as "The Impact of Liberal Policy on Mexico's Northern Frontier: Mission Secularization and the Development of Alta California, 1812–1846," *Colonial Latin American Historical Review* 2:2 (1993), 195–225. This material is reprinted by permission.

Library of Congress Cataloging in Publication Data
Jackson, Robert H. (Robert Howard)
Indians, Franciscans, and Spanish colonization: the impact of the mission system on California Indians / Robert H. Jackson, Edward Castillo.—1st ed.
p.   cm.
Includes bibliographical references and index.
ISBN 0–8263–1570-8 (cl.) 0-8263-1753-7 (pb.)
1. Indians of North America—Missions—California.
2. Franciscans—Missions—California.
3. Indians of North America—Cultural assimilation—California.
I. Castillo, Edward D.
II. Title.
E78.C15J318 1995
979.4'00497—dc20
94-18719
CIP

First paperback printing, 1996

Contents

Figures

Tables

Indians,
Franciscans,
and Spanish Colonization

Introduction

Columbus's voyage of discovery to the New World signified the beginning of complex processes of change among the native peoples encountered by Europeans in the Americas. The Spaniards, perhaps the most fortunate of the European colonizers, discovered gold and silver mines and sedentary village dwellers in central Mexico, Central America, the Andes, and other areas of North and South America. To maximize the profits of the colonial enterprise, the Spaniards created institutions that siphoned off surplus production from Indian communities and harnessed Indian workers to provide labor for the mines, commercial agriculture, and major building projects: the institutions of *repartimiento* and *mita* provided Indian labor, while *tributo* was the most important means of taxing the Indian communities. The fundamental success of the Spanish colonial system was due to its ability to exploit sedentary Indian populations.

On the fringes of Spanish America lived semisedentary and nonsedentary natives, who were not as easily controlled or exploited. Much of the history of the frontier regions of Spanish America is the record of efforts made by colonial officials, including representatives of the Catholic church, to transform native societies into sedentary populations that could provide labor and pay taxes, according to the model developed in central Mexico. Along the northern frontier of Mexico, the mission, a center of religious indoctrination and acculturation, was the institution employed to forge the new colonial society. Staffed by Jesuits and members of the mendicant orders, primarily the Franciscans, the missions were a cost-effective way to prepare different Indian groups for their incorporation into the new colonial order. The missionaries, assisted by soldiers, congregated Indians into communities organized along the lines of those in the core areas of Spanish America, where Indian converts were to be indoctrinated in Catholicism and taught European-style agriculture, leatherworking, textile production, and other skills deemed useful by the Spaniards. The converts would lend their labor to the construction of building complexes organized in the grid plan of the colonial American city.

This book examines the functioning of the missionary program in Alta California, a frontier region in northern New Spain colonized after 1769 under the direction of the Franciscans of the Apostolic College of San Fernando, with particular emphasis on the impact of the mission acculturation program on the Indian populations. This is not a study of the successes of saintly missionaries and brave colonial soldiers, but rather an analysis of the Alta California mission system as an example of a Spanish acculturation program that attempted to modify Indian society and religion, along with Indian responses to that effort. The study places the development of the missions and Indian responses within the larger context of colonial patterns in other parts of Spanish America.

There are two major schools of interpretation regarding the historical importance of the mission system in Alta California, both of which tend to be narrowly focused, with limited reference to the general Spanish American context. The study of California and its Spanish and Mexican periods has largely been carried out within the framework of United States history, with only passing reference to the other parts of Spanish America or the history of the Catholic church. The earliest substantial studies of the Alta California missions were written by critics or defenders of the missions and the Franciscans. In the 1880s H. H. Bancroft published the first serious synthesis of California history in six volumes, as well as a supplement entitled *California Pastoral*.[1] During a period in California of renewed popular interest in the missions, which saw the creation of the romantic mission mystique and the first efforts to restore ruined churches, Bancroft presented evidence of the downside of Indian life in the missions and criticized the Franciscans and the system they created. Bancroft's research workers transcribed and/or annotated thousands of documents concerning California under Spain and Mexico that were subsequently destroyed during the 1906 San Francisco earthquake and fire.

A Franciscan historian, Zephyrin Engelhardt, OFM, responded to Bancroft's view of the history of the missions in a series of books published between 1900 and the early 1930s that can be characterized as church self-history, with very evident eurocentric biases. In a four-volume study entitled *Missions and Missionaries in California*, Engelhardt provided an overview of the development of the missions and attempted to counter many of Bancroft's charges, especially those of cruelty toward the Indians.[2] Engelhardt also railed against the California political leaders and Mexican liberals who ordered the secularization of the missions in 1833, an action he erroneously claimed to have been illegal. Indian converts, the vast majority of the inhabitants of the missions, appear only marginally and almost as shadows in the Franciscan version of history. Engelhardt published detailed individual histories of most but not all of the missions in Alta California. His research drew upon the document collection destroyed in San Francisco in 1906 and other collections, including the holdings of the Santa Barbara Mission Archive-Library, and it remains a useful source of information, in spite of its extreme biases.

The works of both Bancroft and Engelhardt are narrative studies, generally focused on missionaries, colonial officials, and settlers. Although they are present, the Indians who lived in the missions are only supporting actors in a drama defined by Spanish soldiers, bureaucrats, and clerics. The eurocentric focus of the study of the missions changed in the late 1930s and early 1940s with the publication of the first monographs of the physiologist-turned-historian Sherburne F. Cook. Cook used the missions of Baja and Alta California to explore the impact of introduced euroasiatic diseases on Native American populations and analyzed the biological and nonbiological factors that contributed to the demographic collapse of the mission Indians, as well as the fate of California's Indians up to the present century. Cook's first important study on the Alta California missions appeared in the early 1940s in the *Ibero-Americana* series, under the general title *The Conflict between the California Indian and White Civilization.*[3]

Cook's early research on the missions has had a profound impact on the field of California Indian and mission history. He laid out many of the issues that scholars continue to debate today, especially those arising from his characterization of the quality of life of the Indians living in the missions and the causes of the demographic collapse of mission Indian populations. However, after the publication of his first studies, Cook continued to refine his initial conclusions, as he drew upon additional sources of information. This new research resulted in the publication of two important books: *The Population of the California Indians 1769–1770*, which is a collection of previously published and unpublished essays[4]; and a detailed study of the vital rates of eight Alta California missions, based on an analysis of original sacramental registers of baptisms and burials, which appeared in volume 3 of *Essays in Population History*, coauthored with the historian Woodrow Borah.[5]

The issues raised by Cook in his pioneering studies became highly politicized in the 1980s, as a result of the ongoing campaign to canonize Junípero Serra, OFM, the architect of the Alta California mission system. Advocates of the canonization launched a public-relations campaign to win the hearts, minds, and pocketbooks of California Catholics and others. They have attempted to challenge those of Cook's findings that contradict many of the basic assumptions of the Serra "cause," because Cook's conclusions have been used by critics of canonization, frequently out of context.[6] Despite the politicization of the study of California mission history, significant scholarly advances have been made in the last half century, especially in the areas of ethnography and ethnohistory, material culture, and historical demography. Several generations of scholars from different disciplines have taken Cook's basic assumptions and refined or refuted them. Moreover efforts have been made to present a more balanced view of the history of the missions by giving a voice to the Indians who made up the vast majority of their population.[7]

These studies make important contributions to our understanding of the history of the missions and the fate of the California Indians, but at the same time many perpetuate the parochialism that has characterized a century of writing on the missions, both professional and popular. The history of the California missions is generally viewed in isolation from the larger patterns of institutional, economic, social, political, and demographic history in colonial Spanish America that served as the blueprint for colonial frontier policy. The patterns of exploitation developed in the missions were not unique to Alta California, but were simply a warmed-over version of the sixteenth-century colonial policy of *congregación/reducción*, modified by two hundred years of practical experience in missions throughout northern New Spain and the rest of Spanish America. For example, as early as the 1550s Spanish officials in Huamanga in the Andean region congregated the population of 672 villages in 252 villages, in an operation designed to facilitate tribute collection and the organization of labor drafts that was similar to the later congregation in the missions of northern Mexico.[8] As was the case in central Mexico and other areas in Spanish America, missionaries spearheaded the effort to acculturate the Alta California Indians and prepare them for their role in a new colonial order. The fundamental ideas that shaped the Alta California missions were first discussed in the early sixteenth century, as Spanish civil and religious officials grappled with the problem of how to create a colonial society in Mexico, using the labor and subsistence economy of the Indian population to further that goal.

This book examines the history of the Franciscan program in Alta California from a broad perspective; we understand the missions to have been the key institution employed by the Spanish colonial government in Mexico City to recreate the colonial social and political order that already existed in central Mexico. This study focuses on Spanish colonialism in the Alta California frontier region and its impact on the Indians who lived in the missions. The first chapter offers an analysis of the political economy of the missions, which clarifies the relationship between the mission program and the larger goals of the Spanish colonial program and challenges many scholarly assumptions. We demonstrate that the Franciscan missionaries placed considerable stress on subsidizing the cost of the colonization of Alta California by harnessing Indian labor to produce surplus grain to supply the military garrisons. The Franciscans identified and categorized Indians as both potential converts and laborers.

The second chapter examines the acculturation of the Indians in the mission communities; the effort to convert the Indians into a Catholic peasantry engaged in agriculture, stock raising, and artisanry. The impact of acculturation can be measured in several ways: in material culture, religion and world view, and sociopolitical organization. The Indian converts who lived in the missions experienced considerable change, but not always in the ways envisioned by the missionaries. One important factor modifying the course of cultural and social change was the high mortality rates in the mission communities and the almost continuous recruitment of unacculturated Indians into the missions, strengthening the survival of Indian culture. A second factor was the general lack of understanding by many missionaries of Indian religious beliefs and practices. Despite the efforts of the Franciscans, there was considerable Indian cultural retention.

The Indian populations in the mission communities were inviable, that is, they did not grow through natural reproduction. The third chapter examines the causes and manifestations of the demographic collapse of these Indian populations. We conclude that despite recent criticism, many of Cook's basic conclusions regarding demographic patterns in the missions are indeed valid.

The Indians did not passively accept the arrival of the Spaniards, but resisted the mission acculturation program. Indian resistance took several forms: rebellion, flight from the missions, the murder of missionaries, the refusal to carry out orders given by the Franciscans, and the theft or destruction of mission property. The fourth chapter describes the different forms of Indian resistance and rejects the basic premise repeated in recent years by supporters of the Serra canonization campaign that the Indians willingly accepted mission life.

The final chapter outlines the impact of secularization, the conversion of the missions from communities managed by the Franciscan missionaries into towns that were theoretically to be independent municipalities, but that in reality were under the control of administrators appointed by local government officials. Contrary to the impression left by Engelhardt, the secularization process was not only legal but was closely related to political developments in central Mexico. The negative response of many Spanish-born Franciscan missionaries resulted from their continued allegiance to Spain and their rejection of Mexican independence and the liberal reform measures implemented in the 1820s and 1830s that challenged the role of the

Catholic church in Mexico. More importantly, however, the breakdown of rigid social controls led to a massive exodus from the missions by hundreds of Indian converts.

This book, then, offers an interpretation of the history of the Alta California missions that draws upon a long and contentious literature and that incorporates different perspectives. First, however, it is necessary to briefly describe the Indian societies the Spaniards encountered in Alta California.

Indian Social and Economic Organization

Between 1769 and 1823, Franciscan missionaries established twenty-one missions along the coast of California in the territory of different Indian groups, including the Kumeyaay, Luiseño, Kumi'vit/Gabrieleño, Chumash, Salinan, Esselen, Ohlone/Costanoan, and Coast Miwok. The missionaries also resettled converts from other groups, including Cahuilla, Yokuts, and Miwok, among others. The purpose of this brief ethnohistoric overview is to identify general patterns of social and economic organization targeted by the Franciscans for modification or elimination; it is not our intention to present detailed ethnohistoric data on each native group affected by the mission acculturation programs.[9] The Franciscans attempted to restructure the native societies they encountered to further Spanish colonial-policy objectives.

One goal of the Franciscans was to convert the Indians of California into a disciplined labor force to work in agriculture, ranching, and the production of textiles, leather products, and other goods. The model for the acculturation program in the missions was the corporate indigenous community in central Mexico. The economy of the Indian groups living along the California coast did not lend itself to the fulfillment of Spanish policy, however. The basis of the economy was hunting and collecting wild plant foods and, along the coast, fishing and collecting shellfish and other marine foods. Indians practiced skillful food-resource management, such as the burning of grasslands to promote the growth of certain seed-bearing plants. Each tribelet had a clearly defined territory, within which it hunted and collected food.

The Spanish had ideas of gender roles that conflicted with those of California Indian society. Men hunted, waged war, and in some instances helped build tule huts. Women did the mundane tasks of collecting and preparing wild plant foods. The collection and preparation of indigenous foods did not require the same type of sustained work required of Indian converts, and the missionaries resorted to corporal punishment and other methods of social control to discipline the work force.

California Indian social hierarchy was dominated by high-status men and women, whose status derived from wealth. Chumash chiefs, for example, received offerings of food, goods, and beads and ruled individual villages or groups of villages. Their position was inherited patrilineally with the approval of the village, but there were instances of daughters or sisters becoming chiefs. Chiefs enjoyed privileges denied to other villagers, such as having many wives.[10] Other specialists in Chumash society included shamans, generally men, whose principal function was to cure disease.[11]

California Indians were divided into small tribelets, which waged war over resources, social slights, or revenge for witchcraft or murder. For example Ohlone/Costanoans fought among themselves, as well as with neighboring groups such as the Salinans.[12] Ohlone/Costanoan-Salinan hostility probably resulted from trade competition.[13] Similarly interior Chumash villagers raided coastal villages.[14] The Spaniards exploited the political divisions among California Indians to facilitate the establishment of Spanish rule along the California coast. There were several examples of primary resistance against the new Spanish colonial order in the years immediately following the establishment of the missions, but these revolts were organized along the lines of traditional warfare between tribelets or coalitions of tribelets. The mission acculturation program helped break down the distinctions between tribes, but also gave rise to the new forms of resistance explored below.

The history of the development of the Alta California missions, then, is the story of an effort to modify the social, political, and economic organization of the California Indians, as well as to restructure their beliefs and religious practices. The missions initiated profound changes in the lives of the Indians affected by them, changes that we hope will appear in a broader perspective as a result of our study.

I

Political Economy
of the Alta California Missions

Several complementary objectives directed the development of the Alta California mission economies. First was the goal of establishing self-sufficiency in foodstuffs and clothing for the Indian converts. It should be noted, however, that the Franciscans and colonial bureaucrats who shared the prevailing eurocentric attitudes incorrectly assumed that a stable supply of European-style food would serve as a major factor in attracting Indian converts. Secondly the Franciscan missionaries, in an agreement worked out between Junípero Serra, OFM and government officials in Mexico City, agreed to supply surplus grain and clothing to the military garrisons stationed in the region, thus reducing the cost to the royal government of maintaining troops in the province to protect the missions. As the productive capacity of the missions expanded, the military and settlers in Alta California received supplies of foodstuffs and clothing from the Franciscans.

Land and labor were the keys to the functioning of the mission economies. The government assigned a roughly defined territory to each mission for the development of agriculture and ranching. The boundaries of the mission territories were not precise, but it was generally known where the territory of one mission ended and the lands of the next began. Most contemporary documents described the mission territory as running so many leagues north to south and east to west. For example, the lands of La Purísima mission reportedly ran fourteen leagues north to south and six leagues east to west, and embraced some eighty-four square leagues, or 149,000 hectares of land. The lands of neighboring Santa Inés mission covered about 128,000 hectares of land.[1] The size of the territory of each mission varied.

Within the mission territory the Franciscans directed the development of ranches and farms at different locations, which frequently included considerable improvements, such as the construction of irrigation systems and buildings. The San Antonio de Pala *rancho* of San Luis Rey mission consisted of a chapel, which still exists, and other buildings, including granaries.² The Franciscans stationed at San Miguel mission operated six ranches and farms in the mission territory, including Paso Robles, with improvements that included a chapel and residence for the overseer and the Indian workers assigned to the mission. Similarly the missionaries stationed at San Francisco mission began the development in 1786 of a farming station (*labor*) called San Pedro y San Pablo, located in the San Pedro Valley (modern Pacifica). The building complex at the labor included a chapel, several granaries, and storage rooms.³ Some of the ranches and farms were also significant population centers, even following the closing of the missions. In 1790 and 1791, as many as 300 Indian converts lived at San Pedro y San Pablo. In 1839 Paso Robles rancho of San Miguel mission reportedly had a population of 190 converts.⁴

The missions did not monopolize all the land in Alta California. Land disputes occurred between the missions and both the military and settlers. For example the Franciscans stationed at Santa Cruz disputed grazing land with the residents of the Villa de Branciforte after the establishment of the Villa in 1797. The Franciscans argued that they had insufficient pasture for the mission herds, although their claims that the mission herds were dying off is not substantiated by other records. The missionaries and settlers made several compromises, which gave the Franciscans temporary access to pasturage on lands that belonged to Branciforte. The Franciscans at Santa Cruz also attempted to annex lands assigned to the Monterey presidio's horse herd, but they were blocked by the governor.⁵

Labor was the second key element in the development of the mission economies. The viceregal government conceded to the Franciscans stationed in the Alta California missions complete control over mission temporalities, Indian labor, land and agricultural production, textiles, and other artisan goods produced in the missions. The temporalities also included the right to apply corporal punishment and other measures to ensure discipline and social control in the missions.

Both men and women labored in mission farming, ranching, building construction and maintenance, and artisan production. Little direct evidence survives in the documentary record as to the size and gender composition of the mission labor force. According to a 1825 report, some 65 percent of the Indian population of Santa Cruz mission participated in communal projects: 36 percent of the labor force worked in agriculture; 20 percent in the tending of the mission herds; 7 percent in food preparation; and skilled laborers in crafts such as smithing, weaving, and others made up 43 percent of the labor force. Significantly 31 percent of the labor force worked in the production of textiles (mostly woolens) for the use of the Indian population, soldiers in the military garrisons, and local settlers.[6] The use of the labor force may have varied from mission to mission, as did the relationship between the number of Indians enrolled in it and the total population. However, in the 1820s (the last decade of the missions), as the number of recruits dropped off, the age structure of the missions became imbalanced as a consequence of chronically high patterns of infant and child mortality. During that decade a proportionally higher percentage of the total Indian population fell within the ages from which the Franciscans expected the greatest amount of work.

Evidence indicates that the Franciscans were concerned that large-scale flight from the missions by Indian converts would deplete the labor force, and missionaries often categorized converts by their ability to work. For example in 1798, 138 Indians fled from Santa Cruz mission. In reporting the incident, the missionary Manuel Fernandez, OFM, complained that following the flight of the converts, only some 30 to 40 men reported for communal work projects. Three months later, when a small force of soldiers returned 52 of the fugitives, Fernandez classified those brought back by his estimation of their ability to work.[7]

Agriculture

Agriculture was the mainstay of the mission economies. A variety of Old and New World cultigens were grown at the missions, including wheat, barley, corn, *frijol*, chick-peas, and a variety of fruits and vegetables. The length of the agricultural year varied among the different climatic regions in Alta California, but there were generally two crops planted during the rainy season, which lasts from late fall to the end of spring.

The agricultural cycle at San Gabriel mission was typical. The Franciscans had wheat planted following the first rains in the fall, and a second crop in the spring, which included corn and perhaps barley.[8] Reports for San Diego are more complete and note that two varieties of corn, yellow and "small" (perhaps white) corn were planted in the spring and harvested at the beginning of summer.[9] The Franciscans directed the development of extensive irrigation systems, but crops still could be damaged by adverse weather conditions, such as drought or an overabundance of rainfall at critical points in the agricultural cycle. In 1824, for example, heavy rains at San Gabriel mission badly damaged the corn and frijol crops.[10] Even following the construction of irrigation systems, agricultural production and productivity at the missions fluctuated wildly from year to year (see appendix 1).

The Franciscans, who controlled the crops produced at the missions, distributed grain in a number of ways. They set aside grain supplemented by some fresh vegetables and meat for the consumption of Indian converts, although the quantity of food made available to the converts may never be known. In addition grain had to be stored in granaries for the next year's planting. Finally the Franciscans supplied grain to the local military garrisons and settlers for their consumption and as seed. With several exceptions the annual reports do not record the amount of grain stored in the granaries or the amount left for the Indian converts. Several reports for San Gabriel dating from the mid- and late 1780s recorded the amount of grain consumed and the amount placed in the granaries. For example in 1785, 50 percent of the wheat crop from that year was consumed, 50 percent again in 1786, 22 percent in 1787, and 26 percent in 1789. In 1786 29 percent of the corn crop was consumed.[11]

Ranching

The second important economic activity at the missions was ranching. They controlled large herds of cattle and horses and flocks of sheep, which provided meat and raw materials for artisanry such as textiles, the production of large quantities of goods from leather (including shoes), and soap and candles made from tallow. Horses were used periodically to round up the semiwild cattle from the range.

As described above the Franciscans had developed ranches at different sites within the mission territory, which was ideally suited to ranching. With the abundance of land, thousands of head of livestock could be kept on pasture that otherwise could not be exploited because of the limited labor available in the missions. The Franciscans profited from extensive use of the lands assigned to the missions. Even so they complained on occasion about not having enough pasturage for their growing herds and flocks. The case at Santa Cruz mission described above is one example. While the brothers claimed that large numbers of livestock would die if the governor did not assign new pasturelands to the mission, the annual reports show that the number of animals owned by the mission actually increased, despite the failure to obtain the lands they wanted.

Agriculture, ranching, and crafts at the missions were never static, and the orientation of the mission economies changed as a consequence of changing government policies, political events in distant central Mexico, and the opening of Alta California to illegal trade with foreigners. Scholars have debated the nature and significance of changes in the orientation of the mission economies, in some instances in an attempt to define the political economy of the missions and the Spanish colonization of Alta California. A discussion of these changes should help to define the political economy of the missions.

The Transformation of the Mission Economies

The historical geographer David Hornbeck's chronology and model for the development of the economy of the Alta California missions has gained a wide audience through its publication in the Smithsonian Institution's *Columbian Consequences.* Hornbeck maintains that the orientation of the missions shifted, after about 1805, away from the acculturation of the Indians to the large-scale production of grains and great quantities of hides and tallow. According to Hornbeck, with this move to commercial agriculture the Franciscans deemphasized the conversion of Indians and made less of an effort to attract them to the missions.[12] In supporting Hornbeck's interpretation, the archaeologist Julia Costello maintains that the Franciscans consciously decided to grow less grain in the 1820s and early 1830s, in order to shift labor to the slaughter of livestock.[13]

Hornbeck and Costello's model of the political economy of the California missions, and particularly their claims of a shift away from acculturation to commercial agriculture and ranching, does not withstand close analysis. To begin with it ignores a number of factors that influenced the development of the mission economies. For example Hornbeck does not take into consideration the impact of Spanish and Mexican government policy on California economic development, nor does he consider the larger historical context of the colonization of the province. Visitor-General José de Gálvez, the architect of many of the so-called "Bourbon Reforms" in central Mexico, organized the occupation of Alta California with an eye toward keeping as low as possible the costs to the royal government. From the very beginning, it was implicitly, if not explicitly, understood that surplus agricultural produce from the mission economies would help defray the costs of colonization, by reducing the amount spent on supplying food to the military garrisons, an understanding formalized in an agreement between the Franciscans and the viceregal government in the early 1770s. Gálvez's approach to using the missions to further colonial frontier policy can be see in the organization of the 1769 expedition that occupied San Diego. He directed the Franciscans to strip the Baja California missions of all necessary supplies for the expedition and to slaughter hundreds of head of livestock from the small mission herds carefully built up over many years, in order to obtain provisions. The same attitude governed the colonization of Alta California and the development of the mission economies.[14]

The Franciscans subsidized the military and supported the colonization of the province through the sales of food and crude textiles to the military, at remarkably stable prices. In turn the Franciscans received goods from central Mexico that could not be produced locally. Significantly in the first years of the colonization of California, all such transactions were on paper, and the funds for both the military and the Franciscan missionaries came from the same branch of the treasury, in Mexico City.[15]

An analysis of price movements for agricultural goods produced in selected California missions indicates that a true market system did not exist in California until the late 1820s. Tables 1 to 3 summarize prices and production levels for selected grains produced at three missions in northern Alta California: San Francisco de Asís, Soledad, and San Francisco Solano (selected because their account books have survived). If a true market in grains had existed, fluctuations in production levels and shortfalls would have affected price levels, as commonly occurred in the grain markets in the core regions of Spanish America. Numerous studies document the dramatic increases in grain prices following periods of drought and the destruction or damage of crops, only to return to near normal levels with the end of adverse conditions.[16]

An analysis of the statistical relationship between prices and production levels can demonstrate the existence of a market, if prices responded to changing production levels. Correlation and regression show the relationship between secular trends in time series of quantitative data. A strong statistical relationship exists between time series if a change in one variable tracks changes in a second or multiple variables. For example a strong correlation can exist if prices respond to changes in production levels. With the exception of San Francisco Solano in the early 1830s, there is virtually no statistical relationship between fluctuations in production levels and price movements, which in a true grain market would mirror variations in grain production, until the late 1820s, when the hide-and-tallow trade grew in importance (see table 4). The supply to the military of grain and textiles produced in the missions constituted a form of subsidy, and the Franciscans maintained prices at stable levels, despite fluctuations in production levels. The governor periodically published an official price list (*arancel*). The data from extant account books show that the Franciscans followed the price lists in most if not all transactions.[17]

Hornbeck maintains that the expansion of agricultural production and the growth of the livestock herds at the missions constituted a conscious

Table 1. Price (in reales) and Production Levels (in fanegas) of
Selected Agricultural Products at San Francisco Mission,
1807–1823

	Corn		Wheat		Frijol	
Year	Price	Prod.	Price	Prod.	Price	Prod.
1807		125	8	2090		50
1808		100		1580		50
1809		110	12	3224	8	60
1810	12	190	12	3122	20	60
1811	12	7		1472	20	74
1812	12	100	20	3702		55
1813		100		3763	20	40
1814		94		3904	20	62
1815		50		3600	20	26
1816		20		2800	20	24
1817		50		2000		25
1818		120	8	2800		22
1819		0	12	1300		10
1820		1000	12	2000	20	100
1821	12	200		2600		100
1822		600		2800		110
1823	12	200		1372		80

Sources: San Francisco mission account book, San Francisco Archdiocese
Chancery Archive, Colma, California; San Francisco Mission annual
reports, Santa Barbara Mission Archive-Library, Santa Barbara, California; and Mission statistics, Bancroft Library, University of California,
Berkeley.

decision on the part of the Franciscans to deemphasize acculturation in
favor of economic development. Hornbeck's basic assumption is that the
incorporation of Indian converts into a disciplined labor force was incom-
patible with the goal of acculturation.[18] The rich historical literature on colonial Latin America, especially recent studies, demonstrates that the Spanish
colonial state was based upon the exploitation of the Indian population, including corvées that provided cheap labor to Spanish miners, farmers, and
ranchers. The policy of congregación, which formed the basis of the Franciscan
program in Alta California, was designed to resettle a dispersed Indian population into compact communities, for easier extraction of labor and delivery

Table 2. Price (in reales) and Production (in fanegas) of Selected Agricultural Goods at Soledad Mission, 1810–1818

Year	Corn		Frijol	
	Price	Prod.	Price	Prod.
1810	12	400		40
1811	12	300	20	100
1812		200		5
1813	13	300	20	35
1814		400		15
1815		250		40
1816		400		24
1817	12	500	20	195
1818		100	20	140

Sources: Soledad mission account book, The Bancroft Library, University of California, Berkeley; and Soledad Mission annual reports, Santa Barbara Mission Archive-Library, Santa Barbara, California.

Table 3. Price (in reales) and Production (in fanegas) of Selected Agricultural Goods at San Francisco Solano Mission, 1829–1834

Year	Corn		Wheat		Frijol	
	Price	Prod.	Price	Prod.	Price	Prod.
1829	12	300	16	19	20	20
1830	12	300	16	1190	20	0
1831		200		1171		24
1832		300		800		32
1833		90		931		15
1834	16	287	16	873		28

Sources: San Francisco Solano Mission account book, The Bancroft Library, University of California, Berkeley; San Francisco Solano Mission annual reports, Santa Barbara Mission Archive-Library, Santa Barbara, California, and The Bancroft Library, University of California, Berkeley; and mission statistics, The Bancroft Library, University of California, Berkeley.

Table 4. Statistical Tests of the Relationship between Price and
Production at Selected Alta California Missions

Mission	Corn	Wheat	Frijol
		Regression (Adjusted R^2)	
San Francisco	.00	.10	.16
Soledad	-.09	——	.00
San Francisco			
Solano	1.00	.00	.00
		Correlation	
San Francisco	.00	.29	-.07
Soledad	-.52	——	.00
San Francisco			
Solano	-1.00	.00	-1.00

Source: tables 1–3.

of religious instruction. The Spanish view of acculturation entailed changes in Indian belief systems, social organization, and material culture, and the acceptance of the apparatus of colonial labor drafts and tribute. Priests were important agents in the acculturation process throughout Spanish America, and thus preached compliance with the demands of the colonial state.[19]

There was a decline in Indian recruits in the 1820s and 1830s, but not because the Franciscans were no longer stressing conversion, as Hornbeck contends.[20] Hornbeck ignores the important role of Indians as actors in the missionization process and their growing resistance to the Franciscan program in the years after 1810. Resistance took such forms as flight, horse raiding, and rebellion. Moreover Indians living in the Sacramento, San Joaquín, and other interior valleys increasingly resisted military incursions searching for fugitives and new converts.[21]

Hornbeck also argues that during the period of transformation to more commercially oriented economies, there was less food available to attract Indian converts. In other words, Hornbeck implies that Indians entered the missions in large numbers during an earlier period because of the attraction of a secure food supply.[22] This argument supposes that prior to the arrival of the Spaniards, the Indians did not have adequate supplies of food. This view ignores the sophisticated food-resource management skills of the Indians and simplifies the complex set of factors that led to the voluntary and forced incorporation of thousands of individuals. The hypothesized decline in Indian food supplies draws upon Costello's analysis of mission agriculture. Agriculture formed the basis of the mission economies, but as Hornbeck pointed out, production levels declined in the years after 1810 and especially in the 1820s. Did mission agriculture decline, as Costello suggests, because of the shift to other labor-intensive activities such as the slaughter of livestock?[23]

The mission agricultural cycle included the planting of winter wheat and spring corn, in addition to unspecified summer-fall crops.[24] Crop rotation may have been used to limit the impact of the exhaustion of nutrients in the soil, but the decline in the productivity of the land as measured by the ratio of grain sown to that harvested at five missions (San Diego, San Gabriel, La Purísima, San Miguel, Santa Clara) clearly indicates that the Franciscans did not use fertilizers.

Much has been made in recent years about the use of tree rings to determine rainfall levels and drought conditions in specific years; on the basis of evidence from tree rings, Costello discounts drought as a factor in the decline of mission agriculture in the 1820s.[25] Total rainfall is important for the success or failure of agriculture, but the timing of rain at different points in the agricultural cycle is at least as important. Tree rings may indicate normal rainfall during a given year but not the distribution of the rainfall; there may be insufficient rain at critical points during the growth of a given crop. For example the lack of rain for a month or two following the planting of a given crop can destroy or greatly limit the harvest, whereas a more or less balanced rainfall following the first planting, even if somewhat below normal levels, will not necessarily result in crop damage. Finally a prolonged scarcity of rain can lower the sources of irrigation water to the point where crops cannot effectively be irrigated, even with dams for impounding water. Drought therefore cannot be discounted as a cause for fluctuations in mission agricultural production or for its decline.

Other climatological conditions could also effect crops. For example too much rain could delay the harvest or severely damage crops. Frost and hail could also be problems, especially in the northern mission communities. Insects could destroy growing crops, and rodents could damage stored crops, including seed needed for the next planting.

A detailed analysis of agricultural production at the five missions covered for the years 1810 to 1832 (appendix 1) serves as the basis for an evaluation of the causes of the decline of mission agriculture in the 1820s. Those missions were selected because they represent different ecological zones in Alta California, with conditions suitable for a variety of crops produced by the Mediterranean-style agriculture practiced by the Spaniards. The analysis is based on calculations of the ratio of grain sown to crop harvested on a year-to-year basis for wheat, corn, and barley, along with the construction of a yearly index of the amount sown and harvested. The goal is to present a reasonably clear picture of the short- and long-term movements in production levels. The samples represent the years following 1810, by which time agriculture at all five missions was fully developed, and when the demand on surpluses to feed the military was greatest. With only several exceptions, annual reports (the sources for figures on the amount of grain planted and harvested) are not available for the years 1799–1809.

The amount of grain sown provides the clearest idea of intent. In order to test Costello's hypothesis that agriculture was deemphasized after 1810, the mean indices of the amount of wheat and corn planted at the five missions in the years 1810–19 and 1820–29 have been calculated. By focusing on individual missions rather than on composite indices, as Costello does, local variations in agricultural production can be determined. The first case study is of San Diego mission, established in 1769.

Since this mission was located on the edge of a river floodplain, the Franciscans had access to fertile lands for the development of agriculture. Rainfall was the key variable in the successful growing of crops, and irrigation was necessary because of the semiarid climate of the area. The importance of irrigation can be seen in the references in the annual reports to the construction of irrigation systems in the decade from 1810 to 1820 (see table A3.6 in appendix 3). Such systems had a dramatic impact on agricultural production (especially corn), which enabled the Franciscans to plant less corn. The amount of wheat and barley planted after 1810 increased, and the ratio of grain harvested to seed sown remained positive until 1822. After 1823 production levels of all three grains declined, while the amount of seed planted continued at around pre-1823 levels. The evidence suggests that adverse climatological conditions were responsible for the decline in production after 1823, but it may also have been exacerbated by soil exhaustion. The mean index of wheat sown is 140 for the decade 1810–19 and 201 for the years 1820–29, indicating an increase in the planting of wheat. The index for corn reveals a decline, registering 28 for the first decade and 21 for the second. Since expansion of the irrigation system increased the productivity of corn, less corn needed to be planted (see appendix 1).

There was a similar pattern at San Gabriel mission, located in the semiarid Los Angeles Basin, although there is no documented correlation between the growth in productivity and the completion of an irrigation system, as shown at San Diego mission. The amount of seed planted varied from year to year, but there was no marked decline in the plantings, which would support the conclusion that there was a shift away from agriculture. There was a decline in the harvest-to-seed ratio after 1823 for both wheat and barley. The Franciscans encountered such an uneven performance with barley that in some years the grain was not planted at all. However, climatological problems clearly affected both crops after 1823; for example an overabundance of precipitation damaged the 1823–24 crop.[26] Corn harvests did not deteriorate to the same degree as did wheat and barley harvests, which is understandable, because irrigated corn was generally planted toward the end of the rainy season and would be less affected by heavy precipitation than were wheat and barley. The mean index of wheat planted increased between the years 1810–19 and 1820–29 from 81 to 94. At San Gabriel as at San Diego, the Franciscans planted more wheat in the 1820s than in the previous decade. Slightly less corn was planted in the 1820s; the mean index dropped from 141 in the period 1810–19 to 135 in the years 1820–29 (see appendix 1).

A similar pattern can be seen at La Purísima mission. Significantly, after relocation of the mission in 1813, the Franciscans developed new fields and an irrigation system to serve them. This led to short-term increases in productivity and the planting of a smaller amount of seed. The mean index of wheat planted dropped from 84 in the years 1810–19 to 71 in 1820–29; corn dropped from 130 to 123. As at San Diego and San Gabriel missions, there was a decline in the harvest-to-seed ratio after 1823, which again was probably caused by climatological factors.

Agriculture was more tenuous at San Miguel mission, located as it was in a dry section of the fertile Salinas River Valley. Corn production was less successful than at the other missions examined, suggesting the absence of a large-scale or efficient irrigation system. Wheat and barley were doubtless produced through dry farming. As at the other missions, there was a decline in the harvest-to-seed ratio in the 1820s and a similar effort to produce more wheat. The mean index of wheat planted increased from 76 in the years 1810–19 to 109 in 1820–29. The poor performance of corn perhaps convinced the Franciscans to place more emphasis on wheat production. The mean index of corn sown dropped from 20 in 1810–19 to 14 in the following decade (see appendix 1).

The final case study is that of Santa Clara mission, located in the northern reaches of the valley of the same name, near the southern end of San Francisco Bay. The Franciscans developed an efficient irrigation system at Santa Clara in the 1780s, and the productivity of corn was considerably higher than at the missions farther south, as seen in the ratio of grain harvested to seed sown. The Franciscans increased corn production at Santa Clara in the

1820s, as measured by the mean index of grain sown, which shot up from 127 in the years 1810–19 to 197 in the following decade. At the same time, wheat performed poorly, so that the Franciscans planted less of it. The mean ratio of wheat harvested to wheat sown dropped from 16.28 in the years 1810–19 to 10.31 between 1820 and 1829. The wheat harvests were particularly bad in 1822, 1826, and 1829. The mean index of wheat planted dropped from 123 during the first period to 99 during the second (see appendix 1).

The preceding analysis of agriculture at five missions during the years 1810 to 1832 reveals no significant decline in the amount of grain sown, although there was some yearly variation. Local climate conditions seem to have dictated decisions at individual missions to specialize in either wheat or corn. The decline in agricultural productivity at the five missions in the 1820s, as measured by the ratio of grain harvested to seed sown, was apparently caused by climate conditions and perhaps by the exhaustion of the soil, not by a shift away from agriculture, as hypothesized by Costello and Hornbeck. There is also evidence that heavy rains at some missions, such as at San Gabriel in 1824, damaged crops.[27]

Besides arguing for a shift away from agriculture at the missions, Costello and Hornbeck insist on a trend toward slaughtering livestock for the hide-and-tallow trade, an activity that required fewer Indian laborers than crop production did. But was the slaughter of cattle for the hide-and-tallow trade the only explanation for the fluctuation in livestock holdings at the missions, as hypothesized by Costello?[28] Appendix 1 gives the number of cattle, sheep, and horses for the years 1810–32 at the same five missions examined for agricultural production. The numbers represent estimates, however, and it is unclear whether they reflect the total number of animals on the open range or only those rounded up from larger herds. Although the patterns described for the missions examined here may not apply to other missions, they nevertheless explain the functioning of the mission ranching economy.

The size of livestock holdings reported at the five missions fluctuated annually, but generally increased after 1810. Only two missions show clear evidence of a rapid decline in the number of cattle, which suggests over-culling of the herds for hides and tallow. The number of cattle at Santa Clara dropped sharply between 1813 and 1818, then gradually increased after 1819, only to drop once more after 1829. The number of horses steadily declined after 1812, perhaps reflecting Indian raids on the horse herds and the supplying of animals to the military. At San Miguel, however, there was a rapid decline in the number of cattle after the legalization of the hide-and-tallow trade in 1823.

The relative stability of the number of cattle at San Diego, San Gabriel, and La Purísima does not indicate that the Franciscans at these missions were less involved in the hide-and-tallow trade, but rather suggests a more limited slaughter of cattle, designed to avoid depleting the herds.[29] Another possible explanation may be Indian resistance. Raids on the mission horse herds may have limited the ability of Indian vaqueros to round up cattle on the open range.[30]

Two statistical tests, correlation and regression, can be used to assess the relationship between changes in the number of horses and cattle at the five missions (see table 5). A strong correlation between the two variables would suggest that the number of horses available was a key factor in the growth or decline in the number of cattle. A strong statistical relationship, in turn, could be interpreted to mean, among other things, that Indian horse raiding had an adverse short-term impact on the ability of Indian vaqueros to round up cattle on the open range. The strongest correlation between the numbers of cattle and horses exists for San Diego and San Gabriel missions, while the statistical relationship weakens for the missions located farther north. The climate may be one explanation for the difference. The drier climate in southern California may have supported poorer pasturage which would have been depleted more rapidly as cattle increased in number and spread out over an ever larger territory, thereby making mission vaqueros even more dependent on the horse herds. Successful Indian raids on those horse herds would obviously reduce significantly their ability to round up cattle on the range.

Costello, as further reenforcement of the position she and Hornbeck take, argues that the Franciscans suspended construction of mission buildings after about 1805, in order to divert labor to the slaughter of cattle for the hide-and-tallow trade and to commercial agriculture. Extant annual reports record major building projects with varying degrees of detail, so that an evaluation of the relative importance of building during the years 1810-32 can be made.

Table 5. Statistical Tests of the Relationship between Number of Cattle and Horses at Selected Missions, 1810–1832

Mission	Correlation	Adjusted R^2	t
San Diego	.79	.61	5.90
San Gabriel	.84	.69	7.10
La Purísima	.30	.04	1.40
San Miguel	.13	-.03	-.58
Santa Clara	-.21	-.004	-.96

Source: Appendix 1.

Routine maintenance of mission buildings constructed of adobe and roofed with tiles was also required. Buildings had to be whitewashed, in order to protect the adobe walls from rain, while roof tiles had to be periodically adjusted, in order to maintain their effectiveness. The annual reports also indicate instances when individual buildings had become uninhabitable and had to be completely reconstructed.[31]

Depending upon the mission, it could take from ten to thirty years to develop the whole complement of buildings, so that by the period between 1810 and 1832, at a number of the older missions such as San Diego, San Gabriel, La Purísima, and Santa Clara, the building had already been completed. The Franciscans stationed at San Miguel and Santa Inés missions directed major building projects, including the construction of new churches. This is not to say that there was sufficient labor to undertake major new projects or to carry out extensive repairs on buildings damaged by earthquakes and other natural phenomena. For example the Franciscans at La Purísima and Santa Clara had entirely new complexes, including churches, built at new sites. The 1812 earthquake and 1824 Chumash revolt damaged buildings at San Gabriel and Santa Inés that had to be repaired or completely rebuilt. Finally, as at San Diego, older buildings that were no longer usable because of deterioration were replaced. In all instances the Franciscan missionaries, even in the 1820s, were able to mobilize sufficient labor to carry out needed building projects.

It is misleading for Costello to link the completion of building complexes at the older missions to a shift in the orientation of the mission economies, by postulating a transfer of labor to the slaughter of cattle from building projects. Moreover there was considerable building activity between 1810 and 1832, even at the older missions. During that period construction was reported at San Diego for eight years out of twenty-two; at San Gabriel for thirteen years; at La Purísima for nine years; at San Miguel for eight years; at Santa Clara for five years; and at Santa Inés for twelve years. Considerable construction was undertaken at the six missions, including the building of entirely new complexes at two of them.

Contrary to the claims of Hornbeck and Costello, there was no perceptible shift in the orientation of the missions away from agriculture and toward ranching and presumably the export of cattle hides and tallow, even though in 1823, when the trade in hides and tallow was legalized, the mission economies appeared to be booming, producing large quantities of grain, hides, and tallow. This apparent prosperity and success, however, masked the roots of change that would lead to the collapse of the system after 1834.

The size of livestock holdings, especially cattle, grew after 1810; but in some instances, the rapid slaughter of cattle for the sale of hides and tallow resulted in a sharp decline in the number of animals. And as mentioned, Indian horse raiding in some areas may have reduced the number of horses available to the vaqueros, thus hindering the roundup of cattle on the range. In the 1820s climatic conditions and possible soil exhaustion reduced the productivity of mission agriculture, as measured by the ratio of grain harvested to seed planted, following a period of good harvests in the decade 1810–19. This uneven performance by the mission economies occurred during a period of increasing demand for foodstuffs and clothing by the military, following the outbreak of civil war in central Mexico in 1810.[32] The mission Indian population had to absorb shortfalls caused by the decline in productivity and poor harvests at several missions. It can be argued that the standard of living of the Indians in the missions declined in the 1820s.

The Economic Dimension of Mission Development

The cost of the military garrisons constituted the single largest expenditure made by the Spanish colonial government in the occupation of Alta California. In the 1760s royal officials in New Spain had begun to implement the series of fiscal and military changes known as the "Bourbon reforms," which attempted to improve colonial defenses, streamline and improve administration, and reduce costs, while at the same time producing additional revenues that could be remitted directly to Spain. Through a restructuring of the tax system and the establishment of lucrative royal monopolies on such items as tobacco, royal revenues collected in New Spain increased. However, much of the money went to help pay for the cost of Spain's involvement in a series of costly international wars, including the American Revolutionary War (1776–83) and the French Revolutionary and Napoleonic wars (1792–1815). Furthermore expenditures on colonial defense increased with the organization of militia systems built around a core of veteran European soldiers and officers. Finally the government of New Spain initiated an extensive military reform along the northern frontier.

Beginning in 1766, a military mission visited the *presidios* (military garrisons) of northern New Spain, in order to improve frontier defense while at the same time reducing the cost of the garrisons. During the course of the eighteenth century, the size of the frontier army tripled, and the cost of the garrisons more than tripled. In 1701 expenditures for presidios totaled 251,883 pesos; by 1787 the sum had risen to 810,240 pesos. The number of soldiers stationed in the presidios grew from 1,006 in 1724 to 3,087 in 1787. The largest increase in manpower took place between 1764 and 1787. The cost of the garrisons in the Californias is not included in the figures above.[33]

Whereas the presidios located on the northern frontier were easily supplied from central Mexico, Alta California was isolated and initially had to be supplied by sea. Moreover the Baja California missions operated at a level of self-sufficiency and did not produce surpluses for export.[34] The new colony depended on supplies sent from San Blas, a port founded in 1768, west of Tepic.[35]

A basic contradiction existed within Spanish policy in Alta California. An implied Russian and English threat to areas claimed by Spain dictated occupation at a time of bureaucratic and fiscal reorganization designed to reduce administrative and defense costs. One way to economize was to promote self-sufficiency in agriculture, thereby reducing the expensive dependency of the military garrisons on supplies from Mexico. Supplying the military establishment was the critical factor in financing the colonization of Alta California; production of large agricultural surpluses in the missions was a partial solution.

For four years, 1769–73, the Franciscans administered the Alta California missions on the basis of José de Gálvez's initial mandate to occupy the region. By 1773 the Franciscan leadership felt the need to have the colonial role of the missions regularized. For that purpose Father-President Junípero Serra, OFM, went to Mexico City to lay a proposal before Viceroy Antonio de Bucareli. The resulting regulation formed the economic basis for the continued colonization of Alta California. The military establishment, including the guard assigned to the missions that existed in 1773, totaled 131 officers and men, at an annual cost of 55,435 pesos in salaries. However, the actual cost was lowered by paying the salaries in goods shipped from San Blas, at prices inflated by as much as 150 percent.[36]

The key to the economic system was the control the Franciscan missionaries exercised over Indian labor. The Jesuits in Baja California had controlled mission "temporalities" (production and labor), but following the expulsion of the Jesuits in 1767–68 the viceregal government removed the temporalities from the control of the Franciscans. Although Gálvez ordered control of the temporalities returned to the Franciscans in Baja California in 1769, the status of the missions in Alta California remained unclear.[37] In consultation with different government committees in Mexico City, Bucareli decided to give the Franciscans stationed in Alta California control of mission temporalities and the authority to administer corporal punishment and other measures, in order to maintain discipline among the converts.[38]

The military was the principal recipient of surplus agricultural production and clothing from the missions. Data from extant mission account books and reports of *suministraciones* (accounts maintained between the missions and presidios) indicate the variety and in many instances the volume of goods supplied to the military. A study of the relationship between four missions and the military shows that the presidios and guards assigned to the missions to protect the Franciscans received some 5–20 percent of annual agricultural production, although the percentage fluctuated from year to year, based on the size of the crops and the needs of the military. Moreover the Indian populations living at the missions generally absorbed any shortfalls due to poor crops. In 1829, for example, the Franciscans stationed at Santa Cruz and Santa Clara missions did not reduce the supplies provided to the military, despite poor crops in that year.[39]

In exchange for the supplies provided to the military at prices established by an official price list the missionaries received credits to be charged against the royal treasury in Mexico City. A representative of the Franciscan College of San Fernando in Mexico City in turn collected the funds and purchased items requested by the missionaries. Actual cash transactions took place in Mexico City, and the Franciscans also had to pay high transportation costs, which effectively reduced the real amount the royal government paid for supplies provided to the presidios. The system worked smoothly until 1810 and the outbreak of civil war in central Mexico. After 1810 the Franciscans stationed in Alta California continued to send warrants, but received little of what they ordered, because of the disruption of communications and the financial problems faced by the viceregal government.[40] After 1810 the military became completely dependent on supplies provided by the missions.

The Franciscans found a secondary market in the growing settler population in Alta California. Sales took two forms: supplies provided communally at the time of the founding of the three pueblos; and individual transactions with settlers, who maintained accounts with the missions. In 1797 and 1798, for example, Santa Cruz missionaries supplied food and planting seed to the settlers at Branciforte, for a total of 5 fanegas, 3 almudes of corn; 13 fanegas of frijol; 20 fanegas, 6 almudes of wheat; and 2 arrobas, 7 pounds of lard in the first year. In the second year they supplied 50 fanegas of corn; 15 fanegas, 8 almudes of wheat; and 1 arroba, 24 pounds of lard. The Franciscans stationed at San Antonio reportedly contributed Indian laborers to the new community.[41] Settlers, including individuals who worked for the Franciscans as *mayordomos* (overseers), bought quantities of grain, dairy products, alcoholic beverages, shoes and boots, and clothing from the missions.

Franciscans also provided the military and individual settlers with Indian labor. An 1819 document listing Santa Cruz mission converts away from the mission reported six converts working at the Monterey presidio.[42] Fire damage to the presidio in November of 1818, at the hands of Argentine revolutionary Hippolite Bouchard, probably accounts for the presence of the Indians there in 1819, working to repair damage to the presidio buildings.[43]

Access to mission Indians gave settlers additional labor at key points in the agricultural cycle, as well as for other uses, such as building construction. In 1807 residents of the Villa de Branciforte rented the labor of twelve Indians from Santa Cruz mission. José María Pinto had two Indians for a week, and Marcos Briones had one worker for four weeks. In December of 1812, the settler Juan Pinto rented two Indians at a rate of 1.5 reales per day, which amount was entered into the account book as a debt to the mission. In the same year, Serafín Pinto paid 30 reales for Indian laborers. In January of 1813, Joaquín Castro owed the Franciscans at Santa Cruz mission 40 reales for the services of one Indian laborer beginning on December 16 of the previous year, during the sowing of wheat at Branciforte.[44] The employment by colonists of Indians from the missions was a common pattern throughout Alta California.[45]

2

Aspects of Social
and Cultural Change
in the Mission Communities

One of the primary objectives of the Franciscan-directed mission program in Alta California was the transformation of the culture and world view of the Indian converts congregated in the missions. The evidence analyzed here strongly suggests that the Franciscans failed to completely transform Indian culture. As the archaeologist Paul Farnsworth recently argued, "To some extent, Indian culture survived, and the Indians who survived the missions, emerged with a new culture that was neither Spanish nor Indian."[1] Cultural change indeed did occur in the mission communities. However, the Indians who lived in the missions at the beginning of secularization in 1834 had a culture that already combined elements of traditional Indian and Hispanic European material culture and significant survivals from pre-Hispanic religion.

This chapter examines cultural change in the missions, focusing on material culture and religious practices. The analysis of material culture relies upon a limited amount of archaeological and documentary evidence. Although thousands of documents written by Franciscan missionaries survive, very few specifically discuss the culture and lifeways of the Indian residents of the mission communities. The single most important set of documents are the responses written between 1813 and 1815 by the Franciscan missionaries to a questionnaire prepared by the liberal Spanish Cadiz Cortes. The questionnaire, prepared to elicit information for the evaluation of colonial policy, requested specific information on Indian culture and religious beliefs. However, the responses to the questionnaire are not an ideal source of information, for several reasons: variation in the amount of time that respondents had been stationed at the mission they reported on; varying length of responses to the questions; variation in duration of operation of the individual missions; and the inclination of the Franciscans to write positive descriptions of the missions for a potentially hostile government in Spain, which in

1813 was considering a measure to secularize the missions in the New World.[2] The second source of information is based on the archaeological record. Although archaeologists have undertaken a number of studies of mission sites in California, most are descriptive and generally are concerned with locating architectural features.[3] However, patterns of cultural change and persistence can be identified for a handful of missions.

Significant aspects of Indian material culture changed under the direction of the Franciscan missionaries. The 1813–1815 questionnaires clearly document gradual changes in food, clothing, and economy of the Indians living at the missions.[4] For example the Franciscans substituted European and central Mexican cultigens for plant foods traditionally collected by the different Indian groups in California. Meat from domesticated animals replaced meat from wild animals. Although the diet of Indian converts varied from mission to mission, it generally contained some supplementary traditional foods.[5] Lorenzo Asisara, an Ohlone born at Santa Cruz mission in the early nineteenth century, described the diet of the converts living at that mission:

> The Indians at the mission of Santa Cruz, after prayers in the morning at church, received their orders as to their labors at the church door; then they went to breakfast, and had their meal altogether of boiled barley, which was served out to them from two large cauldrons, by means of a copper ladle. This full was the ration to each in a *cora* (a small kind of basket), from which they ate with a shell or the fingers. Some had small gourds into which they received their rations. Boiled barley was all that they had in the mornings. . . . At eleven A.M., the bell was rung to call them together. . . . The dinner consisted of cooked horse beans and peas. At the end of an hour the bell was rung again, and all went to work until about sunset, when each received his rations of boiled corn. Such of the Indians as had families were given meat also.[6]

The Franciscans also introduced the use of European-style clothing, and gradually replaced traditional Indian housing with permanent adobe dormitories for single women of child-bearing age and apartments for Indian families.

The archaeological record shows considerable persistence in Indian material culture at the missions, as measured by the types of artifacts (such as beads) left behind. The analysis of artifacts from Soledad mission shows that the retention of Indian material culture ranged between 30 and 45 percent of the artifacts found at the site, although the degree of retention varied over time, related to patterns of recruitment and demographic collapse. For example around 1810, a period when the size of the Indian population was dropping and few recruits entered the mission, the retention of material culture declined to 30 percent of all artifacts. However, after 1810, when the number of recruits into the mission increased, the retention of material culture increased to 40 percent. In other words the Indians who lived in the missions for a period of time gradually replaced their own material culture with imported European materials. During periods of active recruitment and the resettlement of large numbers of converts at the mission, the use of traditional artifacts increased.[7]

A comparison of the retention of Indian material culture and the intensity of acculturation at Soledad, San Antonio, and La Purísima missions suggests that the size of the population at the individual missions and the rates of congregation of new converts modified patterns of acculturation. The population of Soledad mission was small in comparison to other missions, reaching a recorded high of 688 in 1805.[8] The retention of material culture was greater at San Antonio (established in 1771) and La Purísima (established in 1788) missions.[9] The population at both missions was considerably larger than the population of Soledad mission; in 1805 the population of San Antonio mission was 1,296.[10] Similarly the population of La Purísima totaled 1,520 in 1804.[11]

The process of acculturation appears to have been less successful in the missions with larger populations, because of the sheer numbers of people; that made it difficult for the missionaries to effectively instruct converts in Catholicism and other elements of Spanish colonial culture. Moreover the Franciscans stationed at the more populous establishments continued to congregate large numbers of Indian recruits, who also reintroduced traditional material culture back into the mission communities. Perhaps because they had charge over large numbers of converts, the Franciscans stationed at the more populous missions instituted more intensive acculturation programs in the first years following the establishment of the missions. The intensity of acculturation, as measured by the types of artifacts found at the three missions, was greatest at San Antonio mission and weakest at Soledad. However, the intensity of acculturation declined over time, and later Indian converts retained more of their traditional material culture.[12]

A second objective of the acculturation program in the missions was the conversion of the Indians to Catholicism. The historiography of the "spiritual conquest" of Spanish America, especially Mexico, is rich and provides a context for the discussion of religious changes in the mission communities. In a pioneering study, published in 1933 under the title *Conquête Spirituelle du Mexique*, Robert Ricard argued that Catholic missionaries completed the conversion of the Indian populations of central Mexico during the sixteenth century.[13] Ricard focused on the methods employed in evangelization and equated the establishment of churches and convents with the advancement of the conversion of the Indian populations. Moreover, according to Ricard, the anti-idolatry trials in central Mexico in the 1530s symbolized the triumph of Catholicism over the gods of central Mexico.[14] Much of the focus of older studies of religious change in colonial Mexico and the other parts of Spanish America has been on the activities of the missionaries and their world view.[15]

In recent years scholars have reexamined and questioned the depth of the spiritual conquest of the Indians in Spanish America.[16] The historian Nancy Farriss, for example, stressed the importance of different layers of religious belief among the Yucatec Maya: the highest level of official state religion, controlled by priests with esoteric knowledge and concerned with creation and the role of humans in the cosmos; and the local fertility and rain gods, which regulated the day-to-day lives of Mayan farmers. Moreover Farriss documents the transformation by the Maya of their traditional gods into the Christian pantheon of God, Jesus, and the saints. The care of the saints assumed a central role in the religious life of the postconquest Maya. The emergence of the speaking-cross cult after the failed Maya revolt of 1847 was a logical extension of the appropriation of Christian symbols by the Maya, as the Christian cross became an intermediary between the Maya and the spirit world.[17]

The early missionaries, trained in the monotheistic state Catholicism of early modern Iberia, believed that by having wiped out the state religion of hierarchical Indian societies, they had begun the spiritual conquest. This belief proved to be wrong, and within several generations of the beginning of the spiritual conquest of the Americas, evidence mounted pointing to the persistence of traditional religious practices. For example the famous idolatry trials in the Yucatan peninsula in the 1560s showed that Indian conversion to Catholicism had been superficial at best.[18] Similarly the Taqui Onqoy, an Andean revitalization movement in the 1560s, caught priests who thought that traditional religious practices had been exterminated off guard.[19] Taqui Onqoy reflected the collective desire of highland Andean Indians to return to the pre-Hispanic past, but it also represented, as in the case of the Yucatan idolatry trials during the same years, the persistence of traditional beliefs at the level of the family and the individual, even after the structured state-level religion had ceased to exist. The Indian populations of central Mexico, the Andean region, the Yucatan Peninsula, and other areas of Spanish America incorporated the new religion into their belief systems on their own terms. Similarly the effort of the Franciscans stationed in

Alta California to exterminate Indian religious practices also failed.

The apparent initial success of the first generation of missionaries gave way to a degree of disillusionment in the core areas of Spanish America, with the revelation of the persistence of traditional religious practices. However, the frontier missions provided the zealous with an opportunity to spread God's word and save the heathen. Junípero Serra, OFM, the architect of the Alta California mission system, gave up a comfortable academic career in Europe to work as a missionary in the Americas.[20] Many Franciscans were stationed in the Alta California missions, but with the passage of time, few of them shared Serra's initial evangelical enthusiasm. As the missions developed, the Franciscans were tied into a routine of acting as labor and estate managers responsible for the administration of the mission estates, as well as for periodic reports on their progress. Many of the extant letters discuss mundane issues related to the economies of the missions, such as problems of labor and discipline, Indian resistance, supplying goods to the military garrisons, and the procurement of supplies from central Mexico. There is no parallel in the writings of the Franciscans stationed in Alta California to the discussions of ethnohistory and related subjects among some of the early Franciscans in central Mexico in the sixteenth century, such as Bernardino de Sahagún.

The functions of representing the colonial state, labor and estate management within the political economy of the missions, acting as accountants and bureaucrats, and the apparent lack of interest among the culturally chauvinistic Franciscans toward an Indian culture and religion they felt to be inherently inferior and destined to disappear, partially explain the failure of the Franciscans to document most aspects of the world view and religious practices of the mission Indians. An analysis of the 1813–15 responses to the questionnaire sent by the Cadiz Cortes clearly reveals that many Franciscans had difficulty even in describing Indian religion or connecting ritual practices to religious beliefs.[21] For example the missionaries stationed at San Juan Capistrano wrote that "we do not know whether they adore the moon or sun." Similarly the missionaries at San Antonio reported that "formal idolatry was not known to them, not even in their pagan state, nor after their conversion to the faith. All on that subject said about the savages may be said to be pure superstition."[22] Traditional funeral practices and healing persisted in the missions, and shamans continued to have considerable influence. Dancing, which survived in the missions, formed an important link to religion.[23]

The failure to understand pre-Hispanic Indian religions also can be attributed to the ability of the Indians to erect a "wall of silence" around the

true nature of their religious practices and beliefs.[24] The 1824 Chumash revolt can be understood, in part, as an attempt to protect traditional religion.
The historian James Sandos argues that the effort to root out Chumash religious practices, particularly the ʔantap cult, through the use of confesionarios
(confessional aides), was one of the underlaying causes for the revolt. Fr.
Antonio Ripoli, OFM, stationed in Chumash territory at La Purísima
(1812–15) and later Santa Bárbara (after 1815), learned several Chumash
dialects and observed social relations and ritual. According to Sandos, of all
the Franciscans stationed in Chumash territory prior to the uprising, Ripoli
was the most responsible for the disruption of traditional culture, social and
economic organization, and religion. Fr. José Senan, OFM, stationed at San
Buenaventura, prepared the confesionarios that probed sensitive elements
of Chumash culture, to pierce the "wall of silence."[25]

A final reason for the survival of traditional religious beliefs was the demographic factor. The high death rates in the mission communities meant
that the more acculturated Indians did not survive, especially children born
at the missions. Until near the end of the mission period, the Franciscans
continued to recruit and resettle unacculturated Indians, who replaced the
more acculturated converts who died. The new recruits almost continuously
reintroduced religious practices that had gradually faded as the older converts, who had lived in the missions for some time, died.[26] According to the
missionaries at Santa Inés, "Inasmuch as most of these neophytes have been
raised amidst the superstitions of paganism, there are some, especially old
men and women, who as yet are not undeceived about them."[27]

The impact of the acculturation program in the missions can also be measured by an examination of the economy, social organization, and religious
practices of communities of former mission Indians. A group of converts
fled Santa Bárbara mission following the failure of the 1824 Chumash revolt and established a small community in the Central Valley that survived
until it was wiped out by disease in the late 1830s. The fugitive Chumash
continued to worship church images taken from the mission as sacred ob-
jects, practiced European-style agriculture, and used and traded horses, as
did many valley tribelets.[28]

The fugitive Chumash took the elements of Hispanic culture that served
them, such as agriculture that provided a more secure source of food and
horses that could be slaughtered for meat and gave greater mobility for hunting and warfare. Moreover a type of religious transmission or borrowing
similar to the patterns described by Farriss for the Yucatec Maya occurred.
The description of the use by the Chumash of church images as sacred ob-
jects is similar to the Maya use of the Christian cross in the cult of the speak-

ing cross. A process of selective appropriation of elements of Catholicism probably took place in the missions, although the process in many respects was stillborn because of the high mortality rates that killed off the more acculturated converts.

The impact of Spanish colonization also led to modifications of traditional Indian religion as practiced outside of the mission communities, such as in the case of the Chingichngish religion. Chingichngish was a cultural hero who reportedly first appeared at Pubunga, a Kumi.vit ranchería near modern Long Beach. Chingichngish introduced a new body of knowledge that merged with existing knowledge. The new religion spread to surrounding groups, such as the Luiseño, Cupeño, Kumeyaay, and Chumash. Among the Luiseño, for example, Chingichngish became a new creator figure.[29] One Chumash Chingichngish ceremony was associated with the California condor.[30]

The Chingichngish religion may have been a "crisis cult," a response to the impact of newly introduced diseases. It may also have been influenced by runaway converts, who introduced basic concepts of Christianity. The religion was associated with the use of *toloache* (jimsonweed), a narcotic used to enhance power obtained from altered states. At the core of the religion were formalized rituals carried out in enclosed areas decorated with poles, banners, and the image of Chingichngish.[31] The secrets of the new religion were well guarded.[32]

Traditional and New Indian Leaders in the Missions

As was the case throughout Spanish America, the Franciscans and civil-military colonial officials in Alta California attempted to place Indians they could rely on in positions of power in the mission communities. In the Indian communities of central Mexico, for example, the Spanish government recognized the legitimate economic and political rights of the Indian nobility known as *señores naturales*, but they also created Spanish-style municipal governments headed by *gobernadores/gobornadoryotl/alcaldes* and *regidores*. With the passage of time, the Indian nobility lost control of community government, frequently to commoners, who were brought to power because they cooperated with the Spaniards.[33]

The Indian alcaldes in the Alta California missions played a similar role in managing Indian labor and maintaining discipline. The missionaries at Santa Inés described the alcaldes, who were elected every year, as being subject to the missionaries, except in the area of criminal affairs, where they were subject to colonial civil officials.[34] In describing the punishment administered to an Indian living at Santa Cruz mission in an oral history account recorded in 1877, Lorenzo Asisara, born at Santa Cruz in 1820, described the following role of the alcaldes: "The Father ordered the *alcaldes* to arrest him in order to punish him. . . . He [the Franciscan] ordered that they [the *alcaldes*] take Damaso by force: this [Indian] resisted them and he said to the *alcaldes,* 'Leave me, let the Father grab me and that he himself punish me.' But the Padre insisted that the *alcaldes* do it . . ."[35]

Despite the important role given to the alcaldes by the Franciscans, they faced a serious challenge from traditional Indian leaders, especially chiefs. A number of missionaries commented in the 1813–15 questionnaire on the continued influence of traditional chiefs in the mission communities. The Franciscans stationed at San Carlos (established in 1770) noted that "The missionaries strive to humor them [chiefs], because the contentment of the Indian depends on this."[36] Chiefs still had considerable influence forty years after the establishment of the mission. Similarly the missionaries at San Fernando (established in 1797) wrote that "The Indians respect only those who were the chiefs of their rancherías in paganism . . ."[37]

A second group of traditional leaders, the shamans, also continued to have influence among the Indians living in the missions. The Franciscans stationed at San Antonio (established in 1771) acknowledged that shamans continued to practice in the missions.[38] The missionaries at San Miguel stated that "It is undeniable that the Indians have their healers . . ."[39] Given the high mortality rates in the missions and the lack of European-trained doctors in the province, it is not surprising that Indian converts would continue to turn to shamans for help.

Changes in Gender Roles

There was a clearly defined division of labor along gender lines in pre-Hispanic Indian society. Men engaged in hunting and fishing and at times collected plant foods. However, the collection and processing of plant foods was the primary responsibility of women. Additionally there was a labor division in the production of handicrafts. Women wove baskets as well as clothing; men made goods from wood, bone, horn, and stone. Finally women were responsible for household duties, such as fetching water and wood, and the bulk of child rearing.[40]

Pre-Hispanic Indian society was dominated by men, and the rules restricting specific activities, such as hunting, were stricter for women than for men.[41] Attitudes toward the proper role of women in society and the status of women remained largely unchanged in the missions, although there was some role reversal. Both men and women worked at a variety of tasks in the missions, and the Franciscans achieved considerable success in altering work patterns. Whereas previously women had been responsible for collecting and processing plant foods, men now provided the bulk of the work in the mission grainfields and the mills that processed the grain. Women still did most of the cooking, production of clothing on the mission looms, and similar activities. Men continued to supply most of the labor in the construction of buildings and the procurement of meat; herding mission livestock replaced hunting.

Table 6. Quinquennium Mean Crude-Death Rates in the Alta California Missions

Quinquennium	Mean Population	Mean Crude Death Rate per Thousand Population
1780–1784	3,700	72
1785–1789	6,124	67
1790–1794	9,133	79
1795–1799	12,079	88
1800–1804	16,126	98
1805–1809	19,027	91
1810–1814	19,590	73
1815–1819	20,151	81
1820–1824	20,998	73
1825–1829	19,398	75
1830–1834	16,795	50

Source: "Mission Statistics," manuscript, Bancroft Library, University of California, Berkeley.

3

Demographic Collapse in the Alta California Missions*

The northwestern frontier of New Spain was tied into a system of regional trade. Epidemics spread along established trade routes throughout the larger region, and major outbreaks reached the northern frontier at least once every generation.[1] However, Alta California was somewhat isolated, and fewer epidemics reached the region. Epidemics attacked the missions about once a generation, but cannot account for the chronically high death rates in the mission communities.

The first severe epidemics occurred in the decade 1800–10, and crude death rates were highest during that decade (see table 6 and appendix 2). Data from San Francisco mission gives an indication of the severity of one epidemic during the decade, an 1806 measles outbreak. At the end of 1805, the population of the mission was 1,163. There was a total of 471 deaths during 1806, which indicates a crude death rate per thousand population of 405. At the end of 1806, 886 converts remained at the mission, which was a net decline of 337. Several letters written by the missionaries stationed at San Francisco provide additional information on the impact of the measles epidemic. The outbreak began at San Francisco in March or April. At the end of April, the Franciscans reported that 400 converts were ill.[2] By the end of May, the number of sick Indians had grown to 800, and more than 200 had already died. This indicates a morbidity rate of 69 percent by the end of May, and a mortality rate of around 25 percent.[3] The evidence suggests that later epidemics were not as severe.

* For a comprehensive demographic history and extensive data that extends the points made in this chapter see, Robert H. Jackson, *Indian Population Decline: The Missions of Northwestern New Spain, 1687–1840* (Albuquerque: University of New Mexico Press, 1994).

41

It is necessary to document age-specific mortality during epidemics, in order to evaluate the impact of epidemic outbreaks on native populations. We analyze here the 1827–28 measles epidemic, based upon data abstracted from extant annual reports. Burial figures reflect total deaths during the year of the outbreak at specific missions, either 1827 or 1828. Mortality is divided into two cohorts: children under age nine and anyone older. In non-epidemic years infant- and child-mortality rates in the missions were high, and the same pattern is observed during the measles epidemic, since a proportionally high number of children died. Children under age nine made up 21 percent of the population of fifteen missions, yet accounted for 44 percent of all deaths. On the other hand, 56 percent of the recorded deaths were adults and children over age nine, the cohort that made up 79 percent of the total population of the fifteen missions. The 1827–28 measles epidemic carried off a larger number of adults than died in nonepidemic years, which was a common pattern observed for most Indian populations living in the missions in northwestern New Spain.[4]

The lack of medical attention during epidemic outbreaks probably increased mortality. The general belief held by missionaries that epidemics were a punishment sent by God frequently limited their response to outbreaks. This fatalistic acceptance of the inevitability of disease and God's role in sending contagion led many missionaries to passivity in the face of epidemics; why try to alter God's will? Moreover there was a certain millenarian fundamentalism shared by many missionaries; suffering on earth merely prepared Indian converts for a better life in heaven, in God's grace. These attitudes contributed to a rejection of innovations in medicine that could save lives. In 1781, for example, only three missionaries in Baja California used inoculation by variolation, a technique recently introduced into Mexico, which substantially reduced smallpox mortality. Subsequent death rates at the three missions were low, whereas hundreds of Indians died from smallpox where missionaries refused to inoculate.[5]

Seasonal Mortality

Studies of northern Europe have shown distinct patterns of seasonal mortality associated with a greater number of deaths due to the colder, damper weather in the winter and spring, with related respiratory ailments that claimed the lives of the old and infirm.[6] Was there a similar pattern of seasonal mortality in the mission communities of Alta California?

A sample of 16,552 burials from five Alta California missions shows a frequency of deaths spread evenly by season, the difference between the season with the highest and lowest number of deaths being a mere 3 percent. However, there was some variation between missions located in warmer and in cooler, foggier coastal climates. For example Santa Clara and San Rafael missions, located in warm parts of the greater San Francisco Bay region, evidenced a more even distribution of frequency of deaths. San Francisco and Santa Cruz, on the other hand, both located in cooler and damper microclimates influenced by the cold Pacific Ocean, had a larger percentage of deaths concentrated in the winter and spring. The greatest variation was at Santa Cruz, which is characterized by a cool and damp winter and spring, with 57.9 percent of all burials in these seasons; there was a difference of 12 percent between the seasons of least and greatest mortality.

With the exception of San Francisco and Santa Cruz missions, where cold and damp weather contributed to higher rates of mortality in the winter and spring, respiratory and other ailments of the type that affected the populations of northern Europe were not as important a factor in mortality rates in Alta California. However, cold, damp, and unsanitary housing may have been an important factor in higher rates of mortality in northern Alta California. Adobe housing can be damp in the winter, which would have exacerbated debilitation due to syphilis and other chronic ailments. These illnesses were related more to the living conditions that existed in the missions and were only exacerbated in some mission communities by the weather.

Nonepidemic Causes of Demographic Collapse

In studying the demographic collapse of Native Americans following sustained contact with Europeans in the fifteenth and sixteenth centuries, scholars have identified one obvious cause—epidemics that in a short period of time carried off large numbers of people in dramatic and frequently well-documented episodes. In much of northwestern New Spain, periodic epidemics of contagious disease significantly increased death rates and clearly accelerated the process of demographic collapse, by carrying off adults of child-bearing age, thus reducing the ability of the populations to reproduce. Moreover epidemics increased the frightfully high infant- and child-mortality rates, and in a short period of time virtually destroyed the populations of Indians congregated in the missions.

But relatively few epidemics broke out in the Alta California missions, and the three most serious outbreaks occurred after 1800. How are scholars to explain the chronically high rates of mortality in the Alta California missions and the particularly high mortality among infants, children, and women? The explanation can be found in a reconstruction of the quality of life in the missions. This is not to deemphasize the importance of disease as a cause of high mortality; syphilis was a debilitating disease introduced into Alta California by Spanish soldiers and colonists, and it spread through the Indian populations with devastating effect, as did the mercury often used as a treatment for the disease.[7] Respiratory ailments and illnesses caused by poor sanitation were also factors. However, these diseases were also common in Europe and other parts of Spanish America and did not elevate mortality rates to the same level on a chronic basis as was the case in the Alta California mission communities.

Women and young children were the most vulnerable segment of the mission populations and suffered exceptionally high death rates, out of proportion to their numbers in the total population. Women of child-bearing age were perhaps most at risk. There appears to have been little or no prenatal care, and evidence suggests that the missionaries included women in the mission work force, which would have made pregnancies more dangerous. Moreover the attempt by the missionaries to wipe out much of native culture may have denied young women access to traditional child-care knowledge. Children were stillborn or died shortly after birth, due to the complications of birth or from congenital illnesses such as syphilis. Dehydration also claimed many lives in the first year or two of life. Finally qualitative evidence also suggests that abortion was commonly practiced in the mission communities, and the response by missionaries to apparent or real instances of provoked abortion contributed to the humiliation of Indian women, raised levels of stress, and only exacerbated the social conditions that led women to abort in the first place.[8] The climate of coercive social control that existed in the missions also engendered a negative psychological response among Indian converts and contributed to stress, which reduced the efficiency of their immune systems.

A report written in 1797 by California governor Diego de Borica outlined several causes for the high mortality rates in the California missions.[9] Borica identified four causes: the heavy work load and poor diet of the Indians living in the missions; the practice of locking women and girls, particularly the wives of Indians who had fled from the missions, in unsanitary and damp dormitories at night; poor sanitation; and the loss of liberty and mobility the Indians experienced following congregation in the missions. The following sections examine in more detail the factors that Borica outlined in his report, beginning with a discussion of diet.

Diet, Recruitment, and Depopulation

One of the most controversial and difficult aspects of mission life to document is the quantity and quality of the Indian diet in the missions. Sources for a discussion of the mission diet include contemporary accounts prepared by the missionaries and foreign visitors to the missions and figures on total grain production taken from extant annual reports. There are several deficiencies and biases in both sources. Most accounts written about the missions, particularly by late-eighteenth-century European visitors to the missions and the missionaries themselves, reflect the attitudes of a privileged elite group from stratified hierarchical and race-based societies with preconceived notions about the proper rural social order in Europe and central Mexico and what peasants and the urban poor should and could live on, no matter how unbalanced that diet might be. From this perspective the amount of food provided to Indian converts, when compared to what such observers might think appropriate for a population of a similarly low social status in their native country, could appear to be abundant. Secondly the figures on total grain production have little meaning in regard to the mean food consumption of the Indians living in the missions. As discussed previously the missionaries provided a considerable amount of food to the military garrisons in the province and to settlers, in order to promote the further colonization of the region, and they stored grain against future need; therefore the grain production listed in the annual reports does not directly reflect the amount of food actually consumed by converts.[10]

Scholarly opinion as to the quantity and quality of the Indian diet in the missions varies. Sherburne Cook noted reports of the inclusion of quantities of meat in the Indian diet, but concluded that the mission diet was still deficient, below the optimum in calories and nutritional balance for providing the body with sufficient resistance to disease.[11] In a recent study, Ann Stodder concluded that malnutrition was an important factor in demographic collapse in the missions, and, in conjunction with syphilis, caused lowered birth rates among women.[12] However, Stodder did not provide empirical evidence to substantiate her arguments. In some missions Indians supplemented the food distributed by the missionaries with wild foods obtained through hunting or gathering, and in periods of poor crops or crop failure, they were sent out by the missionaries to collect wild foods. The anthropologist David Huelsbeck argued that wild foods were not a necessary element in the Indian diet, but were in fact a luxury item.[13]

The Indian diet in the missions cannot be quantified. Rough calculations can be made on the basis of grain production, but it must be kept in mind that production levels were greater than the actual amount of grain and produce supplied to the converts. Indians living in the missions consumed a maximum of between 1.6 and 4.1 *fanegas* of grain per person per year, based upon a calculation for a five-year sample (1820–24) of the mean amount of grain per convert in seven missions. The amounts recorded are high because the estimates have not been adjusted to take into account either the grain and produce supplied to the military and settlers or the amount of seed reserved for the next year's planting.

In a recent study of rural Spain in the eighteenth century, the historian Richard Herr estimated the mean consumption by Spanish peasants of wheat per individual per year, which gives the data on mean grain consumption in the Alta California missions some context. According to previously published figures, annual wheat consumption in Spanish cities in the early modern period (sixteenth to eighteenth centuries) ranged from 4.0 to 4.7 fanegas per person, with some variation in the actual quantity consumed between the urban poor, middle class, and wealthy. The Spanish figures are close to estimates for other parts of Europe during the same period; from 5.0 in England, a figure which may have to be adjusted downwards to 3.7 fanegas, to a low of 2.3 fanegas in the Netherlands. Wheat consumption depended on supply, price, and the relative importance of bread in the diet. However, wheat consumption alone does not account for the quantity of different foods in the diet, although the grain certainly was a very important component. On the basis of a detailed analysis of the rural economy of parts of Spain, Herr estimated that a rural family required an income equivalent to between 6.0 and 12.0 fanegas of wheat per individual per year for basic levels of subsistence.[14]

How do Herr's figures compare with grain consumption in the Alta California missions? Herr's calculations attempt to establish a figure upon which to base income and status in rural villages and use wheat as the standard by which to compare income generated from the sale of agricultural produce and other related economic activities. On average each rural family had to dispose of an income equivalent to the value of 6.0 to 12.0 fanegas of wheat when sold on the market to ensure a minimum level of subsistence. This would include goods produced within the peasant household, goods and services purchased outside of the peasant household, and the different taxes and feudal dues paid out to the state, the church, and local elites. These figures do not reflect actual consumption of food, which may have been closer to the estimates for Madrid and other Spanish cities.

The Indians living in the mission communities exchanged labor for food, clothing, and housing in a nonmarket economy, and mission labor can be conceptualized as a form of tribute paid to the state and administered by the missionaries. The missionaries determined the distribution of food and other surpluses produced by the labor of the Indians, using their own criteria as to the amount of food sufficient to guarantee a basic level of subsistence for the Indians, while at the same time also providing for the needs of the military garrisons in the province. Any estimates of mean consumption based upon production figures more closely approximate actual consumption than do Herr's figures, keeping in mind that a considerable surplus from the mission economies went to support the military. Although not conclusive, evidence suggests that mean consumption of staple grains in the missions was lower than consumption in contemporary Spanish cities and in the Spanish countryside. However, as suggested above, there was variation in patterns of consumption in the cities based upon wealth, so conceivably Indians living in the missions may have consumed similar quantities or perhaps even slightly more food than the urban poor.

A second question related to production and consumption in the mission communities is the possible relationship between the resettlement of recruits to the missions and the use of food as an inducement to attract converts. This question in turn is significant within the context of the debate over voluntary or forced resettlement at the missions. If food, a steady diet without seasonal variation, was an important way of attracting Indians living outside of the missions, then forced relocation of Indians to the missions would have been unnecessary. Fifteen-year samples of grain production and the baptism of recruits from San José and Santa Inés missions, both taken during periods of heavy resettlement, have been subjected to two statistical tests, in an attempt to uncover any relationship between grain production (food supply) and the number of recruits brought into the missions. The assumption being tested is that factors other than food supply dictated the success of the missionaries in relocating converts, including the size of the non-Christian population in the region, the number of military expeditions sent to return fugitives and punish or forcibly relocate hostile non-Christians, and levels of resistance by non-Christians, among others. Correlation and regression analyses were used to test the significance of a relationship between two variables. The results show a low level of correlation between the two variables and little statistical significance, as measured by low adjusted r^2 and t statistics. Food supply was therefore not a major determinant in the ability of the Franciscans to relocate Indians to the missions.

Sanitation, Housing, and Overcrowding

Until the nineteenth century, European doctors and scientists did not understand the relationship between sanitation, contaminated water supplies, and the spread of disease. Premodern cities, particularly in the poorer neighborhoods, were characteristically overcrowded, had poor or nonexistent sanitation, and were populated by residents frequently debilitated by chronic ailments. Infant- and child-mortality rates were high, although they did not reach the levels documented for the mission communities of northwestern New Spain.

Housing directly contributed to high rates of infant mortality. The greatest danger for newborns in the first year or two of life was dehydration, caused by diarrhea associated with a number of ailments. A second threshold in the life of a young child was reached when a toddler was placed on the floor for the first time and could catch a different series of illnesses, especially if exposed to unsanitary conditions in houses and dormitories. In the 1797 report, Diego de Borica identified poor sanitation as an important factor in the high death rates observed in the missions, as well as the practice of locking up girls, single women, and the wives of absent or fugitive men, in dormitories at night. Borica described how he entered one such dormitory at an unidentified mission and was forced to leave the building because of the stench of human feces. Moreover other accounts describe the dampness in the dormitories and the inadequate cover provided to the Indians, generally a single blanket. As Borica alluded in his report, this imprisonment was an important form of social control. The missionaries, who felt that the Indians were promiscuous, used the dormitories to protect and control the virtue and virginity of single girls and women. However, incarceration in dormitories disrupted normal social relations between the sexes and in some instances family life as well.

Although incomplete, the chronologies of building construction found in the annual reports prepared by the Franciscans document the building of dormitories, and the importance of these structures as a form of social control. The missionaries directed the construction of dormitories for girls and single or widowed women at the beginning of the development of the mission-building complex, generally within a year or two of the establishment of the missions. Other types of buildings with high priority were temporary chapels and residences for the missionaries. In a number of cases, larger dormitories were built at a later date, to accommodate the growing population of women and girls as the mission populations expanded.

The missionaries stationed at San Luis Rey mission directed the construction of a dormitory for girls and women in 1798. They later organized an agricultural station at San Antonio de Pala, in an interior valley, and settled a substantial Indian population at the new settlement. The Franciscans had a dormitory built at Pala in 1819 for single men and women; the sexes were separated. Dormitories for single men were less common, since the missionaries were less concerned about male virtue and promiscuity. Moreover since they already controlled the population of single women, it was not necessary to duplicate the effort by having dormitories built for single men, thereby taking labor away from other projects deemed to be more important. However, as large-scale flight from the missions increasingly became a problem, dormitories were built to house single men as well. For example a dormitory for men was built at San Juan Bautista in 1815; it became an urgent necessity as the Franciscans stationed at San Juan Bautista resettled San Joaquin Valley Yokuts, a group more inclined to resist the mission regime through flight, since they lived at some distance from their native territory.[15]

Dormitories were not the only form of permanent adobe housing that posed a health problem when coupled with poor sanitation and overcrowding. California Indians generally occupied several semipermanent village sites on a seasonal basis in a specific territory and exploited different food sources. Moreover the Indians built their dwellings of tule grass or other nonpermanent materials and periodically burned the dwellings when they became infested with vermin. Finally population densities in individual villages were low, and sanitation was not a significant problem.

The program of congregation brought large populations together in compact communities, contributing to a major problem of sanitation and water pollution. Moreover the concentration of a large number of people living together in a small space facilitated the spread of disease. Finally, although it was not given a high priority during the initial stage of the development of the mission complex, the missionaries had permanent adobe housing built for Indian families, partially as a means of social control, once the Franciscans began to resettle converts from greater distances.

In the early stage of mission development, Indian families lived in traditional-style housing, generally tule-grass structures. Once the missionaries had constructed the basic buildings, which included a church, a residence for the missionaries, granaries, workshops, housing for the soldiers stationed at the mission and their families, and mills, they directed the construction of adobe houses for Indian families. These houses took several forms; they were either long barracks-like structures with small apartments for individual families, or rows of smaller buildings that housed several families. The record, both annual reports and plat maps prepared following secularization, indicate that at some missions a hundred or more of such housing units were built.[16]

The missionaries also changed the style of dress of mission converts, substituting cotton and particularly woolen cloth for the traditional materials used by the Indians. The common practice was for the Franciscans to distribute a single set of clothing and blankets, which the Indians wore until a new set was issued. Communal laundries were built at the missions, and Indian women made efforts to keep clothing and blankets clean. However, the new-style clothing easily harbored potentially dangerous parasites and could not be discarded with the same frequency as could traditional clothing. Finally the missionaries attempted to establish new standards of dress, which frequently required Indians to wear the new garments. Although not necessarily an important factor in the elevation of death rates, the change in clothing styles and materials is yet another example of the ways in which the social engineering practiced by the missionaries might damage the health of Indian converts.

Labor and Social Disruption

As discussed earlier the mission economies depended upon an abundant labor supply, in order in turn to produce the surpluses that subsidized the cost of colonization of the region. The Franciscans, backed by the small number of soldiers stationed at the missions, imposed a rigid system of coerced and disciplined labor, enforced by the use of corporal punishment and other forms of control. Moreover the mission labor regime instituted a gender reversal in the household economy and forced converts into sustained field labor, building construction, and artisanry such as textile production. Prior to the arrival of the Spaniards, men hunted and engaged in periodic warfare, while women collected and prepared food. The Franciscans put men into sustained agricultural labor resembling the mundane work of women, which generated disaffection and contributed to a general psychological disorientation.[17]

Although not its exclusive objective, the recruitment of new converts throughout the history of the missions served to replenish an unstable yet vital labor supply. The search for new converts took the missionaries to greater distances from the mission communities, and the use of different degrees of force to relocate converts to the missions generated passive and active forms of resistance, including large-scale flight.[18] The missionaries responded to flight by imposing tighter forms of social control, including locking single men and widowers up at night in dormitories.

In the 1790s Diego de Borica recognized the impact on the Indian population of the imposition of an alien labor regime, but a relationship cannot be established between heavy labor, inadequate diet, and malnutrition without a scientific examination of a large sample of skeletal remains from mission cemeteries. The pressure on the labor force intensified after 1810, with the beginning of the war of independence in central Mexico and the collapse of the system that provided essential supplies to the missions and military garrisons. The Franciscans harnessed the mission economies to support the entire colonial system in Alta California, and labor became increasingly important as they expanded production levels to meet the new demands of the military.[19]

The reorganization of the mission economies coincided with the last phase of recruitment; in the northern and central missions, this resulted in the organization of expeditions to the Central Valley and the escalating violence noted above. Converts brought to the missions from a greater distance were more inclined to flee, and the greater demands placed on the mission economies made it imperative for the missionaries to maintain the size of the labor force. Labor demands in the missions may have been heavy in the 1790s, but they became particularly disruptive after 1810.

Acculturation, Changes in Indian World View, and Psychological Dislocation

One of the principal objectives of the missionaries was to transform the Indians's world view and make Indian populations over in the image of the central Mexican peasantry that supported the colonial order with their labor and surplus production, siphoned off through tribute and other taxes. The missionaries attempted to destroy all traditional Indian religious beliefs. However, they did not always have complete knowledge of them, and the Indians may have consciously attempted to keep the Franciscans in the dark about their religion.[20]

A process of syncretism similar to that described by Nancy Farriss in the Yucatan Peninsula may also have occurred in the California missions, although the evidence is contradictory.[21] A segment of the converts were either brought into the missions as young children or were the sons and daughters of converts born in the mission communities. If they survived for a reasonable period of time, the young children would be heavily indoctrinated, whereas adults may have acquired a veneer of Christianity and possibly incorporated some Christian beliefs and practices into their world view. Moreover with the high rates of mortality and resettlement of large numbers of recruits in the mission communities, all converts were exposed to a large number of people who continued to practice their traditional religion. This is not to say that the missionaries did not try to stamp out the more open or visible Indian religious practices, such as dances. The missionaries stationed at Santa Clara mission in fact identified dancing as one of the principal vices of the Indians and probably made efforts to eliminate the practice.[22] The personality of individual missionaries also determined their willingness to go forward with the effort to wipe out Indian religion. In 1816, for example, the missionaries stationed at San Francisco mission staged a traditional Indian dance for the leaders of a visiting Russian expedition, which seems to indicate that they did not view traditional dance in the same light as their colleagues stationed at Santa Clara mission.[23]

Also an important factor in the rigor of the campaign to wipe out traditional Indian beliefs was the ability of the converts to prevent the Franciscans from finding out about their world view and any covert religious practices. Corporal punishment was one key element used in the effort to convince converts to abandon their religious practices. The Franciscans probably experienced mixed results in their witch hunts (the missionaries identified shamans as *hechizeros,* or witches), but the result was another forced change that contributed to the violent wrenching of the Indians from one culture to another, with little thought given to the psychological consequences.

Dances and other communal religious practices cemented social relations and provided a distraction from repeated daily activities. Some aspects of Iberian Catholicism, such as passion plays, contained outward signs of pomp that attracted the Indians. The socializing benefits of Catholic practice, however, were balanced by the stark reality of the brutality of the mission regime, which depended on the use of corporal punishment to maintain order, exacerbated by the impact on the converts of seeing friends and family members dying by the hundreds from painful diseases they did not understand, or physically deteriorating from syphilis and other chronic ailments.

Contemporary accounts describe a melancholy attitude among many converts, symptomatic of the general psychological dislocation caused by the routines, living conditions, and high rates of morbidity and mortality in the missions. The general depression among the Indian population manifested itself in several forms. Stress, which must have been high, weakens the immunological system, contributing to the phenomenon described by some observers as natives giving up the ghost and simply lying down to die.[24] Induced abortion was a second response. Social disruption and psychological dislocation, results of the extreme paternalism practiced in the missions, left the Indians ill-prepared to deal with the new conditions that existed in California following the closing of the missions in the mid-1830s, and undoubtedly explain what Anglo-American settlers in the region interpreted as the shiftlessness of the Indians.[25]

Case Studies of Demographic Collapse

This section offers detailed case studies of the manifestations of Indian demographic collapse in six missions located in central California: San Carlos, San Luis Obispo, Santa Cruz, Soledad, San Juan Bautista, and San Miguel.

The Franciscan missionaries stationed at San Carlos mission (established in 1770) recruited converts from the Carmel River basin, parts of the Salinas Valley, and nearby coastal areas from the 1770s through the first decade of the nineteenth century. The Indian population increased in size until the last phase of active recruitment occurred in the 1803–7 quinquennium, during which period the missionaries baptized 108 converts, 71 in the year 1806 alone. After 1807 only 24 more converts came to the mission, and the population of the mission began a steady decline. The numbers reached a recorded maximum of 876 in 1795, dropped to 747 in 1800, 550 in 1808, 381 in 1820, and a mere 165 in 1834, on the eve of the secularization of the mission.

Indian women at San Carlos mission bore children, and birth rates were moderate to high. The mean crude birth rate per thousand population was 51, and the gross reproduction ratio averaged 3.00. However, death rates were consistently higher than birth rates, averaging 90 per thousand population. The mission population experienced a net decline of 62 percent per generation as indicated by a mean net reproduction ratio of 0.38. Finally mean life expectancy was low, averaging 7.6 years at birth. Data for the last quinquennium analyzed here show a marked improvement in the vital rates of the mission population, with a lower crude death rate and higher gross reproduction ratio, net reproduction ratio, and life expectancy. The improvement can be attributed to a shift in the age and gender structure of the population, with some out-migration from the mission following the implementation of a program to emancipate more-acculturated Indians, as outlined below.

The Franciscans established San Luis Obispo mission in 1772, in a well-watered valley located roughly halfway between San Gabriel and San Carlos mission, among the northern Chumash. The Franciscans also recruited Salinan converts. The congregation of converts was almost continuous from the foundation of the mission through the first years of the nineteenth century, and in the year 1803, 239 non-Christians received baptism, which was the single largest number of conversions in a given year. During the period of continuous active recruitment of converts, the population of the mission fluctuated, but it grew to 961 in 1804, the largest recorded population. The numbers dropped after 1804; they stood at 203 in 1833. There was a last phase of the baptism of non-Christian Indians in 1834 and 1835. In two years 169 Yokuts from the San Joaquin Valley received baptism, although it is not clear whether the Yokuts settled at the mission or went to work on nearby ranches.

Overcrowding appears not to have been as serious a problem at San Luis Obispo as at other missions, although the mission population was still not viable. Birth rates were high to moderate, but they declined beginning in the first decade of the nineteenth century, following a severe mortality crisis and a drop in the number of converts moving to the mission. The crude birth rate averaged 37 per thousand population and the gross reproduction ratio was 2.00. With the exception of the ten years between 1780 and 1789, death rates were consistently higher than birth rates, averaging 76 per thousand population. The population actually grew through natural reproduction until 1789, but then declined at a mean rate of 84 percent, as indicated by an average net reproduction ratio of 0.16 between 1790 and 1834. Mean life expectancy at birth averaged 22.8 in the 1780s but then dropped to an average of 5.9 over the following forty-four years. The rapid decline of the population was partially related to a severe epidemic in 1802.

In the 1790s the Franciscans expanded the number of missions in Alta California. In the summer of 1791, they established Santa Cruz mission, on the northern shore of Monterey Bay, at a site that proved to be among the deadliest for Indians congregated into the missions, due in part to the cool and damp weather, which exacerbated the problems associated with higher population densities. The resettlement of Indian converts occurred in two phases: the conversion of the local Ohlone population, largely completed about 1810, and the recruitment of Yokuts from the San Joaquin Valley, from 1815 to 1826. There were 523 Indians at the mission in 1797, its largest recorded population. The numbers dropped to 358 in 1816, but then rapidly increased to 519 five years later, as a result of the recruitment of Yokuts. The population then declined after 1821 and totaled 238 in 1834, when the Mexican government began the process of secularization.

Crude birth rates at Santa Cruz mission were low compared to other mission populations, averaging 29 per thousand population, with a mean gross reproduction ratio of 1.20. The highest crude birth rates (of 44 and 38 per thousand population) occurred in years of active recruitment of Yokuts, which increased the number of women of child-bearing age in relation to the total population. Crude death rates were extremely high, averaging 109 per thousand population, and the net reproduction ratio was low, with a mean figure of 0.04. The average rate of decline was 96 percent over a generation, and mean life expectancy at birth averaged a mere 2.3 years.

In the same summer of 1791, the Franciscans established Soledad mission, in the Salinas Valley. Records for Soledad mission are incomplete; the burial registers are missing, but patterns of mortality can be reconstructed for most of the history of the mission from extant annual and biennial reports, which record totals of burials. Data for the years 1794–98 and 1803–32 are used for the purposes of the present analysis. The Franciscans stationed at Soledad mission converted and congregated the local Esselen-Salinan population in the 1790s and first two decades of the nineteenth century, then congregated nearly 200 Yokuts from the San Joaquin Valley. The population of the mission reached a recorded high of 688 in 1805 but fluctuated and declined in subsequent years. There were 436 Indians living at the mission in 1820 and 350 in 1834, on the eve of secularization.

Demographic patterns at Soledad mission closely paralleled those at Santa Cruz. The crude birth rate was moderate to low, averaging 28 per thousand population, and declined in the early years of the nineteenth century. The gross reproduction ratio averaged only 1.25. Mortality was chronically high, averaging 107 per thousand population, and the net reproduction ratio of 0.03 indicates a rate of decline of 97 percent over a generation. The high mortality was reflected in a low mean life expectancy at birth of only 2.0 years.

San Juan Bautista mission, established in 1797 in the San Benito Valley, had patterns similar to those of Santa Cruz and Soledad missions, with some variations. There were two distinct phases of expansion in the size of the mission population, related to recruitment: a first period between 1797 and 1807, when the Franciscans congregated the local Ohlone population; and another from 1819 to 1823, with the congregation of Yokuts from the San Joaquin Valley. During the first phase of expansion, the number of Indians living at the missions reached a high of 1,112 in 1805, and the population was 1,248 in 1823, following the congregation of the Yokuts. The numbers dropped after 1823, standing at 858 in 1834.

Crude birth rates at San Juan Bautista were moderate to high, averaging

43 per thousand population, and the mean gross reproduction ratio was 1.63. Crude death rates were high, averaging 98 per thousand population, and the mean net reproduction ratio of 0.13 indicates a rate of decline of 87 percent. The average mean life expectancy at birth was 5.0 years.

Later in the summer of 1797, the Franciscans established San Miguel, in the southern reaches of the Salinas Valley. As was the case at San Juan Bautista mission, there were two periods of expansion of the mission population, related to recruitment efforts: from the foundation of the mission until 1814, when the Franciscans congregated the Salinan population, and in 1834 and 1835, when 254 San Joaquin Valley Yokuts received baptism. The numbers fluctuated, but they reached a maximum recorded figure of 1,078 in 1814. The population then declined, reaching 599 in 1834, on the eve of secularization.

Birth rates at San Miguel mission were moderate to high, but the population was not viable, because of consistently high mortality. Mean crude birth and death rates were 41 and 70 per thousand population respectively, and the average gross and net reproduction ratios were 2.10 and 0.31. Although not as high as at several of the missions farther to the north, the mean rate of decline of 69 percent over a generation still spelled virtual extinction for the Indian population congregated at the mission. Mean life expectancy at birth was as high as 13.5 years and averaged 10.2 years, which indicates that levels of health were somewhat better here than at the other missions in the region.

Gender and Age Structure

The mission populations had unbalanced gender and age structures, due to high mortality among young children and women of child-bearing age. The mission populations had a nearly balanced age structure during periods of active congregation of converts, as in the 1790s, but then became unbalanced in periods of limited congregation. For example there were more than two males for every female at Santa Cruz and Soledad missions. In the long run the deficit of women limited the ability of the mission populations to reproduce and manifested itself in the declining crude birth rates documented above.

The gender imbalance can be further illustrated by comparing the number of females as a percentage of the total population over time and the population of females as related to the number of baptisms of girls and women over time. Santa Cruz mission, one of the missions with the greatest gender imbalance in the 1830s, is selected for the purposes of this analysis. In 1797 females made up 47 percent of the population of the mission. The percentage of females dropped in subsequent years, reaching a low of 31 percent in 1832. It should be pointed out that increases in the percentage after 1797 occurred during periods of active recruitment of large numbers of converts, with decreases during periods of less active congregation. Between 1791 and 1832, the Franciscans stationed at Santa Cruz baptized 1,133 females. In that same year only 87 women and girls lived at the mission, a mere 8 percent of the accumulated total of female baptisms from the date of the establishment of the mission. In a period that roughly corresponds to two generations, the relative and actual number of women brought into the mission declined.

High rates of infant and child mortality were a second factor that substantially reduced the viability of the mission populations. As shown in the individual case studies presented above women bore children, but those children died in frightful numbers. By the 1830s adult males made up the single largest group in the mission populations; ironically the age and gender imbalance contributed to the ability of the Franciscans to control a sufficiently large labor force to produce the surpluses that supported the military garrisons in the province during the difficult years of the Mexican wars of independence (1810–21) and to construct the impressive building complexes that are most closely associated with the missions. The age structure tended to be more balanced during periods of active congregation, when the missionaries resettled entire families and large numbers of children. The number of children then dropped, when the missions approached the condition of being closed communities. *Párvulos,* children under age ten, made up 18 percent of the population of twenty missions in 1810, following the first phase of congregation in most of the missions. It increased to 21 percent in 1832, after a second period of congregation around 1820. The increase in the percentage to 29 percent in 1839 can be attributed to the exodus of adult males from the missions, following secularization.

A detailed examination of changes in the age structure at Santa Cruz mission further illustrates the problem of the imbalance in the age structure. In 1798 children under age ten numbered 121 and made up 24 percent of the total population. The number of children then dropped, until the large-scale congregation of Yokuts around 1820, when it increased to 90 (19 percent of the population) in 1823, only to decline in the late 1820s and early 1830s. There was always a large number of families, primarily because of the Franciscan policy of remarrying widows and widowers as quickly as possible. Family size was small, but the average family size (total population divided by the number of families) in this case is somewhat misleading. Because of the high mortality rates, there was also a large number of orphans and a proportionally large number of adult men, which tends to inflate the average family size.

Demographic Patterns in a Comparative Context

The vital rates of Indian populations living in the missions can be compared with those of contemporary non-Indian populations, in this case the soldier-settler populations of the four military garrisons established in Alta California and the Franciscans who staffed the missions. The soldiers and settlers at the four presidios in the province (San Diego, 1769; Monterey, 1770; San Francisco, 1776; and Santa Barbara, 1782) lived in similar conditions to the Indians in the missions, and had similar diets. Families living at the presidios reproduced vigorously, and the life expectancy of children was high. Mean life expectancy averaged 31.4 between 1790 and 1834.[26]

Similar data do not exist for the Franciscans, but several characterizations can be made. Between 1769 and 1848, 138 Franciscans were stationed in the Alta California missions, plus another 4 in the ill-fated Colorado River missions destroyed in 1781, during an Indian uprising. The mean period spent in Alta California was about sixteen years. Fifty-seven Franciscans (40 percent) spent less than ten years in Alta California, including the four stationed in the Colorado River missions; thirty-six (25 percent) were in the province from ten to twenty years, and forty-nine (35 percent) were there for more than twenty years. Altogether sixty-two of the Franciscans (45 percent) died in Alta California, not counting the four missionaries killed in the Colorado River missions. The mean age at death for those who died in the missions was fifty-eight years.[27]

The non-Indian population of Alta California evidenced vital rates considerably different from those of the Indian population. On average the children of the soldiers and settlers living at the presidios survived into adulthood, whereas the average Indian child born at the missions did not. Even when cases of assassination are included in the sample, the mean age at death of Franciscan missionaries was high, and quite a few Franciscans lived into their sixties and seventies, including Junípero Serra, OFM, the architect of the Alta California mission system, who died in 1784 at the age of seventy. The difference in the vital rates of the Indian and non-Indian populations in the missions strongly suggests that, as argued above, living conditions unique to the missions were important factors in the process of indigenous demographic collapse.

Many Franciscans later stationed in Alta California first worked in the Baja California missions between 1768 and 1773. Fr. Lasuen, who later headed the Alta California missions, was stationed for five years at San Francisco de Borja in Baja California. Lasuen directed the construction of the adobe buildings that are now in ruins, located to the right in this photograph of the stone structures built under the direction of the Dominicans, who replaced the Franciscans. (Photograph from the collection of Robert H. Jackson)

The Indians brought to live in the missions worked on a number of projects, including the construction of extensive building complexes. This 1883 sketch by Henry Chapman Ford shows the ruins at the first site of La Purísima mission (established in 1787), destroyed by an earthquake in 1812. (Courtesy The Bancroft Library, University of California, Berkeley)

The ruins at the first site of La Purísima mission a century after Ford sketched them. The standing walls were a part of a church completed in 1802. (Photograph from the collection of Robert H. Jackson)

Opposite, below: Edward Castillo demonstrates the thickness of the walls found at the first site of La Purísima mission. (Photograph from the collection of Robert H. Jackson)

The "mystique" of the California missions: the attraction of the restored mission buildings visited each year by thousands of tourists, who identify the historical missions with the restored or rebuilt mission structures that they visit. Shown here are the buildings at the second site of La Purísima mission restored between 1936 and 1939 by the Civilian Conservation Corps. (Photograph from the collection of Robert H. Jackson)

*Opposite, below:*A design painted on the wall of a building at San Juan Capistrano mission by an unknown artist. (Photograph from the collection of Robert H. Jackson)

The Santa Cruz mission adobe: a wing of cell-like rooms built to house Yokuts families relocated to Santa Cruz mission from the San Joaquin Valley in the early 1820s. (Photograph from the collection of Robert H. Jackson)

This early image of the Monterey Presidio (c. 1791), by José Cardero, illustrates the elaborate fortress-like military presence that made possible the colonization of Alta California by Franciscan missionaries. Indian workers, usually forced labor-prisoners, are seen working in the foreground. (Courtesy the Honeyman Collection, The Bancroft Library, University of California, Berkeley)

The elaborate flicker feather headdresses and feathered top-knots of mission San Francisco neophytes are highlighted in this lithograph done in 1822 by Louis Choris. As this and other illustrations demonstrate, some tolerance for ceremonial dancing was exhibited in some missions where the padres did not perceive any suspected paganism might be implied. (Courtesy The Bancroft Library, University of California, Berkeley)

par Marlet   3   det por L.t

habitants de Californie.

A mixed group of mission San Francisco neophytes of Costanoan and Coast
Miwok tribes as depicted in a Louis Choris lithograph in 1822. The woman
with a garland in her hair is a member of the North Bay Coast Miwok
Numpali. (Courtesy The Bancroft Library, University of California, Berkeley)

Opposite, below: Louis Choris, French artist
on the 1816 Russian expedition of Lt. Otto
Von Kotzebue's visit to Alta California, drew
this ink and watercolor sketch of Costanoan
Indians in the vicinity of mission San Francisco. The inscription reads: *"Costumes de
danse de guerre des habitans de la
Californie."* The body painting and elaborate
flicker feather headdresses are typical of
north central California ceremonial regalia.
This, in fact, may not have been a war dance
regalia. (Courtesy the Honeyman Collection,
The Bancroft Library, University of California, Berkeley)

68

Habitants de Californie.

Three males and two females neophytes from mission San Francisco. Notice details of female tattoos and coiffeur styles. The somber countenances on these Costanoan Indians reflect the culture shock and stress of the mission's program to rapidly transform the hunting and collecting peoples into a disciplined labor force. French artist Louis Choris made this disturbing observation that is amply reflected in this 1822 lithograph: "I have never seen one smile, I have never seen one look one in the eye." (Courtesy The Bancroft Library, University of California, Berkeley)

This lithograph published in 1822 was taken from an original watercolor executed by Louis Choris in 1816. It depicts Indians of the San Francisco Bay crossing the Golden Gate in their amazingly buoyant and stable tule boats. (Courtesy The Bancroft Library, University of California, Berkeley)

Opposite, top: A group of neophytes at mission San Francisco. In this watercolor by Louis Choris done in 1816, we can note various hair styles and especially female upper body and facial tattoos, indicating a female who had undergone puberty initiations prior to induction into the mission's labor regime. Such practices were strictly forbidden to females once baptized. (Courtesy The Bancroft Library, University of California, Berkeley)

Opposite, below: Ink and watercolor by Louis Choris in 1816 show Costanoan and Bay Miwok neophytes playing a traditional gambling game. These Indians are wearing textile breechcloths and blankets given to neophytes at the time of their baptism. Note the sticks used to keep score and the shell bead money being wagered. These gambling games are accompanied by singing and are still being enjoyed today. Often decried as a vice by the padres, historical records indicate an uneven tolerance for these amusements existed from mission to mission. (Courtesy The Bancroft Library, University of California, Berkeley)

Central Valley Yokut neophytes receiving catechism from an Indian
convert. The staggering death rate in the missions meant a continuous
demand for new laborers, especially after New Spain became para-
lyzed by the independence movement of 1810 and failed to supply
Alta California. Only a handful of padres bothered to learn the native
languages, which left religious instruction to other Indians. Often
conversion consisted of the rote memorization of a series of prayers
and Franciscan rules. (Unsigned work from Soule, Gihon, and
Nesbet's, *The Annals of San Francisco*, 1855)

4

Resistance and Social Control
in the Alta California Missions

The initial reception of the Franciscans by the California Indians was any-thing but hospitable. The Franciscans reported what they considered to be thefts of goods by local people, and on August 15, 1769, a group of warriors from local rancherías attacked the Spanish encampment and attempted to pillage the ship *San Carlos*.[1] Two years later, on October 10, 1771, Indians attacked the recently established San Gabriel mission.[2] These two incidents marked only the beginning of Indian resistance to the Spanish colonization of Alta California, resistance that can be categorized as primary and second-ary, passive and active.

Primary resistance was the first offered to the incoming Spaniards. It gen-erally was localized, and only rarely did village leaders form larger, intervil-lage coalitions. Primary resistance was organized along the lines of traditional Indian warfare; village chiefs and influential shamans led attacks on the Span-ish soldiers and Franciscan missionaries.

Secondary resistance occurred a generation or two following the estab-lishment of the missions and involved Indians born in the missions and In-dian converts who had lived at the missions for varying periods of time. However, because the Franciscans continued to bring Indians to live at the missions until the 1820s and in some instances the 1830s, there was gener-ally no clear discontinuity between the two forms of resistance. Neverthe-less distinct patterns do emerge, including one example of a revitalization movement that attempted to reinvigorate traditional religion in the face of stepped-up efforts by the Franciscans to identify and wipe out elements of Indian religious belief.[3] Traditional village chiefs and shamans were no longer important organizers of resistance. Rather Indian alcaldes, leaders elevated to positions of prominence in the mission communities by the Franciscans, frequently broke their ties with the missionaries and organized opposition to the mission regime.

Active resistance was generally violent and took several forms. The least common was large-scale revolt, consistent with patterns observed in other parts of colonial Mexico, where localized, short-lived uprisings were more common.[4] More common were flight, raids on mission herds of livestock by fugitives from the missions allied with non-Christian villagers, and isolated attempts to murder missionaries. Passive resistance is more difficult to document, since it generally was not recognized as being an act of resistance by the missionaries and civil-military officials who recorded much of what is known about life in the missions. Examples of passive resistance from other colonial societies, such as the Caribbean plantation-slave colonies, in the form of noncooperation, such as work slowdowns and the theft or destruction of equipment, are also documented for the Indian residents of the Alta California missions.[5]

Primary Resistance

The first expedition to establish a permanent colony in Alta California, in 1769, encountered hostility from the Indians living between Velicata, the northernmost mission community in Baja California, and San Diego. Once established in San Diego, the Spaniards had trouble with the local Kumeyaay. On August 15, 1769, Kumeyaay warriors attacked the Spanish camp and only tempered their resistance once they had been "punished" by the soldiers stationed at the new settlement. The Spaniards interpreted the attack as an effort to wipe out the settlement and steal the goods brought from Baja California.[6] An alternative explanation, however, places the early resistance to the Spanish presence in the San Diego region in a different context. The Spaniards were stealing Kumeyaay food resources without offering compensation, and the livestock brought from Baja California destroyed food resources. Moreover the Kumeyaay saw the Franciscans as powerful and dangerous shamans.[7] Sexual abuse of Kumeyaay women by soldiers was also a factor. Fr. Luis Jayme, who died during the 1775 attack on the San Diego mission, described the friction between the Kumeyaay and Spaniards. Fr. Junípero Serra, father-president of the missions, described similar behavior toward Kumi.vit women in the San Gabriel Valley.

At one of these Indian villages near this mission of San Diego, which said village is very large, and which is on the road to Monterey, the gentiles therein many times have been on the point of coming here to kill us all, and the reason for this is that some soldiers went there and raped their women, and other soldiers who were carrying the mail to Monterey turned their animals into their fields and there ate up their crops. Three other Indian villages have reported the same thing to me several times.

In the morning, six or more soldiers would set out together, with or without the permission of their corporal, on horse back, and go to the distant rancherías, even many leagues away. When both men and women at sight of them took to their heels—and this account comes from the father, who learned of it from many declarations and complaints of the gentiles—the soldiers, clever as they are at lassoing cows and mules, would catch Indian women with their lassos to become prey for their unbridled lust. At times some Indian men would try to defend their wives, only to be shot down with bullets.[8]

From the very beginning of the colonization of Alta California, there was friction between the Franciscans, soldiers, and settlers on the one hand, and Indians on the other, especially the traditional political and religious leaders. In the fall of 1771, shortly following the establishment of San Gabriel mission in the Los Angeles Basin, Kumi.vit leaders attacked the mission twice, largely in response to the rape of Kumi.vit women by soldiers assigned to protect the Franciscans. The soldiers killed one important Kumi.vit chief and placed his head on a pole as an example to the other Indians.[9]

There were also problems at other missions. In 1776 the Ohlone-Costanoan resisted the establishment of a mission at San Francisco, until selected Indians were flogged and threatened with execution.[10] In the same year, Indians set fire to the tule roofs of the buildings at San Luis Obispo mission.[11] On the night of November 5, 1775, a coalition of Kumeyaay villages attacked San Diego mission, killing three people, including one Franciscan.[12] In 1779 the missionaries stationed at San Gabriel uncovered yet another plot organized by a recent convert to destroy the mission.[13]

The overt hostility of the Indians throughout much of coastal California during the first years of the Franciscan mission program slowed the rate of the establishment of new missions and created a reliance on soldiers to protect the Franciscans. For example the Franciscans delayed establishing San Luis Obispo mission until 1772, because of a shortage of soldiers. The soldiers to be stationed at San Buenaventura mission were instead sent to San Luis Obispo, and the Franciscans did not establish San Buenaventura until a decade later, in 1782.[14] In the early 1770s, each of the missions was heavily protected by soldiers, who enjoyed a significant technological superiority over local Indian warriors, since they were armed with firearms and swords and lances made of steel, wore body armor that deflected arrows, and rode horses. In 1771 there was a total of seventy soldiers and Baja California Indians stationed at five missions, plus the contingent sent in the following year to San Luis Obispo; fifteen at San Diego; fourteen at San Carlos, eight of whom were soldiers; twelve at San Antonio; twelve at San Gabriel; and seventeen to be assigned to San Buenaventura but later sent to protect San Luis Obispo.[15] Once the overt threat of Indian attack had declined, fewer soldiers were stationed at the missions. Similarly an Indian uprising on the fringes of Spanish California also slowed the settlement of the region. In 1781 the Yuma revolted and destroyed several missions established on the Colorado River by Franciscans from the Apostolic College of Santa Cruz de Querétaro. The Yuma revolt cut off the only practical overland route between Alta California and the settled areas of northern New Spain that could have supplied colonists for the settlement of Alta California.[16] As a result it was even more difficult and expensive to transport large numbers of settlers to the area.

An analysis of one effort to dislodge the Spaniards from California sheds further light on primary resistance in Alta California. In 1785 a Kumi.vit convert living at San Gabriel mission organized a coalition of converts and non-Christian Indians to destroy it. The coalition leaders enlisted the aid of a powerful female shaman named Toypurina. The soldiers stationed at the mission discovered the plot and captured the principal leaders of the attack, including Toypurina. In 1786 Spanish officials exiled her to San Carlos mission, after she had received baptism, and punished other participants.[17]

The trial record provides important details on the motives for the revolt and the pressures placed on Toypurina to accept baptism.[18] The leaders of the failed attack responded to a series of questions structured in such a way as to reveal how extensive the conspiracy was, who organized the attack, and the source of the weapons used by the Kumi.vit, which indicated their ability to offer further resistance to the Spaniards. The military officials who conducted the questioning clearly wanted to learn the full extent of the conspiracy, in order to prevent future attacks on the mission. Moreover soldiers publicly flogged eight leaders of the attack, making an example of them, and exhorted the assembled converts not to offer further resistance to the Spanish and the Franciscans. The public flogging of Indians involved in the revolt was a ritual designed to restore Spanish domination, a practice repeated numerous times throughout Spanish America.

The interrogation of Toypurina through a soldier who acted as interpreter provides insight into the motives for the attack. In her statement Toypurina reported that she ". . . was angry with the Priests and others at the Mission for having come to settle in her country."[19] We can infer from this statement that Toypurina and the other leaders of the attack were attempting to defend an established way of life, including their social and political organization, all of which the missionaries threatened to overturn. Indeed traditional shamans such as Toypurina lost considerable status and authority as a result of their inability to cure the newly introduced diseases that were claiming the lives of thousands of Indian converts.

The defeat of the Toypurina revolt and other similar incidents was but one aspect of the Franciscan-directed process of social engineering in the mission communities, which entailed a complete restructuring of power relations. The eclipse of traditional leaders and the strengthening of the mission system led to the emergence of a new group of resistance leaders, some of whom were raised to positions of power within the mission communities by the Franciscans themselves.

Secondary Resistance

Within a few years of the establishment of the first mission communities in Alta California, patterns of Indian resistance changed. A new group, Indian alcaldes appointed by the Franciscans, emerged to replace shamans and traditional village chiefs as leaders of armed resistance. More importantly converts living in the missions voted with their feet to reject mission life. Large-scale and individual flight, as well as that of family groups, became a common form of resistance, which taxed the ability of the Franciscans to maintain social control. Finally individual missionaries became targets of murder or attempted murder.

Large-scale armed revolt occurred infrequently in the mission communities. The most important was the 1824 Chumash revolt, which involved Indians living in Santa Inés, La Purísima, and Santa Bárbara missions, all of which had homogeneous populations. For something more than a month, Indian rebels occupied La Purísima and Santa Inés missions and unsuccessfully resisted a military expedition sent to restore order.[20]

The approach of the Argentine revolutionary and privateer, Hippolite Bouchard, in 1818, prompted the Franciscans stationed at La Purísima and Santa Bárbara to organize the Indians into militia units consisting of archers, infantry, and cavalry lancers, to defend the California coast. While the Indians did not have an opportunity to fight at that time, it was reported that they took to the training with a great deal of enthusiasm. Six years later they had an opportunity to test their new military skills.

The Chumash revolt occurred as the result of a number of factors. The historian James Sandos pointed out the increased efficacy of the bilingual confessionarios, whom local missionaries used to probe the degree to which mission residents retained pagan beliefs and practices. Almost simultaneous with the death of Fr. Senan, whose linguistic skills threatened the secret world of the ʔantap cult, there appeared a twin-tailed comet in the night sky. According to Chumash traditional astronomy and religious beliefs, such an unusual occurrence foretold of great changes to come. With the approach of the annual Easter confessions, which proved so intrusive and threatening, tension among the residents of the missions reached a flash point. The routine beating of a Santa Inés Indian on February 21 proved to be the spark that touched off the last great antimission revolt among the California Indians.

A significant number of Chumash fled deep into the pagan interior of the lower San Joaquin Valley, beyond Mexican control. In response to entreaties to return, the leaders of the fugitive community responded that "We shall maintain ourselves with what God will provide us in the open country. Moreover, we are soldiers, stonemasons, carpenters, etc., and we will provide for ourselves, by our work."[21]

Flight from the missions was by far the most common form of active resistance and also entailed the least amount of risk for the Indian converts. Moreover in most missions that had populations drawn from different ethnic groups, it was generally difficult to overcome preexisting hostilities between villages and tribelets to organize revolts, and the Franciscans carried out an effective policy of divide and rule in the missions. A comparison with another Spanish colonial frontier, the Yucatan Peninsula in southern Mexico, helps explain the importance of flight as a form of resistance and why relatively few revolts occurred within the missions. The historian Nancy Farriss argues that few major revolts occurred in the Yucatan Peninsula because an open frontier and territory beyond effective Spanish control existed. It was easier and certainly less risky for disgruntled Yucatec Maya to run away to territory not controlled by the Spaniards than it was to try to organize an armed revolt. In effect the open frontier in the Yucatan Peninsula and neighboring areas served as a safety valve for the anger and frustration of Indians living under Spanish control.[22] Another difficulty facing fugitive Indians was the still-powerful cultural mandate that forbid tribesmen from entering the territory of neighboring tribes and using their food resources. Those non-Christian villages still able to maintain their independence found it dangerous to harbor fugitives in their villages, since doing so meant risking the wrath of military expeditions sent to recapture the fugitives and to punish or take hostages from the villages that sheltered them. Moreover fugitives might be carriers of lethal diseases.

An open frontier similar to the one in the Yucatan Peninsula in fact existed in Alta California. Indian converts easily escaped into the interior valleys east and north of the strip of territory controlled by the Spaniards along the California coast. Once in the interior, fugitives from the mission communities organized alliances with interior tribelets to resist Franciscan recruitment efforts more effectively, and, after about 1800, to raid the herds of livestock, especially horses, in Spanish territory.[23]

One of the most audacious alcaldes turned renegade was the Mission San José Licquisamne Yokuts called Estanislao. This gifted and charismatic leader grew disenchanted with mission life and in 1828 lead hundreds of native followers deep into the upper San Joaquin Valley. Estanislao established a fortified village and issued the following message to Narciso Duran, the missionary stationed at San José: "We are rising in revolt . . . We have no fear of the soldiers, for even now they are very few, mere boys . . . not even sharp shooters." From this fortified village ringed with deep trenches, Estanislao waged guerrilla warfare against mission stock. He counted among his followers fugitives from Santa Cruz, San José, and San Juan Bautista missions, in addition to Cipriano, a renegade alcalde from Santa Clara, with his own followers. Following a series of Mexican military expeditions, however, Estanislao and his followers surrendered and returned to the missions.[24]

Many if not most instances of fugitivism involved individuals, nuclear families, or small extended families. However, there were instances of large-scale flight from missions. For example in 1795 and 1796, 280 and 200 converts, respectively, fled from San Francisco mission. In 1798 a total of 138 converts fled from Santa Cruz mission. In 1805 200 fled San Juan Bautista. In 1824, following the failed Chumash revolt in La Purísima, Santa Inés, and Santa Bárbara missions, an alcalde from Santa Bárbara mission led 453 Indians into the interior, where they established a community that incorporated elements of both aboriginal and Spanish cultures.[25]

Fugitivism depleted the mission labor force and contributed to the growing level of resistance by Indians living beyond the area of effective Spanish and later Mexican control. Sherburne Cook recorded a sample of ninety-four legal cases involving converts and non-Christian Indians, specifying the class of offense and punishment. Of the total number of cases, twenty-three (25 percent) involved flight from the missions, protection of fugitives, or the failure to report fugitives to Spanish or Mexican officials. Eighteen (19 percent) of the cases were related to stock raiding. Civil-military authorities, along with the Franciscans, imposed stiff penalties for fugitivism and stock raiding, generally flogging or imprisonment, often with hard labor.[26] The military also mounted punitive expeditions into interior areas, with the goal of capturing fugitives, especially individuals and groups involved in the raiding of mission herds, and punishing non-Christian groups that hid fugitives and/or actively engaged in livestock raiding.[27]

A final form of violent Indian resistance was the assassination of individual missionaries. The best-documented case is the murder in 1812 of Fr. Andrés Quintana at Santa Cruz mission by a group of converts who reportedly feared punishment by his order.[28] In 1801 Fr. Francisco Pujol, stationed at San Antonio mission, died of possible poisoning, and two missionaries at San Miguel (Fr. Baltasar Carnicer and Juan Martin), as well as a colleague also stationed at San Antonio, Marcelino Cipres, all fell ill from a possible poisoning.[29] In 1811 Fr. Panto, stationed at San Diego mission, was poisoned by his personal cook, Nazario, who had been subjected to 124 lashes over a twenty-four hour period.[30]

Some scholars have disputed the significance of the reported poisonings. Following Maynard Geiger, Doyce Nunis argued that Indian converts did not poison missionaries. Rather the latter frequently fell ill because they ate or drank from metal plates and cups.[31] However, civil and religious officials inevitably suspected poisoning when a missionary died or fell ill under questionable circumstances.[32] The anthropologist Florence Shipek provides some useful insight into the assassination of missionaries. Indians generally viewed the Franciscans as powerful shamans or witches. In aboriginal society witches might appropriately be poisoned.[33] Franciscan missionaries would thus be poisoned when the Indians felt that the Franciscans' magic no longer benefited them; in a similar fashion, the village chiefs who supported the 1785 uprising at San Gabriel mission threatened to kill the female shaman Toypurina, following the failure of the revolt.

Social Control in the Mission Communities

The different forms of Indian resistance, and especially fugitivism, threatened the successful development of the colonial order in Alta California, especially the development of the mission economies. The process of social, cultural, and religious change in the missions also depended upon the maintenance of discipline. The missionaries implemented measures based upon contemporary social standards, in order to ensure discipline and to wipe out what the Franciscans perceived as vice. Finally the missionaries attempted to eradicate all vestiges of traditional religious practices, including most dances.

From the very beginning, the Franciscans attempted to limit the mobility of converts of working age, although with varying degrees of success. In 1771 the mission buildings inside the compound at San Diego included a dormitory for Christian converts.[34] As the Franciscans developed building complexes, they included dormitories for single women, girls, and the wives of Indian men absent from the missions. In most cases dormitories were among the first buildings constructed (see Appendix 3).[35]

Lorenzo Asisara, an Indian born at Santa Cruz mission in 1820, described in an oral history account taken in 1877 how the dormitories were used to control the Indian population. "One night he [Fr. Ramón Olbes, OFM] took in his own hands the key of the *jayunte* [dormitory] to lock up the single men . . . He had a list of all those who were inside the *jayunte,* in order to know if some were absent and who it was."[36]

In 1806 the German naturalist Lansdorff described the San Francisco mission, including the provisions made for widows and single girls:

> All the girls and widows are in separate houses, and are kept at work under lock and key; they are only sometimes permitted, by their superiors, to go out in the day, but never at night. As soon, however, as a girl is married she is free, and lives with her husband in one of the villages of Indians belonging to the mission . . . About a hundred paces from the buildings called the mission, lies one of the villages or barracks for the Indians, which consist of eight long rows of houses, where each family lives entirely apart from the rest.[37]

The Russian explorer Otto von Kotzebue, visiting Santa Clara mission in 1824, described one dormitory as a large building resembling a prison, without windows and only one carefully secured door. He goes on to say that, "these dungeons are opened two or three times a day, but only to allow the prisoners to pass to and from church. I have occasionally seen the poor girls rushing out eagerly to breathe the fresh air, and driven immediately into the church like a flock of sheep by an old ragged Spaniard armed with a stick. After mass, they are in the same manner hurried back to their prison."[38]

Hugo Reid, a settler living in the Los Angeles area who married a Kumi.vit woman raised at San Gabriel mission, discussed one additional aspect of the use of dormitories and of the segregation of segments of the Indian population.

> The infants were then baptized, as were also all children under eight years of age; the former were left with their mothers, but the latter kept apart from all communication with their parents [in dormitories]. The consequence was, first, the women consented to the [rite of

baptism] and received it, for the love they bore their off-spring; and finally the males gave way for the purpose of enjoying once more, the society of wife and family.[39]

In the first years of operation, during the period of development of the mission building complexes, Indian converts lived in traditional brush-and-thatch structures. However, the Franciscans eventually replaced traditional dwellings with permanent adobe housing units for couples. Permanent housing afforded a greater degree of control over the converts, which was enhanced by the building of walls to surround the villages.

In addition to attempting to control the mobility of converts and ensure that they attended mass and worked at the tasks assigned to them, the Franciscans also tried to control one type of behavior that has been labeled a form of resistance—abortion and infanticide (see also chap. 3).[40] Reid noted that "They necessarily became accustomed to these things [being raped by Spanish soldiers], but their disgust and abhorrence never left them till many years later. In fact every white child born among them for a long period was secretly strangled and buried."[41]

The missionaries themselves wrote about the problem of abortion. For example in 1813, the missionaries stationed at Santa Clara mission noted that the dominant vices among the Indians living at the mission were "first fornication, second theft, fighting, and the dance [*danza o baile*], and in the women abortion."[42]

Some missionaries suspected that infertile women practiced abortion and treated these women in harsh ways. The account of Lorenzo Asisara describes one such example. The missionary Ramón Olbes, examined the reproductive organs of a man and woman who had been unable to have children. When the woman resisted the examination, Olbes had her sent to be flogged and then had her carry a small wooden doll that represented an unborn child in front of the mission church for nine days. The woman's husband was shackled and made to wear horns in front of the church. Lorenzo Asisara left a graphic description of the incident, most likely as related to him by his father:

> Fr. Olbes cried out [after the woman resisted his examination] and the interpreter and the alcalde entered to help him. Then Olbes ordered that they take her and give her fifty lashes. After the fifty lashes he ordered that she be shackled and locked in the nunnery [dormitory]. Finishing this, Fr. Olbes ordered that a wooden doll be made, like a recently born child; he took the doll to the whipped woman and ordered her to take that doll for her child, and to carry it in front of all the people for nine days. He obligated her to present

herself in front of the temple with that [doll] as if it were her child, for nine days . . . The vicious father [Olbes] made the husband of that woman wear cattle horns affixed with leather. At the same time he had him shackled. In this way they brought him daily to mass from the jail. And the other Indians jeered at him and teased him.[43]

Hugo Reid, A Scotsman who settled in the Los Angeles area and married a Kumi.vit woman, described a similar treatment for Indian women at San Gabriel mission:

> Having found out the game practiced in regard to destroying the children born to the whites, he [Fr. José María Zalvidea] put down all miscarriages to the same cause. Therefore, when a woman had the misfortune to bring forth a still-born child, she was punished. The penalty inflicted was shaving the head, flogging for fifteen subsequent days, irons on the feet for three months and having to appear every Sunday in Church on the steps heading up to the altar, with a hideous painted wooden child in her arms![44]

The Franciscans, generally working through intermediaries such as the soldiers stationed at the mission or Indian alcaldes, used floggings and stocks and shackles to maintain discipline and their own notions of morality in the mission communities. Although the Franciscans and civil officials, as well as a few modern scholars, have trivialized the impact of corporal punishment, the use of shackles and flogging to control the behavior of the Indians could and did have a demoralizing affect on converts. Floggings were particularly devastating. In addition to the physical pain of a flogging, the individual flogged also experienced public humiliation and in some instances a loss of status. For example the flogging of a high-status person could cause disaffection among other converts and thereby reduce the status of the individual flogged.[45]

An early account written by a French naval officer, who visited San Carlos mission in 1786, describes the use of corporal punishment:

> Corporal punishment is inflicted on the Indians of both sexes who neglect the exercises of piety, and many sins, which in Europe are left to Divine Justice, are here punished by irons and the stocks.
>
> Women are never whipped in public, but in an enclosed and somewhat distant place that their cries may not excite a too lively compassion, which might cause the men to revolt. The latter, on the contrary, are exposed to the view of all their fellow citizens, that their punishment may serve as an example. They usually ask pardon for their fault, in which case the executioner diminishes the force of his lashes, but the number is always irrevocable.[46]

On the use of corporal punishment Lansdorff observed that "Disobedience is commonly punished with corporal correction . . ."[47]

California governor Pablo Vicente de Sola (1815–22) supported the use of corporal punishment in the missions. Sola noted that, in his opinion, reprimands were not sufficient punishment for public sins and the vice of fornication, and he pointed out that adult Indians were to be given only twelve to fifteen lashes.[48]

The accounts dictated at the end of the nineteenth century by former residents of the missions, as well as the oral history passed through several generations of families until recorded by ethnologists in the early decades of the present century, all record the use of corporal punishment; and the use of corporal punishment in the missions remained as one of the most salient and strongest memories that many Indians had of life in the missions. Kitsepawit, also known as Fernando Librado, born at San Buenaventura mission in 1839, dictated the following account of corporal punishment in the missions to the ethnographer John P. Harrington:

> In those days punishment for the Indians was performed in a jail
> just east of the tower of Mission San Buenaventura. In one of the
> rooms there were the punishment stocks. There were two kinds of
> stocks in that room. One was shaped of wood to cover the foot like
> a shoe. It was made from two pieces of wood which opened, and the
> entire foot was placed into it from toe to heel. These pieces of wood
> were joined to a ring which went about the knee, and from this ring
> straps were attached to a belt that went around the waist of a person.
> Weights were fastened to the straps. As punishments the priests
> would work men and women in the fields with these weighted
> wooden shoes. The priests also sometimes shackled the feet of the
> Indians, or shackled two Indians together at the same time. I remem-
> ber how the Indians were treated unjustly by the order of the
> priests. There were also whippings.[49]

Pablo Tac, a Luiseño born in 1822 and taken to Rome, where he died in 1841, left an account that records the following details concerning corporal punishment: "With the laborers goes a Spanish majordomo and others, neophyte alcaldes, to see how the work is done, to hurry them if they are lazy, so that they will soon finish what was ordered, and to punish the guilty or lazy one who leaves the plow and quits the field keeping on with his laziness."[50]

Julio Cesar, also born at San Luis Rey mission, dictated an account to one of H. H. Bancroft's workers that also mentions the use of corporal punishment in the missions. However, Julio Cesar's account presents a different perspective from Tac's, since he also described conditions following the secularization of the missions:

When I was a boy the treatment given to the Indians at the mission was not at all good. They did not pay us anything, but merely gave us our food and a breechclout and blanket, the last renewed every year, besides flogging for any fault, however slight. We were at the mercy of the administrator, who ordered us to be flogged whenever and however he took a notion. Pio Pico and those who followed him were despots, and in addition Señor Pico required us to carry our hats in our hands whenever we met him as long as we remained in sight.[51]

The regimented and extremely paternalistic life-style in the mission communities, coupled with the impact of depopulation and other factors, definitely demoralized the converts. Hugo Reid wrote, based on his experience in the Los Angeles area, of the apparent psychological dislocation of the Indian converts: "At first surprise and astonishment filled their minds; a strange lethargy and inaction predominated afterwards. All they did was to hide themselves as best they could from the oppressor."[52] The missionaries themselves commented on the apparent submissiveness of the Indians living in the missions. In 1814 the missionaries living at Santa Cruz wrote that "the Indians of this Mission . . . profess . . . the virtue of obedience . . . It is certain that the gardener, if he knew his job very well, would put the plant in the ground with the roots up if the Father so ordered. And when he wants to punish them, he need do no more than order them to undress in order to execute it, and they receive their lashes."[53] However, social control in the missions did not always guarantee the success of the Franciscans' objectives, or even their lives. Only two years before writing the passage quoted above, Indian converts at Santa Cruz mission killed the missionary Andrés Quintana.

These views, especially of former mission Indians, contrast with the vision of the scholars who are apologists for the Franciscan mission regime and Spanish colonization in general in California, with all its negative consequences for thousands of Indians. A series of interviews entitled "The Serra Report," released in 1986 by Monterey Bishop Shubsda for public-relations purposes, summarized the interpretations of a handful of scholars who represent an older, eurocentric and triumphal view of the experience of California Indians in the missions. One such view, espoused by the historian Harry Kelsey, stresses the material benefits and substantial improvement in the standard of living realized by the Indians in the missions, implying the underlying premise that the Indians were culturally backward: "The Indians were delighted to come into the missions. They had been living on the bare edge of existence. Until they came to the missions they didn't know from one month to the next or one day to the next what they were going to eat."[54]

The historian Doyce Nunis further underlines the civilizing role of the missions as a justification for their policies, by painting a misinformed and distorted caricature of California Indian social relations:

> Up until that time [the establishment of the missions], the Indians had no sense of fidelity to each other, there was no spirit of loyalty. There was no spirit of commitment. You stayed together out of necessity rather than out of appreciation. In other words, they had no sense of a social compact, in the strongest sense of the word . . . The Chumash are really quite exceptional. But, they were a gathering people. They had no sense of morality. They participated in free love. Well, of course, the Franciscans would put a taboo on that, that taboo lasted until our time. Today it's gone, more or less. And so, I think you've got to realize that many of these Indians truly were born again.[55]

The Franciscans may have felt that they were civilizing the Indians brought to live in the missions, and that they were materially as well as spiritually benefiting the converts. While it is not our intention to further debate the merits of this attitude toward California Indians, we do want to point out that the Franciscan missionaries achieved the goals of social and cultural change applauded by apologists such as Kelsey and Nunis only in the face of resistance and by the physical enforcement of social control.

5

Mission Secularization
and the Development of Alta California
in the 1830s and 1840s

In the 1820s and 1830s, Mexican liberals and conservatives debated the future of the country, often in a violent fashion.[1] Among the issues central to the liberal-conservative debate was the continued role of the church in Mexico. In 1833 a short-lived liberal government, led by vice-president Valentín Gómez Farias passed legislation that attacked the economic base of the Mexican church, which proved to be only the first round in the effort to confiscate church wealth.

Much of the historiographic discussion of the anticlerical liberal policies of the 1820s and 1830s focuses on events in central Mexico and the important political arena of Mexico City, as well as the ideological content of liberalism.[2] However, the impact of 1833 liberal legislation has received little attention from scholars. Legislation enacted in the late 1820s and in 1833 profoundly modified and in a number of instances destroyed functioning missions in northern Mexico. From the point of view of liberals, the mission was an anachronism that needed to be eliminated, in order for the frontier to progress and to integrate the Indians. One of the laws passed in 1833 mandated the secularization of the frontier missions, including the granting of emancipation to Indian converts living under the control of the missionaries, and the legal obligation to distribute lands, livestock, buildings, and other communal property among the surviving Indian converts, under the supervision of state-appointed administrators. Many frontier missions elsewhere had already been partially or completely secularized prior to that time, so that the 1833 law had its greatest impact on the Franciscan missions in Alta California. Moreover any discussion of secularization must be placed within the context of continued concern among government politicians over the sparse population of the frontier regions coveted by the expansive United States and the implementation of colonization laws, which often contradicted the letter if not the intent of legislation governing the economic and political organization of the missions.[3]

In the 1820s and 1830s, three fundamental ideas influenced Mexican liberal reformers: English utilitarianism, with its emphasis on the rights of the individual; the goal of eliminating corporate privilege and incorporating the Indians into Mexican society; and a desire to liquidate corporate wealth and promote economic modernization and development.[4] The multiple objectives of liberal reformers had a direct bearing on the secularization of the Alta California missions. José Mora, the most influential liberal ideologue of the 1820s and 1830s, argued that the missions that continued to operate in northern Mexico following independence perpetuated the paternalism of Spanish colonial policy, which degraded Indians and prevented them from entering the "rational world." Moreover the special legal status of "Indians" under the Spanish *Laws of the Indies* and their social segregation deprived them of the skills to carry out the "social transactions of life." Finally, according to Mora, the missions perpetuated the notion of communal property among Indians, by not teaching them the value of individual property.[5]

In addition to the issue of integration, the liberals attacked the corporate privilege of the regular orders and the wealth of the church, including the holdings of the regular clergy.[6] At the national level, the Pious Fund of the Californias, an endowment set up in the early eighteenth century to fund the establishment of missions in Baja California and administered by the royal government following the expulsion of the Jesuits in 1767, came under attack.[7] In Alta California, local politicians supported the secularization of the missions, in order to gain access to their lands and goods. Moreover there was a growing anti-Spanish sentiment in Mexico in the late 1820s, which led to decrees in 1827 and 1829 calling for the expulsion of all Spanish-born people living in Mexico, including missionaries stationed in the frontier missions.[8] Spanish-born Franciscans in Alta California were not expelled by local officials, however, because the bulk of the Franciscans still serving in the missions were Spanish-born.

Several legal precedents existed for the secularization of the missions: the 1767 expulsion of the Jesuits from the Spanish empire, a secularization law passed in 1813 by the liberal Spanish Cortes and reissued for Mexico in 1821, and an effort to secularize the missions in the mid-1820s.[9] However, the changing fortunes of liberal reformers in Spain and Mexico led to the suspension of the efforts to close the missions. In 1814, following his return from exile in France, King Ferdinand VII suspended all legislation enacted by the liberal Cadiz Cortes and threw many prominent liberals into prison.[10] The liberal Spanish Cortes, restored in 1820, following a military coup that forced the king to reinstate the 1812 constitution, reinstituted the 1813 secularization law. However, a conservative counterrevolution in Mexico in 1821 led to independence and a suspension of the secularization law.[11]

Proclerical conservative politicians dominated Mexico during much of the first federal republic (1824–35) and prevented the secularization of the frontier missions in Mexico, including the Alta California missions. In late 1832 Antonio López de Santa Anna, in alliance with liberal politicians, staged a coup that overthrew the conservative regime that had controlled Mexico since 1829. Santa Anna, the consummate apolitical military *caudillo*, became the new president of the country, and the liberal Valentín Gómez Farías was elected vice-president. Santa Anna retired from Mexico City to return to his hacienda in the state of Veracruz on several occasions in 1833, leaving Gómez Farías in charge of the government. During four periods as interim-president of the republic, Gómez Farías, fearing the growing strength of the proclerical forces in the country and Santa Anna's own gradual shift away from liberalism, pushed a series of anticlerical laws through congress.[12]

A number of specific laws affected the legal and financial status of the frontier missions. Legislation of August 17, 1833, ordered the secularization of the missions in Baja and Alta California, although as a consequence of the division of powers between the federal and state or territorial governments, local officials in California were made responsible for the implementation of the law. A related law of August 31, 1833, confiscated the property and goods in Mexico belonging to the missions located in the Philippines; and in October of the same year, a second law provided for the sale at auction of the goods and property confiscated after August 31. The antimission legislation was one element of a broader anticlerical program, which included the suspension of the legal obligation to pay the tithe supporting the secular clergy, the closing of the church-run Universidad de México, the organization of a national library (housed in a structure confiscated from a church-run school ordered closed in the same year), the suspension and later the prohibition of the sale of all church-owned property, and the suspension of the civil obligation to follow church vows taken by men and women entering regular orders and the secular clergy.[13]

In 1834 proclerical politicians and their supporters in the army began plotting to overthrow the government headed by Gómez Farías, and in February and March rumors of an impending antiliberal revolution multiplied. At the same time, Santa Anna began giving indications that he would return to Mexico City and take a more active role in the government. Under growing pressure Gómez Farías left the vice-presidency on April 24, 1834, and Santa Anna resumed the presidency. Radical liberals in congress prolonged the regular session, which was due to end on April 15, but under pressure from Santa Anna, both the Chamber of Deputies and the Senate suspended but did not cancel the current session. Santa Anna called the deputies and senators back to cancel most of the anticlerical laws passed in the previous year and then closed congress at the end of May, after he failed to get a quorum in either house. The closure of congress marked the end for the time being of liberal rule in Mexico.[14] A new coalition of pro-clerical centralist politicians, supported by the clergy and military, dismantled the federalist system in Mexico in 1835. However, the political changes in central Mexico did not modify the implementation of the secularization law in Alta California.

Beginning in 1834 local government in Alta California dismantled the paternalistic authority the Franciscans had exercised over the converts living in the missions and appointed secular administrators for the missions. However, secularization did not bring about an immediate change in the legal status of the converts living in the missions; their emancipation was a gradual rather than an immediate process. Moreover much of the land, buildings, and other property of the missions did not pass into the hands of the converts. Most of the Indians living in the missions in 1834 simply used the breakdown of the Franciscan regime as an opportunity to leave.

Emancipation, 1826–1840

Until emancipation Indian converts were legally defined by the state as wards of the Spanish crown and later the Mexican government, and mission property and lands were theoretically held in trust for the converts under the administration of the Franciscans. However, the Alta California missions were not ready for secularization after more than sixty years, since, as the Franciscans continuously pointed out, the mission populations still included large numbers of converts still only marginally acculturated.

The implementation of the secularization decree in Alta California, beginning in 1834, did not signal an immediate change in the legal status of many converts living in the mission communities. The legal emancipation of the mission Indians, their conversion from the status of state wards to free citizens, began in the late 1820s, but it was not completed until after 1840. However, the breakdown of social control in the missions in the 1830s, with the transition from missionary control to that of state appointed administrators, contributed to an exodus of Indians from the missions.

Prior to 1834 the Mexican government had experimented with a loosening of social controls in the missions, by emancipating a small number of acculturated converts. Emancipation had a dual meaning; not only were the Indians freed from the control of the missionaries, but they were also legally able to take their place in Mexican society as free citizens, with the right to settle where they pleased. In concrete terms one of the most immediate changes brought about by emancipation was the right to refuse to labor on communal projects in the missions and not to be subjected to whippings and other forms of corporal punishment and imprisonment on the orders of the missionaries. The first emancipation decree, of July 25, 1826, emancipated a small number of converts living in the mission communities within the jurisdiction of San Diego, Santa Bárbara, and Monterey presidios. In 1828 the government extended the initial emancipation decree to missions in the jurisdiction of San Francisco presidio, excluding the recently established San Rafael and San Francisco Solano missions. The initial emancipation plan also included a scheme to establish a community of free Indians near San Fernando mission in the Los Angeles Basin, which was never carried out.[15] Most if not all of the emancipated Indians migrated to the emerging towns in the province. For example emancipated Indians settled in the growing town of Monterey and nearby ranches, as reported in the annual reports prepared by the missionaries stationed at San Carlos mission.[16]

The impact of the presecularization emancipation decrees can be measured by documenting changes in the number of Indians living at the seven nonmission settlements in Alta California prior to 1834. There was an increase in the number of Indians living at the seven communities, from 154 in 1825 to 427 in 1830, and then a decline from 435 in 1832 to 406 two years later. Los Angeles was the single largest center of nonmission Indian settlement, due to the larger number of Indians emancipated in the southern missions. In 1825 a mere 23 Indians reportedly lived at Los Angeles, but the number increased to 311 by 1828.[17]

A close examination of the patterns of Indian settlement at Monterey presidio and Los Angeles sheds further light on the short-term impact of the 1826 and 1828 emancipation decrees and on which segments of the mission populations left the missions. Between 1827 and 1828, the Indian population at both settlements increased, with the greatest increase occurring at Los Angeles. However, the numbers gradually declined in subsequent years, as Indians subsequently left the immediate vicinity of the town. The Indian population of Monterey nearly doubled between 1827 and 1828, but did not reach the presecularization high of 110 until 1831. The majority of the Indians leaving the missions in the late 1820s were adult males. At Los Angeles, for example, adult males constituted 22 percent of the total Indian population in 1825, but the number increased to 64 percent in 1828. Similarly the percentage of adult males in the Indian population of Monterey ranged from 49 percent to 72 percent between 1828 and 1837. Where the adult males went who left Los Angeles between 1829 to 1834 is not known, although many probably went to work on ranches being organized in the region.[18]

The second stage of emancipation came in May of 1833, at the beginning of the local debate over the secularization of the missions. Governor José Figueroa (1833–35) provisionally decreed the emancipation of a larger number of the converts still living primarily in the southern missions, over the objections of the Franciscans. The 1833 decree set into motion a social experiment at San Juan Capistrano mission (established in 1776). In October of the same year, the governor emancipated all of the Indians living at the mission and created a *pueblo de indios*, a formal town inhabited by converts, with a municipal government. The governor justified this experiment on the grounds that the Indians at the older establishment were sufficiently acculturated to take their place in society. The creation of the pueblo de indios entailed the distribution of mission lands to the Indians, generally lands they were already exploiting for their own subsistence needs. In the following year, the provincial government initiated the secularization of San Juan Capistrano mission and appointed a civil administrator to manage the Indians. The return of the Indians to a form of subjugation similar to the social controls previously exercised by the Franciscans disrupted the development of the Indian pueblo. In the late 1830s, the Indians at San Juan Capistrano complained about the administrator, especially his attempts to get the Indians to work for his personal benefit. Moreover the Indians complained about the alienation of mission lands and goods into the hands of local settlers. Growing discontent led to desertions from the community. In 1834 861 Indians lived at San Juan Capistrano; by 1840 the number had dropped to some 500, of whom only about 100 were residents of the pueblo de indios. Finally the provincial government dissolved the Indian pueblo, in July of 1841, and distributed its lands among a small number of Indians and local settlers, in an effort to promote the development of a more stable community.[19]

At many of the other missions, the immediate result of the 1833 emancipation decree was to reduce the labor force available to the missionaries, since most of the newly liberated converts refused to work under the same coercive mission labor system. For example the Franciscans stationed at San Luis Rey mission reported, in June of 1833, that most of the recently emancipated converts refused to work on communal mission projects.[20] The Franciscans also bitterly complained about the breakdown of the social controls that were necessary for the smooth functioning of the mission economies and acculturation programs.

The presecularization emancipation decrees freed many Indians living in the missions, but most Indians who continued to live at the missions after 1834 retained the status of state wards, under the control of the administrators appointed under the terms of the 1833 secularization decree. Moreover the 1826, 1828, and 1833 decrees had more of an impact on the Indians living in the older southern missions and did not substantially alter the status of converts living in the north. For example the majority of Indians living at Santa Cruz mission (established in 1791) continued to work between 1835 and 1840 in communal labors, under the direction of the state appointed administrators.[21] At the same time, the unauthorized exodus of converts from the missions in 1835 and 1836, as the civil administrators took charge of the missions, alarmed local officials. A May 25, 1836, decree issued by interim governor Mariano Chico (1836) attempted to stop the out-migration, with only limited success; but it probably delayed the further emancipation of Indians still living in the missions, particularly in the more recently established northern missions.[22]

In 1839–40 the territorial government sent the Anglo-California settler and rancher William Hartnell on an inspection tour of the missions. Hartnell recorded a number of complaints from Indians in the diary and official report prepared following his inspection of the missions. Although the surviving copy of the diary and report is incomplete, it does record the requests for emancipation presented by Indians at several missions.[23] Moreover a number of emancipated Indians continued to live at the missions, such as the twenty-two emancipated adults (11 percent of all adults) Hartnell found at San Buenaventura (established 1782). Indians still living at Soledad (established 1791), Santa Cruz (established 1791), San Francisco (established 1776), and San Rafael (established 1817) missions, in the northern part of the province, petitioned for their emancipation and the distribution of remaining communal property. At San Rafael mission Hartnell specified that the "old Christians," the more acculturated converts, were the ones who requested emancipation.

Although incomplete the evidence does indicate that at least a limited emancipation was granted to the Indians who still lived at the missions in 1840, following Hartnell's inspection tour. According to one document, Governor Juan Bautista Alvarado (1836–42) emancipated the Indians at Santa Cruz mission in 1840.[24] Guadalupe Vallejo, brother of the commander of the northern military district, Mariano Vallejo, emancipated the Indians of San Rafael mission, which he administered. Writing in December of 1840, the Franciscan stationed at the ex-mission of San Rafael complained that Vallejo's emancipation decree had caused most of the Indians to leave.[25]

Exodus

Official reports written both by the Franciscans still assigned to the ex-missions after 1834 and by other government officials decried the exodus of Indians from the missions after 1834. Most of the surviving annual reports on the status of the missions prepared in 1840 by the Franciscans comment on the dispersion of the mission populations and identify different patterns of out-migration. For example Jesús González, OFM, stationed at ex-mission San José, noted that "almost the majority [of the Indians that formerly lived in the mission] are wandering with the Gentiles, [in the] Ranches, and [the other] Missions."[26] The Franciscan stationed at San Antonio wrote that "[i]n the number of [Indians listed in the census] is included those who are wandering in the Ranches, or [have] fled to the *tulares* . . ."[27] José Quija, OFM, stationed at San Rafael, wrote that, "On October 26, Sor. Don Guadalupe Vallejo [emancipated] all of the Neophytes of this Mission, with whose permission they could go where they wanted, as a consequence of which the Mission has remained only with my servants . . . the rest have gone to various ranches and some to the *gentilidad* . . ."[28]

Contemporary sources record an exodus away from the area of effective Mexican control on the coast; resettlement of Indians as laborers on the ranches being carved out of former mission lands; and migration to the emerging towns in the province. Most of the converts who remained under Mexican jurisdiction probably went to work, on a seasonal or permanent basis, on the growing number of cattle ranches as *vaqueros*, agricultural laborers, skilled craftsworkers, cooks, and household servants. The majority of the converts probably left the missions in search of employment, although some may have been directly recruited from the missions. A census from around 1840 of the population of ex-mission Indians at San Antonio, for example, records that one Sr. Aguilar took two Indian families (six individuals) to the former San Luis Obispo mission. The census provides little information beyond this, but Aguilar may have taken the Indians to work for him.[29]

Former mission Indians found work on the ranches from the late 1820s and early 1830s and were extremely mobile. A detailed census of the jurisdiction of the municipality of Monterey, which included ranches in the Salinas and Pajaro valleys, lists Indian converts and non-Christian Indians seized on military and paramilitary raids to the San Joaquin Valley living on a number of ranches. William Hartnell had eighteen former mission Indians living on his Rancho Patrocinio, the largest number on any of the ranches in the jurisdiction. All told there were fifty-nine former mission Indians and four non-Christian Indians living on nine ranches. The Indians working on the Salinas Valley ranches had migrated a considerable distance. There were individuals listed in the census from Santa Clara mission in the San Francisco Bay area, as well as La Purísima, Santa Inés, San Fernando, and San Gabriel missions in the south. In the early stages of the process of secularization, Indians were a significant but not the dominant source of labor on ranches in the Monterey area, and a number of ranches did not even employ Indian workers. Social and economic differentiation in nineteenth-century Spanish and Mexican California led to the growth of an incipient mestizo working class, and much of the labor on the ranches was provided by these non-Indians.[30]

Former mission Indians also migrated to the growing towns, where they either lived in rancherías located on the outskirts and served as a pool of temporary laborers or found permanent employment and lived in the households of prominent settlers as servants, cooks, etc. In 1836 for example, six former mission Indians and one non-Christian lived in Monterey town.[31] By 1839 the exodus of Indians from the missions in general and to the towns in particular caused considerable alarm among civil officials, who wanted the Indians to remain in the missions. In 1839 and 1840, William Hartnell received complaints about the flight of the Indians and resulting labor shortages from the administrators of San Diego, San Luis Rey, and San Juan Capistrano missions. Many of the absent Indians were in Los Angeles. On June 11 and 14 of 1839, Hartnell wrote to the prefect of Los Angeles, asking that fugitive Indians be returned to San Luis Rey and other missions.[32]

Finally there was a limited pattern of migration from the northernmost missions alluded to by Hartnell in his inspection diary. The division of the region north of San Francisco Bay into Spanish-Mexican and Russian spheres of influence did not disrupt established trading patterns between coastal and interior tribelets. In the 1830s the Franciscans stationed at San Rafael mission reported numbers of the Indians under their charge absent at the Russian settlement at Ross, trading with the local Indians and the Russians, and they documented one instance of a local Indian woman who married an Aleut, went to the Russian colony in Alaska, and later settled at San Rafael mission.[33] Indians from San Rafael and perhaps San Francisco Solano mission also went to work for the Russians at Fort Ross, as agricultural laborers.[34]

How many former converts left the missions in the twelve years following the initial implementation of the secularization decree? There are post-secularization population counts and estimates that can serve as the basis for calculations of the scale of the exodus from the missions, although these population figures are not as accurate as the censuses prepared during the period of Franciscan administration of the missions. The very fact that converts left the missions in large numbers or left settlements around the missions on a seasonal basis to work in the towns or ranches made it difficult to prepare accurate censuses, and the numbers reported at the missions varied from year to year. For example William Hartnell recorded a population of 70 Indians at Santa Cruz mission in 1839, while the Franciscan stationed there counted 102 in the following year. Other evidence suggests that as many as 148 to 160 Indians lived in the Santa Cruz area in 1840.[35]

San Juan Bautista missionary José Anzar succinctly described the problems of trying to enumerate the Indians who the Franciscans and mission administrators considered to be residents of the missions in 1840. "It is not possible to take an exact count of the number of Indians because [they are] all very dispersed in the other missions and as fugitives in their land."[36] San José missionary Jesús González added that "The Indians that are [enumerated] above are not currently congregated here . . ."[37]

The general trend was one of a decline in the numbers of Indians remaining in the neighborhood of the former missions, due both to disease (especially a severe smallpox outbreak in 1838) and out-migration. In 1842 some 4,300 Indians were counted at and in the immediate neighborhood of the twenty-one ex-missions, less than a third of the number of Indians in the missions immediately prior to secularization in 1834. However, the post-secularization population estimates do not provide a suitable basis for a calculation of the relative importance of out-migration and high mortality rates as causes for the decline of the population of Indians living in and around the ex-missions.

An earlier study used a computer-generated projection of the vital rates of the population of the twenty-one Alta California missions to calculate the rate of decline, had secularization not led to large-scale exodus.[38] The projection showed that the population of the missions would have continued to decline at a rate of about 4 percent per year; in total numbers, there would have been some 11,845 converts in 1840 and 9,321 in 1845. Censuses in 1839 and 1842 reported substantially lower Indian populations at the former missions, 7,246 in the former year and 4,372 in the latter. On the basis of this projection, it was estimated that some 60 percent of the Indians living in the missions left between 1834 and 1842. The mean annual rate of out-migration was 8.6 percent between 1834 and 1839 and 5.6 percent from 1839 to 1842.

A significant number of former converts lived at the missions or in their immediate neighborhood following secularization, and at some locations they continued to work until 1840 in communal labors at the missions, under the direction of the state-appointed administrators. These administrators attempted to maintain the same coercive forms of social controls as had existed during the Franciscan regime, including the use of corporal punishment.[39] Many of the converts who remained at the missions under the control of the administrators agitated for emancipation, as mentioned above, as well as for the distribution of lands and other communal mission property that they were entitled to, under the terms of the 1833 secularization decree. Moreover the Indians complained about the granting of ranches to non-Indians from mission lands.[40] The process of the distribution of former mission lands and goods to ex-mission Indians varied, but distinctions can be made between those mission communities where the government attempted to establish Indian pueblos (as at San Juan Capistrano) and other missions, where prominent local settlers retained control over the secularization process and distributed mission lands and goods to only a small number of Indians, on an individual basis. The course of secularization at Santa Cruz mission is illustrative of the majority of cases where the government did not attempt to establish Indian pueblos.

The Indians living at Santa Cruz remained under the control of the appointed administrators until emancipated in 1840 by governor Alvarado. Prior to 1840 the converts complained on numerous occasions about administrator abuses. For example Russian born José Bolcoff, placed in charge of the ex-mission in the late 1830s, reportedly took roof tiles and other building materials for use on the structures being built on his own lands.[41] Much of the mission lands and movable goods had been lost prior to 1840, but enough remained to reward the more acculturated Indians who had remained at and near the ex-mission and worked on the ranches and town growing up around it. Twenty-five Indians owned small plots of former mission lands in the years 1834–49, including ten individuals who communally exploited a parcel known as "San Pedro Regalado" as late as 1847. However, most of the Indian landowners sold their lands to Mexican and Anglo-American settlers in the 1840s, 1850s, and 1860s.[42] Similarly Indians received sections of mission buildings, particularly residences in the dormitories built under the direction of the Franciscans to house Indian converts. The recipients of sections of buildings sold their interests to Mexican and Anglo-American settlers in the 1840s and 1850s.[43]

The Indians who remained at the missions received lands and other mission property. However, others reaped the benefits of some sixty years of development of the mission estates. The following section documents the decline in the assessed value of the mission estates based on inventories and the appropriation of mission land and livestock by a new class of ranchers.

The Decline of the Mission Estates

The mission estates consisted of the buildings (including the church) at the main village and surrounding ranches and agricultural stations, church equipment, tools, looms, land, and livestock. The local politicians who took control of the secularization process appropriated much of the wealth of the mission estates, especially land, livestock, and equipment. The buildings themselves, improperly maintained because of a lack of labor, or exposed to the elements because of the removal of roof tiles for use elsewhere, deteriorated rapidly. The net result was a rapid decline in the value of the mission estates (see table 7).

By 1845 little remained of the mission estates other than a few buildings from the complex of buildings at the mission sites and small parcels of land nearby. The value of the eight missions dropped from an estimated 548,110 pesos in the mid-1830s, to 73,755 pesos in 1845, a decline in value of 86 percent. Much of the loss in value was due to the granting of former mission lands as ranches to prominent settlers and the expropriation, sale, or slaughter of the livestock herds.

In the first decades of the nineteenth century, the sale of cattle hides and tallow supplied primarily from the mission herds became increasingly important in the economy of Alta California. Moreover wool was consumed in large quantities in the production of textiles used to clothe the Indians living in the missions, the military garrisons, and the civilian population, thus reducing the dependence on imports of coarse woolens (but not fine textiles).

In the administration of the former missions, livestock became the asset most easily liquidated to provide supplies, particularly clothing, for the Indians remaining under the control of the civil administrators and for the payment of other obligations, such as salaries. Moreover the owners of the ranches being carved out of former mission lands took mission livestock to start up their ranching operations. Raids by hostile Indian groups from the interior, including a growing number of former residents of the mission communities who had escaped from Mexican-controlled territory, reduced the size of the horse herds. Finally with the dispersion of the Indian population following secularization, there was insufficient labor to round up the thousands of head of semiwild range cattle that made up the bulk of the mission herds.

Estimates of the numbers of cattle, sheep, and horses recorded in annual reports and the 1839 Hartnell report are used to document the decline in the mission herds between 1830 and 1839 (tables 8–10). The greatest decline occurred in the cattle herds and flocks of sheep. Data on the number of cattle

Table 7. Value of Mission Estates (in pesos) at Secularization and in 1845

Mission	Value of Mission Estate at Secularization	Value of Mission Estate in 1845
San Carlos	46,022	8,269
La Purísima	61,976	25,845
Santa Cruz	85,494	975
Soledad	40,424	2,494
San Juan Bautista	138,973	7,860
San Miguel	82,806	5,875
San Fernando	35,978[a]	2,150
Santa Inés	56,437	20,287
Total	548,110	73,755

[a] Does not include lands and livestock.

Sources: Zephyrin Engelhardt, OFM, *Missions and Missionaries of California* (San Francisco, 1913–15), 3:534; Zephyrin Engelhardt, OFM, *Mission Nuestra Señora de la Soledad* (Santa Barbara, 1929), pp. 41–42; Thomas Savage, "Records in the Parish (ex-Mission) Church of Santa Cruz, Cal. Copies and Extracts by Thomas Savage for the Bancroft Library 1877," Bancroft Library, University of California, Berkeley; Zephyrin Engelhardt, OFM, *La Concepción Purísima de María Santísima* (1932), p.57; Zephyrin Engelhardt, OFM, *San Juan Bautista: A School of Church Music* (Santa Barbara, 1931), pp. 57–58; Zephyrin Engelhardt, OFM, *San Miguel Archangel: The Mission on the Highway* (Santa Barbara, 1929), p. 36; Zephyrin Engelhardt, OFM, *San Fernando Rey, The Mission of the Valley* (Ramona, 1973), pp. 50–51; Zephyrin Engelhardt, OFM, *Mission Santa Inés Virgen Martir and Its Ecclesiastical Seminary* (Santa Barbara, 1932), p. 43; and Pico Papers, Bancroft Library, University of California, Berkeley.

reported at thirteen of the twenty-one missions show a decline of 74 percent in the size of the herds in the five years between 1834 and 1839; the rate of decline varied from mission to mission. For example the San Gabriel mission herds dropped by 96 percent, whereas the Santa Clara mission herds declined by only 57 percent during the same period of time. Sheep experienced a similar decline in numbers, caused in part by a lack of workers to tend them. The overall figures for thirteen missions show a decline of 61 percent in the same five years. Finally the horse herds did not experience the same decline in numbers; figures for thirteen missions show a drop of only 2 percent over five years.

Hartnell's correspondence from the late 1830s provides examples of the ways in which the mission administrators disposed of mission livestock, particularly cattle. Settlers who received land grants obtained loans of animals to start their private herds, with the obligation to return the animals when their herds were sufficiently large. However, with changes in mission administrators, the growing control over the provincial government by the emerging landed elite, and the attempted sale of the missions in 1845 by the Pico brothers, it is doubtful whether animals lent to ranchers were ever returned. In August of 1839, Hartnell wrote to Manuel Jimeno Casarín to discuss governor Alvarado's order to lend five hundred head of cattle belonging to San José mission to José Castro.[44] Individuals also received licenses from mission administrators to slaughter range cattle on former mission lands for their hides.[45] Finally mission administrators sold cattle and sheep to buy clothing and other supplies for the missions, or they transferred animals to local settlers to satisfy outstanding debts against the mission administrations.[46] Some losses of livestock can be attributed to poor administration, the outright seizure of animals to add to the growing private herds, or to slaughter for hides. For example in July of 1839, Hartnell wrote the administrator of San Luis Rey mission, Pio Pico, to ask for an explanation for the disappearance of mission property, which included livestock not accounted for in mission accounts, and the name of the administrator during the period when the property disappeared.[47] Finally some former mission Indians did receive livestock; the Indians living at the pueblo de indios established at Los Flores collectively owned 384 cattle, sheep, horses, and goats, worth 867 pesos 6 reales.[48]

The concern of the newly independent Mexican government over the potential loss of its northern territories led to the passage of colonization laws in 1822 and 1824, designed to attract Mexican and foreign-born settlers to the frontier. One important element of the colonization policies was the concession to local governors of the authority to grant land. In the twelve years following the beginning of secularization, different regimes in California granted hundreds of thousands of acres of land to settlers in large tracts embracing thousands and in some cases tens of thousands of acres, much of the land previously undeveloped by the Franciscans or merely used as pasture for livestock. The Indians who remained at the missions follow-

Table 8. Numbers of Cattle Belonging to Selected Missions, 1830–1839

Mission	1830	1832	1834	1839
San Antonio	4,000	6,000	2,000	1,442
San Gabriel	23,500	16,500	26,000	1,062
San Luis Obispo	2,200	2,500	3,000	1,672
San Francisco	4,200	5,000	6,927	758
San Juan Capistrano	10,800	9,500	8,000	494
Santa Clara	9,000	10,000	13,000	5,560
San Buenaventura	4,500	4,050	4,500	3,068
Santa Bárbara	2,500	1,800	3,400	1,735
La Purísima	13,000	9,200	6,200	3,824
Santa Cruz	3,000	3,600	3,070	35
Soledad	4,000	6,000	6,000	544
San Miguel	3,840	3,710	4,222	990
Santa Inés	7,200	7,200	7,000	2,720
Total	91,740	85,060	93,319	23,904

Sources: Annual Reports, Santa Barbara Mission Archive-Library, Santa Barbara, California; "Mission Statistics," Bancroft Library, University of California, Berkeley; and Hartnell Mission Reports, Bancroft Library, University of California, Berkeley.

Table 9. Numbers of Sheep Belonging to Selected Missions, 1830–1839

Mission	1830	1832	1834	1839
San Antonio	10,000	10,500	11,000	2,612
San Gabriel	14,400	8,500	6,548	1,045
San Luis Obispo	1,000	5,424	3,400	2,500
San Francisco	2,000	3,500	4,122	1,272
Santa Clara	8,000	9,500	15,000	6,500
San Buenaventura	3,200	3,000	2,800	1,670
Santa Bárbara	3,400	3,200	2,624	2,250
La Purísima	6,000	3,500	6,458	1,300
Santa Cruz	4,827	5,211	4,721	1,026
Soledad	5,257	6,200	5,000	,865
San Miguel	7,428	8,282	5,796	3,800
San Luis Rey	25,136	26,100	14,600	5,960
Santa Inés	2,100	2,100	2,000	2,180
Total	92,748	95,017	84,069	32,980

Sources: See table 8.

Table 10. Numbers of Horses Belonging to Selected Missions,
1830–1839

Mission	1830	1832	1834	1839
San Antonio	944	774	500	306
San Gabriel	2,100	1,200	1,300	1,701
San Luis Obispo	1,200	700	700	1,200
San Francisco	914	1,000	1,301	967
San Juan Capistrano	135	110	50	448
Santa Clara	755	730	1,200	353
San Buenaventura	360	340	582	799
Santa Bárbara	560	480	349	609
La Purísima	275	1,000	1,200	1,532
Santa Cruz	276	400	325	127
Soledad	960	740	200	32
San Miguel	980	700	817	249
Santa Inés	280	390	400	382
Total	9,739	8,564	8,924	8,705

Sources: See Table 8.

ing secularization generally lost out in the scramble for land despite their protests, and the more developed tracts of former mission lands were the most attractive.

It would be incorrect to speak of mission lands with clearly defined boundaries; rather they formed territories in which the Franciscans oversaw the development of agriculture and ranching. Several examples demonstrate the nature of land tenure at the height of the mission regime. In the 1820s, for example, the Franciscan stationed at Soledad mission in northern Alta California noted that the mission lands extended north to south in the Salinas River Valley and east to west between the Santa Lucia and Gabilán mountains, which border the valley. It was understood that the Soledad mission lands were bounded on the northwest by the lands of San Carlos mission and on the south by the lands of San Antonio mission. Boundaries were not precise, but it was generally known where the lands of one mission ended and the lands of another began. Within the mission territory were a number of ranches identified in contemporary records by the rough distances between them and the number of livestock run at each of the ranches.[49] Similarly the missionaries stationed at Santa Cruz ran livestock at four ranches that stretched eleven leagues north to south, from Punto Año Nuevo to the San Lorenzo River, and three leagues east to west, from the ocean to the crest of the Coast Range. Most of the ranches were located on the narrow coastal plain north of the mission.[50] Finally La Purísima mission territory reportedly stretched across eighty-four square leagues, or some 149,000 hectares of land.[51]

The number of ranches and the amount of land granted in the 1830s and 1840s has been documented. It is our intention here rather to focus on Indian responses to the granting of former mission lands. William Hartnell received complaints from Indians at several missions. The case of San Miguel mission is illustrative. The Franciscans operated a number of ranches in the mission territory, including Paso Robles, Asunción, Aguaje, San Simeón, Santa Rosa, and Santa Isabel. Improvements at ranch sites included corrals and adobe structures, and most of the crops at the mission were grown at two of the ranches.[52] Paso Robles was perhaps the most important of the ranches in 1839, with a resident population of 190, engaged in the production of wheat and barley, stored in a large granary at the site. San Simeón and neighboring Santa Isabel, where most of the mission fields were located and the flocks of sheep pastured, had a population of 59. Buildings still in use included a large granary built in 1810, a chapel, and a residence for the Indian workers and the overseer assigned to the ranch. La Asunción had an orchard, and Santa Rosa was the site where most of the mission cattle and horses ran, although wild cattle could be found at several locations. Hartnell found only 112 Indians still living at the mission site itself. Several individuals petitioned for and eventually received title to the ranches of San Miguel mission, over complaints made to Hartnell by the Indians still engaged in agriculture and ranching at the disputed sites.[53]

The Spanish colonial governors had granted grazing concessions to a small number of individuals, but it was only after 1822 that local officials made titled land grants. The government also granted specific lands to the three pueblos of San José (1777), Los Angeles (1781), and Branciforte (1797), and set aside lands for the use of the military, such as pasturage for the presidio herds. However, expansion outside of the pueblo lands was impossible, as illustrated by two incidents at Branciforte. In 1803 a retired soldier named Marcelino Bravo unsuccessfully petitioned for lands in the nearby Pajaro Valley. The governor in Monterey turned down the petition, because the missions in the area and Monterey Presidio already had title. In 1817 the settlers at Branciforte had to negotiate with the missionaries at Santa Cruz mission to obtain the use of grazing lands for the growing number of livestock they owned.[54] Altogether there were some 800 land grants made in Alta California between 1822 and 1846: 20 grants made in the ten years from 1822 to 1832, another 90 between 1832 and 1836, and about 690 from 1837 until the Anglo-American conquest of Alta California began, in 1846.[55]

Table 11. Credits and Debts of Selected Alta California Missions at Secularization (in Pesos)

Mission	Date of Accounting	Credits	Debts
San Antonio	September 10, 1835	18,642	11,197
San Gabriel	November of 1834	11,154	8,271
San Francisco	July 28, 1835	2,542	7,222
Santa Bárbara	September 1834	14,953	1,000
La Purísima	March 1, 1835	3,613	1,218
Santa Cruz	December 1, 1835	3,338	4,979
Soledad	August 12, 1835	442	0
San Luis Rey	August 22, 1835	49,619	9,300
Santa Inés	July 1836	1,892	5,474
Total		106,195	48,661

Sources: Zephyrin Engelhardt, OFM, *San Antonio de Padua: The Mission in the Sierras*, Ramona, 1972, p. 65; Zephyrin Engelhardt, OFM, *San Gabriel Mission and the Beginnings of Los Angeles* (San Gabriel, 1927), p. 177; Zephyrin Engelhardt, OFM, *San Francisco or Mission Dolores* (Chicago, 1924), p. 241; Zephyrin Engelhardt, OFM, *Santa Barbara Mission* (San Francisco, 1923) p. 171; Zephyrin Engelhardt, OFM, *Mission La Concepción Purísima de María Santísima* (Santa Barbara, 1932), p. 57; Zephyrin Engelhardt, OFM, *Mission Nuestra Señora de la Soledad* (Santa Barbara, 1929), pp. 41–42; Zephyrin Engelhardt, OFM, *San Luis Rey Mission* (San Francisco, 1921), p. 98; and Zephyrin Engelhardt, OFM, *Mission Santa Inés Virgen y Martir and Its Ecclesiastical Seminary* (Santa Barbara, 1932), p. 43; and Thomas Savage, "Records in the Parish (ex-Mission, Church of Santa Cruz Cal. Copies and Extracts by Thomas Savage for the Bancroft Library 1877," Bancroft Library, University of California, Berkeley.

Credit and Debt

Until 1834 the Alta California missions produced the largest surpluses in the developing regional economy, and they became the principal creditors to the military and especially prominent settlers. Mission administrators carried active and passive debts against the missions, but in the long run there was little prospect of debts owed to the missions being collected, especially in the 1840s, when local politicians representing the emerging ranch-owning class gained firm control over the government and hence the administration of the ex-missions. On the other hand, as shown in Hartnell's reports and correspondence from 1839 and 1840, individuals with claims against the mission estates, especially the administrators, ensured the prompt payment of their claims.[56]

Table 12. Unpaid Debts Owed to Selected Alta California Missions, 1837–1840

Mission	Date of Accounting	Amount in Pesos
San Diego	June 30, 1840	2,668 p 2 r
San Carlos	October 5, 1839	160 p 2 r
San Antonio	August 6, 1839	499 p 3 r
San Gabriel	April 30, 1840	3,231 p 2 r
San Luis Obispo	July 31, 1839	987 p 6 r
San Francisco	May 13, 1840	2,615 p 1 r
San Juan Capistrano	July 22, 1840	1,556 p 7 r
Santa Clara	May 15, 1840	3,940 p 3 r
San Buenaventura	August 25, 1840	4,918 p 2 r
Santa Bárbara	June 9, 1840	1,479 p 5 r
La Purísima	July 25, 1839	3,696 p 5 r
Santa Cruz	April of 1837	593 p 4 r
Soledad	November 5, 1839	1,297 p
San José	April 22, 1840	4,621 p 3 r
San Juan Bautista	March of 1837	357 p 4 r
San Miguel	August 1, 1839	283 p 5 r
San Fernando	June 19, 1840	2,391 p
San Luis Rey	August 16, 1840	15,656 p 7 r
Santa Inés	February 1, 1840	2,079 p 3 r
San Rafael	June 1, 1840	1,967 p 6 r

Source: William Hartnell, "Razón de los créditos pasivos de las diferentes Misiones de la Alta California," Pico Papers, Bancroft Library, University of California, Berkeley.

In 1834 the missions were owed a considerable amount of money by the national government, for supplies provided to the military and by individual settlers. For example Santa Cruz mission was owed 3,338 pesos 1 real. The mission owed 4,979 pesos, primarily to merchants, individual ships, the Russian-American Company, and the military commissary in Monterey, for the purchase of manufactured goods not produced at the mission.[57] Immediately prior to secularization, nine missions were owed a total of 106,195 pesos by the military, individual settlers, and merchants and ships' captains. The outstanding debts of the same nine missions reached 48,661 pesos, leaving a net balance of 57,534 pesos (see table 11).

Foreign merchants were a source of credit, but the accumulated capital of the missions financed the expansion of the Alta California economy in the

1820s and 1830s and the creation of ranches in the 1830s and 1840s. The transfer of capital took place in the form of cash earned from the hide and tallow trade and, as seen above, in the loan of livestock, tools, etc. At the same time, the debts of the missions grew, primarily as a result of the salaries paid to the administrators and their assistants, and as a consequence of the decline of mission income as their economies contracted in the second half of the 1830s, following the large-scale exodus of converts, the decline in mission livestock, and the nonpayment of debts owed to the mission estates. Meanwhile local settlers still used the missions as sources of credit. During his inspection of the missions in 1839 and 1840, William Hartnell prepared an account of the unpaid debts owed to twenty of the twenty-one mission estates (a total of 55,003 pesos 4 reales), which constituted another form of capital transfer, since the debts remained unpaid. San Luis Rey, administered by Andrés Pico, was owed a total of 15,656 pesos 7 reales, or 29 percent of the total (see table 12).

Conclusions

The impact of the social reorganization and acculturation of the California Indians who lived in the missions can be judged in several ways: by the narrowly defined objectives of colonial policy and by the changes, both positive and negative, experienced by the Indian converts. The second also relates to the larger question of motives, for example the different motives of individual and large groups of natives to embrace mission life: what did the Spaniards offer that attracted Indians?

Spanish and later Mexican policymakers attempted to secure control over the northern frontier of New Spain to serve as a buffer against potential foreign attacks on the all-important mines. In order to achieve this goal, policy makers tried to control local Indian populations, provide an adequate defense against foreign attack and hostile Indians, attract settlers to help defend the frontier and develop the economy, and tap the labor and any surplus production to contribute to economic development. To a certain degree the California missions contributed to the political and economic objectives of the Spanish and Mexican governments. Indian labor was used to construct buildings in the presidios, and in some instances in the *pueblos,* and produced grain and other foods as well as textiles and leather goods consumed by soldier and settler alike. Labor and goods provided to the presidios substantially reduced the cost to the government of maintaining military garrisons on the distant frontier.

The question of why Indians entered the missions is more complex. Certainly coercion played a role in the relocation of Indians to the missions, as did the long-standing practice in frontier missions of bringing children or children and women to the missions to serve as leverage over parents in the first instance, or men in the second. What other factors motivated Indians to live in the missions? The interpretation that a steady food supply was a key pull factor to the missions is overly simplistic and reductionist, and to a certain extent discounts the sophisticated Indian food resource management skills. In light of the persistence of traditional Indian material culture in the missions, the attraction of European goods can be discounted.

While there is a tendency in mission historiography to focus on one or two push-pull factors that played a role in motivating Indians to move to the missions, we must consider multiple factors. Indians viewed the missionaries as powerful intermediaries to the spirit world. Political/war leaders certainly saw the Spaniards, especially soldiers, as useful allies. Low status individuals may have seen opportunities for social, political, and economic advancement in the missions.

The impact of mission life on Indian converts also varied. The rhetoric of the Serra canonization campaign and the quincentenary of Columbus's voyage to America, with the cynical resurrection in some circles of the "Black Legend" for strictly political motives, has to a certain degree clouded the issue of the impact of Spanish colonization on the native populations of the Americas. However, the evidence speaks for itself. Obviously, the day-to-day lives of the Indians changed dramatically. In housing, clothing, diet, and economy, Indian converts in the missions lived more like the sedentary peasants of central Mexico, although the California missions more closely approached the utopian ideal of primitive Christian communities that influenced several generations of Franciscans in the Americas.

The acculturation programs in the missions represented a give-and-take of cultural elements by Indian converts, which can best be seen in religion and world view. As was the case in other regions in the Americas, California Indians appear to have incorporated elements of Catholicism into their religious beliefs and practices on their own terms. The case of the fugitive Chumash community in the Central Valley after 1824 is illustrative of this. Ornaments taken from mission churches assumed considerable spiritual power, perhaps as intermediaries to the spirit world. Spanish colonization of California also modified existing religious practices, and gave rise to new beliefs and cults such as Chingichngish.

That many Indian converts found mission life unacceptable is shown by different forms of resistance to the mission regime including revolt, flight, and efforts to murder Franciscan missionaries. The Indians living in coastal California attempted to expel the unwanted visitors who allowed their animals to destroy valuable food producing plants without offering suitable compensation. This early resistance failed to overcome the political fragmentation of the coastal tribelets, but the weakening or elimination in the missions of political distinctions facilitated the organization of anti-mission conspiracies such as the one that led to the 1824 Chumash revolt, and large-scale flight.

Horrific mortality rates in the missions were the most important consequence of the congregation of Indians. Epidemic and endemic disease exacerbated by unhealthy living conditions caused chronically high mortality that in most years was higher than birth rates. To replenish the mission populations and labor force, the missionaries had to constantly resettle new converts. The obligation to supply the military with food and clothing placed considerable pressure on the Franciscans to resupply the labor force.

The policy of *congregación* contributed to high death rates in the missions in several ways. Bringing Indians to live in compact communities made it easier for disease to spread. Moreover, unsanitary conditions existed in the mission communities, especially in the dormitories for girls and women. Spaniards understood the relationship between sanitation and disease, but a policy of social control in the missions overrode concerns over poor sanitation. Moreover, although medical doctors in the eighteenth and early nineteenth centuries did not understand the pathology of diseases such as smallpox and measles that frequently reached epidemic proportions, many of the first generation of Franciscan missionaries stationed in Alta California including Junípero Serra had already observed the lethal consequence of a severe measles epidemic in the Baja California missions in 1768–69.[1] In the sixteenth century, when missionaries first observed the impact of epidemics on Indian populations, idealistic Franciscans rationalized disease as God's will.[2] Late eighteenth and early nineteenth century Franciscans, who were both pragmatic administrators as well as spiritual leaders and teachers, carried forward colonial policy despite the consequences for the Indian converts living in the missions. Indian demographic collapse in the missions was not intended but was intentional, since Franciscan *congregación* continued despite the negative impact on Indians even though one civil official, governor Diego de Borica in the 1790s, identified the problem and suggested solutions never implemented by the Franciscans.

At the end of the Mexican period in California in 1846, the Indian population of the coastal areas south of San Francisco Bay was substantially reduced in size, and disease, warfare, and recruitment to the missions reduced the size of the population of the areas on the fringes of the coastal strip controlled by Mexico. The American conquest of California in 1846 accelerated Indian population decline as miners, farmers, and ranchers settled throughout the territory carrying disease with them and waging war and in some instances virtual genocide to win control of Indian land. According to one estimate, there were as many as 71,000 Indians in California in 1848. The numbers dropped precipitously over the next decades. In 1852, there were an estimated 60,000, and 15,377 in 1900 according to the federal census of that year. The greatest decline occurred in the thirty years after 1850. Since 1900, California's Indian population has grown through natural increase and migration from other states.[3]

Alta California on the Fringes of Spanish America

As in other parts of Spanish America, the colonization of Alta California relied on the exploitation of the native population. However, California was located on the fringes of New Spain, and developed in ways different from central Mexico. A major problem throughout the Spanish and Mexican periods was the difficulty in attracting settlers, which left the Franciscans to control labor and land in the province. The continued control of Indian labor and land in turn retarded settlement and economic development, leaving the missions the dominant institution in the province until 1834. The settler population grew and the economy diversified only following the secularization of the missions after 1834, but by then it was too late to preserve California for Mexico.[4] In the 1840s, a large American community lived in California that materially contributed to the conquest of the province in 1846–47 during the Mexican-American War.[5]

Decisions made by officials in Mexico City in the early years of the colonization of Alta California contributed to the failure to settle the province. The agreement made in 1773 to return mission temporalities to the Franciscans in return for supplying the military, gave the Franciscans control over Indian land and labor. As mission agricultural and textile production expanded, the Franciscans supplied more of the clothing and food consumed in the presidios. The subsidy by the missions of the military garrisons in California during a period of a general colonial fiscal reorganization in New Spain made further colonization possible, but also prevented the development of markets for goods produced by settlers.[6] Until the 1830s, service in the presidios was the most attractive career for the majority of settlers, especially young men living in the three *pueblos* (San José, established 1777; Los Angeles, established 1781; Branciforte, established 1797) that had a limited land base.[7]

The problems faced by the settlers living in the Villa de Branciforte were typical. In 1797, the Branciforte *vecinos* received a grant of some 4,300 acres south of the San Lorenzo River that could not be easily irrigated. Monterey presidio and the Franciscan missionaries stationed at Santa Cruz and San Carlos missions controlled most of the farm and pasture land north and south of the Villa, although the vecinos apparently did have pasture lands farther south in the Pajaro Valley. Branciforte land soon became crowded by livestock, and settlers began to leave when it became clear that new lands were not available. In 1803, for example, a group of retired soldiers living at Branciforte unsuccessfully petitioned for new farm lands in the Pajaro Valley. After 1803, the number of people living at Branciforte dropped.[8]

Two factors contributed to the recovery of Branciforte after 1820. The growth of the hide and tallow trade and the culling of Branciforte cattle herds provided goods for export, and the depletion of the herds perhaps relieved pressure on community lands. In 1826, Branciforte vecinos owned 4,872 head of cattle, but apparently slaughtered nearly 4,000 animals over the next year. In 1827, only 946 cattle remained.[9] During the 1820s the population of Branciforte doubled.[10] Trade created other economic opportunities. The growth of Monterey, the provincial capital and trade center, created demand for lumber supplied primarily from redwood stands near Branciforte.[11] The second factor was the secularization of the missions, that made mission lands available to settlers who created ranches stocked from former mission herds.[12] The break-up of the mission estates and creation of ranches spurred economic growth in the Santa Cruz area and the rest of California.

The closing of the missions ushered in a new phase of development in California characterized by rapid changes for Indian and non-Indian alike. Local Mexican officials envisioned a society dominated by an elite of ranchers. This economic vision clashed with the Anglo-American frontier ethic that stressed the egalitarian self-sufficient farmer who owned 160 acres. Under Mexican rule California remained a sparsely populated frontier territory despite efforts to promote colonization. The discovery of gold in 1848 following the American conquest of California led to the rapid populating of California and statehood in 1850, and conflicts between Mexicans and Anglo-American settlers over land. Indians in the coastal area where missions previously operated were increasingly marginalized and identified by Anglo-Americans as being a part of an unwanted and despised Mexican underclass. Yet, despite the pressure for change, small numbers of Indians who had lived in the missions retained a separate identity and as best as possible attempted to preserve their culture.

Appendix I
Grain Production and Numbers of Livestock Reported at Selected Alta California Missions

This appendix contains a sample of grain production (wheat, corn, and barley) and the numbers of cattle, sheep, and horses reported at seven of the twenty-one missions, abstracted from several sources. The basic documentary source for information on economic activity in the Alta California missions is the annual report prepared by the Franciscan missionaries, which summarized the spiritual and temporal results at each mission during the calendar year. The father-president of the missions generally prepared a summary of the figures contained in the individual annual reports, a source which many scholars have consulted because of its ease of use, but the original annual reports contain important details that can help to explain the patterns recorded. For example annual reports at times explain the cause for a drop in grain production or a decline in the number of a certain type of livestock.

Two sets of annual reports exist. The Archivo General de la Nación in Mexico City has a fairly complete set of annual reports that dates from the late 1770s to 1798. The Santa Barbara Mission Archive-Library preserves a second set that dates from 1810 to 1832, except for San Juan Capistrano, and a few reports from the 1770s. In addition to the two archives mentioned above, copies of reports may be preserved in the set of records kept at each mission. The Franciscans kept what was generally called a *libro de padrones*, which either contained detailed censuses or a complete copy of each annual report for the mission. I used the libro de padrones of San Gabriel mission in the preparation of the tables contained in this appendix.

There is a ten-year gap in the set of annual reports between 1799 and 1809; nevertheless the gap does not exist for San Carlos mission, and the San Gabriel mission libro de padrones contains copies of all of the annual reports prepared, including those for 1799–1809. A complete set of annual reports existed in what had been the archive of the Alta California civil government, until it was destroyed during the 1906 San Francisco earthquake and fire. However, H. H. Bancroft had figures on grain production and numbers of livestock prepared in the 1880s. Bancroft's tables are preserved in the Bancroft Library, University of California, Berkeley.

Table A1.1: Grain Production at San Diego Mission, 1775–1832 (in fanegas and almudes)

Year	Wheat Sown	Wheat Harvested	Corn Sown	Corn Harvested	Barley Sown	Barley Harvested
1775		155				11
1777			No Harvest			
1778	12f 6a	44	1f 2a	0	8a	13
1779	12	450	2f 8a	80	3f 9a	114
1780	16f 8a	160	2f 7a	18	10f 7a	44
1781	24	800	2f 8a	74	20	700
1782	25	0	——	0	18	0
1783	27f 10a	200	1f 11a	0	36f 3a	84
1784	24	800	1f 4a	74	20	700
1785	43	367	2a	0	13	70
1786	46	808	2	0	20	305
1787	23	648	0	0	18	770
1788	62	420	4	12	20	127
1789	50	387	2f 8a	20	15	400
1790	34	203	0	50[a]	12.5	900
1791	50	3021	9a	52	15	1437
1792	60	3503	7a	72	30	1850
1793	77	4070	7a	68	30	1983
1794	54	1050	.5f	1.5f	21	230
1795	62	340	2a	0	20	30
1796	36	1460	2a	2	20	340
1797	66	2554	2a	10	24	603
1798	71.5	1028	0	0	26	525
1799	101.5	4176	4	25	25.5	1872
1800	160	1060	0	0	50	600
1801	150	700	0	0	38	400
1802	133	680	0	0	38	370
1803	132	600	.5f	7	33	100
1804	143	700	6	400	24	200
1805	137	924	5	113	32	150

Year	Sown	Harvested	Sown	Harvested	Sown	Harvested
1806	140	1428	4	158	66	1250
1807	148	800	3	70	99	900
1808	153	1800	3	70	100	1700
1809	155	193	3	40	98	——
1810	160	200	48	600	103	200
1811	168	2800	7	680	138	2600
1812	216	2168	20	500	125	1700
1813	187	300	5	400	119	350
1814	228	1800	6	320	115	2000
1815	247	1700	8	250	161	800
1816	250	2800	6	600	134	1800
1817	250	3040	9	1156	180	3400
1818	260	4124	10	1056	190	3510
1819	277	2770	12	1300	190	1300
1820	311	1720	14	1100	280	800
1821	320	7080	18	2120	304	4621
1822	200	2620	10	340	45	940
1823	320	1320	12	140	230	364
1824	350	2700	8	320	250	1370
1825	429	2623	9	600	150	1120
1826	425	1243	9	250	173	824
1827	418	2218	9	250	360	1036
1828	229	2120	11	342	189	1800
1829	220	854	12	524	156	156
1830	271	2836	10	516	124	856
1831	324	2946	9	470	152	1120
1832	260	1500	8	25	150	650

[a] Corn produced from plants planted in 1789.

Table A1.2: Grain Production at San Carlos Mission, 1774–1834
(in fanegas and almudes)

Year	Wheat		Corn		Barley	
	Sown	Harvested	Sown	Harvested	Sown	Harvested
1774	——	125	8a	150	3a	20
1775	6	253	10a	114	——	107
1778	——	338	——	27	——	508
1781	64	300	2	0	25	200
1782	50	835	6	371	20	670
1784	25	633	5	720	17	700

Table A1.2: continued

Year	Wheat		Corn		Barley	
	Sown	*Harvested*	*Sown*	*Harvested*	*Sown*	*Harvested*
1785	24	89	5	160	33	350
1786	24	440	8	167	22	969
1787	22	300	3	50	25	1215
1788	32	447	7.5	0	28	1342
1789	47	937	8	704	37	1150
1790	69.5	692	11	820	62.5	675
1791	71	221	11	150	52	536
1792	73	231	16	1400	60	204
1793	68	333	14	700	55	476
1794	62	657	12	500	48	608
1795	57.5	15	19.5	350	51.5	52
1796	81	230	17	400	65	297
1797	94	1800	25	800	55	1728
1798	60	200	11	1000	10	300
1799	150	800	15	1724	50	800
1800	56	500	21	1600	81	1025
1801	68	500	18	1200	82	1050
1802	60	240	12	600	80	1000
1803	30	200	7	200	70	1000
1804	50	900	5	220	60	1900
1805	51	2200	4	100	60	900
1806	56	827	6	25	55	900
1807	100	464	9	41	30	400
1808	40	433	1	9	50	744
1809	65	844	1	18	58	861
1810	84	682	8a	5	60	860
1811	80	865	2	70	80	975
1812	72	540	2	30	45	500
1813	65	770	2	40	7	260
1814	60	200	2	4	33	320
1815	53	511	2	24	50	400
1816	61	642	2	8	61	900
1817	54	825	1	50	61	310
1818	55	715	1	50	51	970
1819	70	750	2	60	16	800
1820	100	672	8a	25	0	0
1821	96	720	8a	80	12	100
1822	96	377	8a	6	20	323
1823	80	500	1	0	30	600

1824	70	214	8a	25	35	800
1825	68	469	3a	22	30	489
1826	80	321	1	40	40	420
1827	60	189	1	24	40	318
1828	50	400	2	0	31	475
1829	50	168	0	0	31	240
1830	50	450	1	18	40	930
1831	50	200	1	0	15	215
1832	45	188	1	3	15	196
1833	52	403	0	0	29	520
1834	50	287	0	0	38	621

Table A1.3: Grain Production at San Gabriel Mission, 1771–1834
(in fanegas and almudes)

	Wheat		Corn		Barley	
Year	Sown	Harvested	Sown	Harvested	Sown	Harvested
1771	6a[a]	0	0	0	0	0
1772	9a[a]	6	0	0	0	0
1773	5f 9a	80	10a[b]	105	0	0
1774	5	48	1f2a	240	0	0
1775	8	109f 2a	2	440	1f 2a	34
1776	11	219f 6a	2f 9a	450	0	0
1777	2a	55	5f 9a	840	0	0
1778	10f 17a[c]	350	7f 7a	837	0	0
1779	21f 1a[c]	263	2f 9a	1200	0	0
1780	27	640	10	1070	0	0
1781	40	475	13	1200	0	0
1782	50	170	10	460	0	0
1783		700	1	1100	0	0
1784	66	1701	12	1575	0	0
1785	80	1500	11	1000	0	0
1786	87	1730	14	700	0	0
1787	126	2050	14	1200	0	0
1788	85	1380	13	1100	0	0
1789	130	3084	14	1700	0	0
1790	160	2375	13	1600	0	0
1791	178	3700	16	1600	0	0
1792	200	2730	17	1600	0	0
1793	159	1990	13	400	0	0
1794	200	2400	12	800	0	0

Table A1.3 continued

1795	179	2600	12	1300	0	0
1796	218	4500	19	1000	0	0
1797	264	3300	19	300	0	0
1798	254	2800	12	500	0	0
1799	285	3000	15	800	0	0
1800	250	4000	20	2000	0	0
1801	268	3696	30	1897	0	0
1802	282	3800	17	1200	0	0
1803	282	4100	19	2500	0	0
1804	110	2600	8	1600	0	0
1805	130	1600	12	500	0	0
1806	300	4800	16	2400	0	0
1807	280	7000	9	1500	0	0
1808	80	1700	5	1000	0	0
1809	150	3700	14	2000	0	0
1810	230	4300	8	1300	0	0
1811	202	6500	12	4200	0	0
1812	200	5000	12	3000	0	0
1813	220	50	0	0	0	0
1814	92	700	14	3400	3	50
1815	270	5400	12	2100	3	92
1816	280	1200	26	6500	4	40
1817	160	4600	25	8000	4	50
1818	50	1800	0	0	4	60
1819	165	3500	4	1600	4	25
1820	165	1000	9	3200	0	0
1821	237	11000	18	7000	0	0
1822	100	800	14	3000	0	0
1823	330	3000	7	1500	0	0
1824[d]	393	2036	7	600	21	105
1825	270	2700	5	1600	0	0
1826	245	1000	8	1000	0	0
1827	103	1200	12	2200	3	19
1828	137	2200	8	1100	8	124
1829	185	1000	20	100	4	30
1830	200	2300	7	2200	16	90
1831	250	1400	6	400	2	12
1832	200	180	8	55	20	60
1833	80	1100	2	200	14	60
1834	110	2000	5	500	9	300

[a] Winter wheat planted in November-December, without the benefit of irrigation.
[b] Spring crop planted in March, April, and May, with the benefit of irrigation.
[c] Both irrigated and unirrigated wheat; after 1778, wheat crop irrigated.
[d] Crop damaged and 600 f. of beans lost.

Table A1.4: Grain Production at Santa Clara Mission, 1778–1832
(in fanegas and almudes)

	Wheat		Corn		Barley	
Year	Sown	Harvested	Sown	Harvested	Sown	Harvested
1778		76		135	—	5
1779		182		200	—	111
1782		711		70	—	55
1786	44	307	8	310	0	0
1787	48	1100	9f9a	700	4	31
1788	49	1200	8f3a	750	0	0
1789	50	1450	3	800	0	0
1790	32	1030	8.5f	600	0	0
1791	64	1400	5	900	0	0
1792	64.5f	1450	13	620	0	0
1793	100	1800	10f 8a	650	0	0
1794	87	2000	12.5f	600	0	0
1795	100	1400	10f 6a	1400	0	0
1796	196	3245	7	1000	8	12
1797	195	5000	10	400	0	0
1798	129	2000	6	300	0	0
1799	186	3000	2.5f	2	0	0
1800	125	2000	5	700	0	0
1801	124	2000	2	400	6	100
1802	129	2000	2	300	8	400
1803	134	2000	3	8000	4	200
1804	160	3000	3	600	4	200
1805	173	2800	3	600	4	200
1806	180	3000	3	300	6	200
1807	78	1400	.5f	80	4	80
1808	175	2500	4	600	6	180
1809	193	2000	2.5f	400	8	100
1810	158	2500	3	500	27	1200
1811	180	2600	2	350	8	200
1812	175	3000	2	600	10	200
1813	200	3500	3	1500	9	1000
1814	209	3300	4	800	11	1150
1815	215	3600	4	900	15	300
1816	205	3450	5	800	12	150
1817	185	3080	4	100	15	300
1818	200	3200	5	1200	12	300
1819	208	3300	6	500	15	200
1820	220	3000	6	700	20	400

1821	208	3600	6	550	18	900
1822	195	1400	6	450	20	700
1823	108	1800	7	650	20	460
1825	188	2190	6	400	18	300
1826	187	809	7	300	18	600
1827	200	2000	6	400	15	200
1828	185	3500	7	550	10	500
1829	80	272	8	600	25	0
1830	85	2220	7	500	30	2000
1831	95	2400	4	60	5	60
1832	110	3900	4	400	2	175

Table A1.5: Grain Production at La Purísima Mission, 1789–1832 (in fanegas)

	Wheat		Corn		Barley	
Year	Sown	Harvested	Sown	Harvested	Sown	Harvested
1789	15	331	2	357	0	0
1790	25	530	3	521	0.5	16
1791	76	800	4	653	0	0
1792	61	602	4	891	0	0
1793	55	1102	6	200	0	0
1794	68	1254	2	549	0	0
1795	96	308	3	502	0	0
1796	75	1250	2	15	0	0
1797	65	1700	2	0	0	0
1798	92	1900	0.5	38	0	0
1799	92	2500	1	15	1	70
1800	69	1200	1	160	0	0
1801	165	1600	10	130	0.16	8
1802	96	1000	1	160	0.16	5
1803	161	500	1	125	0	0
1804	230	3000	3	130	0	0
1805	140	3000	2	100	0	0
1806	300	1200	3	200	10	50
1807	400	1000	3	400	10	50
1808	177	2000	5	450	3	10
1809	175	1800	6	600	6	60

1810	200	3000	4	506	13	360
1811	180	3000	4	450	25	800
1812	150	3000	1	50	0	0
1813	150	3600	7	2000	100	2000
1814	100	200	6	2000	0	0
1815	180	2000	6	400	3	50
1816	123	2500	8	10	18	600
1817	157	2800	8	1000	39	500
1818	250	3000	2	200	12	200
1819	180	2900	6	900	6	200
1820	208	2435	4	0	0	0
1821	240	4000	6	400	13	334
1822	150	1587	7	900	0	0
1823	150	1500	4	200	0	0
1824	112	1100	4	120	0	0
1825	90	2000	5	200	3	30
1826	150	2000	4	80	0	0
1827	120	2000	4	800	12	60
1828	102	1000	7	200	15	58
1829	90	300	4	400	10	80
1830	50	500	4	300	12	50
1831	70	700	4	100	14	56
1832	60	500	4	100	11	45

Table A1.6: Grain Production at San Miguel Mission, 1798–1832 (in fanegas)

	Wheat		Corn		Barley	
Year	Sown	Harvested	Sown	Harvested	Sown	Harvested
1798	20	228	10a	20	0	0
1799	44	850	1a	12	.5f	14
1800	42	900	1	400	0	0
1801	59	797	1.5f	500	1	20
1802	70	1600	2	200	0	0
1803	103	2000	2	150	0	0
1804	73	2100	1	19	0	0
1805	134	2554	1.5f	30	0	0
1806	134	4700	2	30	0	0
1807	119	1309	2	100	8	70

Table A1.6 continued

1808	100	1272	1.5f	200	3	60
1809	147	240	2	200	16	2
1810	145	3157	22	250	37	1402
1811	71	1200	3	300	12	266
1812	100	302	2	270	9	26
1813	140	1993	0	0	19	74
1814	164	1000	.53	370	19	9
1815	96	1623	.50	198	35	417
1816	95	1650	.53	127	18	200
1817	105	1256	.53	38	0	0
1818	91	1441	1	71	12	195
1819	99	700	12	200	26	40
1820	160	949	2	70	29	29
1821	183	2813	1	13	24	259
1822	131	400	6	23	34	20
1823	131	1400	6	23	34	20
1824	159	1200	2	12	8	12
1825	290	1769	3	14	7	340
1826	98	1345	1	20	32	63
1827	190	997	1	4	33	349
1828	146	771	3	300	38	361
1829	90	142	5	15	50	0
1830	60	706	6	50	33	818
1831	100	599	1	36	39	51
1832	90	285	6	276	40	674

Table A1.7: Grain Production at Santa Inés Mission, 1804–1832 (in fanegas)

Year	Wheat		Corn		Barley	
	Sown	Harvested	Sown	Harvested	Sown	Harvested
1804	37	800	2	250	0	0
1805	72	1040	2	180	0.16	4
1806	95	259	3	200	0	0
1807	58	157	4	380	1	17
1808	56	500	4	500	0.5	1
1809	62	700	5	600	0	0
1810	70	1400	6	1200	20	160

1811	115	3000	6	3000	0	0
1812	90	3400	5	3000	0	0
1813	47	2000	3	1000	0	0
1814	34	1000	4	1000	4	60
1815	100	2000	4	400	4	50
1816	60	1200	3	300	4	60
1817	140	2500	8	2600	0	0
1818	150	900	5	2000	3	200
1819	90	2000	2	1000	13	600
1820	100	900	4	1200	0	0
1821	100	3600	5	600	13	800
1822	60	1500	5	1000	0	0
1823	80	1000	6	1000	0	0
1824	60	600	3	400	12	300
1825	150	2400	4	800	11	200
1826	92	1047	2	700	0	0
1827	51	1200	3	400	0	0
1828	58	1200	4	140	0	0
1829	58	200	11	800	0	0
1830	104	1800	6	500	1	16
1831	50	800	6	400	0	0
1832	106	1282	5	300	0	0

Table A1.8: Livestock Reported at San Diego Mission, 1776–1832

Year	Cattle	Index (1810=100)	Sheep	Index (1810=100)	Horses	Index (1810=100)
1776	102	3	304	3	54	12
1777	138	5	244	3	86	18
1778	106	4	343	4	64	14
1779	198	7	450	5	112	24
1780	250	8	630	7	104	22
1781	500	17	1,100	11	256	55
1782	366	12	818	9	188	40
1783	415	14	900	9	209	45
1784	320	11	802	8	142	30
1785	558	19	727	8	262	56
1786	605	20	936	10	278	59
1787	708	24	1,025	11	284	60
1788	1,003	33	1,600	11	354	75
1789	1,192	40	1,875[a]	——	384	82
1790	1,306	44	1,583	16	437	93
1791	2,063	69	2,136	22	494	105
1792	2,503	83	2,426	25	568	121
1793	3,325	111	3,114	32	620	132

Table A1.8 continued

1794	3,516	117	2,600	27	669	142
1795	3,618	121	2,390	25	761	162
1796	3,220	107	2,713	28	544[b]	116
1797	5,000	167	4,020	42	693	148
1798	5,260	175	4,873	51	860	183
1799	5,836	195	5,080	53	600	128
1800	6,000	200	6,000	62	877	187
1801	6,050	201	6,020	63	843	179
1802	6,050	201	6,000	62	900	192
1803	5,000	167	3,000	31	780	166
1804	4,387	146	5,408	56	778	166
1805	4,415	147	5,519	57	796	169
1806	4,458	149	5,640	59	850	181
1807	4,538	151	6,760	70	640	136
1808	4,362	145	9,260	96	696	148
1809	3,000	100	8,740	91	480	102
1810	3,000	100	9,625	100	470	100
1811	2,900	97	9,132	95	406	86
1812	3,128	104	9,344	97	458	98
1813	3,240	108	9,260	96	438	93
1814	3,560	119	9,662	100	528	112
1815	4,234	141	10,400	108	601	128
1816	3,700	123	10,200	106	650	138
1817	4,816	161	12,570	131	760	162
1818	6,224	208	14,674	153	850	181
1819	7,111	237	16,711	174	730	155
1820	8,120	271	14,512	151	870	185
1821	8,436	281	17,000	177	1,060	226
1822	9,245	308	19,000	197	1,174	250
1823	8,120	271	18,024	187	969	206
1824	8,536	285	19,000	197	845	180
1825	8,120	271	19,420	202	665	142
1826	8,620	287	18,620	193	830	177
1827	9,120	304	16,284	169	987	210
1828	8,136	271	16,566	172	1,063	226
1829	8,200	273	15,120	157	917	195
1830	7,630	254	16,120	168	1,050	223
1831	6,220	207	17,624	183	1,196	255
1832	4,500	150	13,250	138	220	47

[a] Includes goats.
[b] Non-Christian Indians ran off a part of the mission horse herds.

Table A1.9: Livestock Reported at San Carlos Mission, 1775-1834

Year	Cattle	Index (1810=100)	Sheep	Index (1810=100)	Horses	Index (1810=100)
1775	101	5	——	——	19	5
1778	248	12	48	1	64	16
1779	254	12	51	1	64	16
1783	500	24	110	2	110	27
1785	600	29	160	3	172	42
1786	600	29	180	3	200	49
1787	609	29	196	3	170	42
1788	710	34	303	5	199	49
1789	1027	49	735	12	230	57
1790	1082	52	900	15	281	69
1791	1193	57	1140	19	272	67
1792	1460	70	1254	21	309	76
1793	2000	95	1600	27	524	129
1794	2300	110	1577	26	610	150
1795	2362	113	1137	19	701	173
1796	2280	109	1205	20	913	225
1797	1417	68	1740	29	850	209
1798	730	35	3200	53	950	234
1799	900	43	3000	50	910	224
1800	1200	57	4000	67	950	234
1801	1200	57	5000	83	972	239
1802	1200	57	6000	100	975	240
1803	1600	76	6000	100	940	232
1804	2000	95	6000	100	900	222
1805	2000	95	7000	117	900	222
1806	2000	95	7000	117	1024	252
1807	2100	100	7000	117	594	146
1808	2150	102	7000	117	466	115
1809	2300	110	7000	117	354	87
1810	2100	100	6000	100	406	100
1811	2100	100	4000	67	334	82
1812	2200	105	3500	58	313	77
1813	2360	112	2300	38	294	72
1814	2400	114	2513	42	290	71
1815	2400	114	2527	42	390	96
1816	2500	119	2600	43	410	101
1817	2800	133	2700	45	420	103
1818	2900	138	2400	40	420	103
1819	3000	143	4000	67	450	110
1820	3000	143	4000	67	430	106
1821	3000	143	4000	67	483	119
1822	2230	106	4000	67	360	89
1823	2240	107	5000	83	400	99

Table A1.9 continued

1824	2000	95	5400	90	508	125
1825	1500	71	5450	91	570	140
1826	2000	95	5400	90	580	143
1827	2000	95	5050	84	620	153
1828	1200	57	4450	74	640	158
1829	1440	69	3200	53	320	79
1830	2150	102	3800	63	440	108
1831	2050	98	4400	73	470	116
1832	2100	100	3300	55	410	101
1833	1943	93	4805	80	474	117
1834	1981	94	4927	82	490	121

Table A1.10: Livestock Reported at San Gabriel Mission, 1780–1832

Year	Cattle	Index	Sheep	Index	Horses	Index
		(1810=100)		(1810=100)		(1810=100)
1780	450	5	500	5	100	14
1781	500	5	820	9	69	10
1782	600	6	968	10	96	13
1783	750	8	1,300	14	84	12
1784	900	9	1,500	16	150	21
1785	1,200	12	2,040	22	141	20
1786	1,540	16	3,200	34	156	22
1787	1,850	19	2,900	31	204	28
1788	2,200	22	3,200	34	239	33
1789	2,890	30	3,578	38	413	57
1790	3,800	39	4,980	52	411	57
1791	4,523	46	6,276	66	471	65
1792	4,750	49	7,250	76	615	85
1793	5,050	52	8,500	90	630	88
1794	5,500	56	9,050	95	785	109
1795	5,800	59	9,200	97	915	127
1796	6,090	62	10,546	111	960	133
1797	6,200	63	11,350	120	1,160	161
1798	6,060	62	11,500	121	1,210	168
1799	6,000	61	11,000	116	1,120	156
1800	5,900	60	12,100	127	1,080	150
1801	6,000	61	12,500	132	1,290	179
1802	7,500	77	13,040	137	1,360	189
1803	9,500	97	13,000	137	1,630	226
1804	8,000	82	13,000	137	1,985	276
1805	8,000	82	9,000	95	2,018	280
1806	8,050	82	10,000	105	1,274	177
1807	9,500	97	10,000	105	1,605	223

1808	9,600	98	10,000	105	1,045	145
1809	8,000	82	9,000	95	918	128
1810	9,800	100	9,500	100	720	100
1811	11,000	112	10,000	105	850	118
1812	12,000	122	10,000	105	810	113
1813	13,000	133	11,000	116	920	128
1814	13,500	138	10,000	105	580	81
1815	13,600	139	10,300	108	639	89
1816	12,900	132	10,500	111	560	78
1817	13,000	133	10,300	108	630	88
1818	15,000	153	11,000	116	830	115
1819	16,000	163	13,000	137	888	123
1820	15,000	153	12,000	126	456	63
1821	14,000	143	13,000	137	600	83
1822	13,848	141	12,900	136	598	83
1823	13,625	139	12,100	127	609	85
1824	13,304	136	11,000	116	510	71
1825	13,895	142	7,068	74	525	73
1826	15,900	162	10,000	105	724	101
1827	18,400	188	14,000	147	2,400	333
1828	26,300	268	13,500	142	2,035	283
1829	25,000	255	15,000	158	2,000	278
1830	23,500	240	14,400	152	2,100	292
1831	20,500	209	13,554	143	1,700	236
1832	16,500	168	8,500	90	1,200	167

Table A1.11: Livestock Reported at Santa Clara Mission, 1779–1832

Year	Cattle	Index (1810=100)	Sheep	Index (1810=100)	Horses	Index (1810=100)
1779	187	3	44	4		
1782	418	7	158	2	42	2
1786	398	6	700	7	69	4
1787	1,264	20	550	6	155	8
1788	1,550	25	720	7	169	9
1789	1,990	32	800	8	178	9
1790	2,413	38	800	8	230	12
1791	3,000	48	800	8	391	21
1792	4,200	67	800	8	610	32
1793	4,200	67	1,300	13	——	——
1794	4,200	67	1,000	10	628	33
1795	4,100	65	1,350	14	680	36
1796	3,100	49	2,100	21	750	39
1797	3,025	48	3,000	30	520	27

Table A1.11 continued

1798	3,000	48	3,150	32	500	26
1799	3,200	51	4,000	40	570	30
1800	4,000	63	5,000	50	789	41
1801	4,000	63	5,000	50	1,000	52
1802	5,000	79	6,000	60	1,700	89
1803	5,000	79	7,000	70	2,200	115
1804	6,000	95	7,000	70	2,599	136
1805	6,050	96	7,000	70	2,312	121
1806	7,000	111	9,000	90	2,349	123
1807	7,000	111	9,000	90	2,300	120
1808	6,900	109	9,000	90	2,095	110
1809	6,260	99	10,000	100	2,312	121
1810	6,321	100	9,999	100	1,910	100
1811	6,550	103	10,250	103	2,800	147
1812	6,400	101	10,300	103	2,320	122
1813	6,120	97	10,000	100	1,250	65
1814	5,200	82	9,500	95	1,285	67
1815	5,200	82	10,100	101	1,260	66
1816	4,900	78	10,200	102	1,140	60
1817	4,000	63	10,500	105	1,080	56
1818	3,120	51	10,200	102	925	48
1819	3,500	55	11,100	111	850	45
1820	4,300	68	12,000	120	850	45
1821	4,500	71	13,000	130	795	42
1822	5,500	87	15,000	150	850	45
1823	6,050	96	13,000	130	795	42
1825	7,200	114	14,000	140	840	44
1826	9,336	148	14,000	140	845	44
1827	10,000	158	12,000	120	860	45
1828	14,500	229	15,500	155	850	45
1829	13,000	206	14,000	140	725	38
1830	9,000	142	8,000	80	755	40
1831	9,000	142	7,000	70	780	41
1832	10,000	158	9,500	95	730	38

Table A1.12: Livestock Reported at La Purísima Mission, 1788–1832

Year	Cattle	Index	Sheep	Index	Horses	Index
		(1810=100)		(1810=100)		(1810=100)
1788	94	1	191	2	53	5
1789	124	2	371	4	74	7
1790	169	2	464	5	88	8
1791	232	3	603	6	106	10

1792	311	4	626	6	105	10
1793	380	5	1,142	11	168	15
1794	451	6	1,587	16	171	16
1795	607	8	1,503	15	182	17
1796	700	9	2,200	22	208	19
1797	900	11	3,300	33	228	21
1798	1,016	13	3,700	37	244	22
1799	1,400	18	4,000	40	264	24
1800	1,600	20	4,000	40	298	27
1801	2,000	25	4,300	43	338	31
1802	2,640	33	5,400	54	370	34
1803	3,230	40	5,400	54	357	33
1804	3,736	47	4,967	50	398	36
1805	4,372	55	6,800	68	440	40
1806	5,000	63	6,000	60	640	58
1807	5,000	63	7,000	70	780	71
1808	7,000	88	10,000	100	890	81
1809	10,000	125	11,000	110	1,445	131
1810	8,000	100	10,000	100	1,100	100
1811	7,000	88	9,000	90	1,080	98
1812	4,000	50	12,000	120	1,150	105
1813	5,000	63	12,000	120	1,160	106
1814	8,000	100	12,000	120	1,160	106
1815	8,000	100	12,000	120	1,110	100
1816	8,500	106	11,000	110	1,217	111
1817	8,500	106	11,500	115	1,300	118
1818	9,000	113	12,000	120	1,300	118
1819	9,000	113	12,000	120	1,110	101
1820	9,500	119	12,600	126	1,305	119
1821	11,000	138	11,000	110	1,344	122
1822	10,000	125	11,000	110	1,463	133
1824	10,500	131	10,000	100	1,445	131
1825	6,000	75	8,365	84	330	30
1826	10,100	125	6,150	62	1,200	109
1827	10,202	128	9,000	90	——	——
1828	10,200	128	9,000	90	1,000	91
1829	8,000	100	6,000	60	1,000	91
1830	13,000	163	6,000	60	——	——
1831	10,500	131	7,000	70	1000	91
1832	9,200	115	3,500	35	1000	91

Table A1.13: Livestock Reported at San Miguel Mission, 1797–1832

Year	Cattle	Index (1810=100)	Sheep	Index (1810=100)	Horses	Index (1810=100)
1797	130	3	535	5	76	14
1798	150	3	105	1	76	14
1799	202	4	1,000	9	80	15
1800	203	4	1,570	14	160	30
1801	302	6	2,451	22	232	43
1802	606	13	3,099	28	283	52
1803	809	17	3,233	29	342	63
1804	1,000	21	4,000	36	465	86
1805	1,400	30	6,309	57	450	83
1806	1,712	36	7,012	64	324	60
1807	3,000	64	8,098	74	426	79
1808	4,000	85	9,000	82	502	93
1809	4,000	85	11,000	100	488	90
1810	4,700	100	11,000	100	540	100
1811	6,000	128	13,000	118	400	74
1812	6,300	134	13,500	123	535	99
1813	6,000	128	12,000	109	638	118
1814	7,528	160	13,584	124	756	140
1815	8,000	170	13,502	123	922	171
1816	8,077	172	13,467	122	773	143
1817	8,600	183	12,500	114	911	169
1818	7,139	152	12,718	116	984	182
1819	8,000	170	14,079	128	1,220	226
1820	8,100	172	14,000	127	1,255	232
1821	9,000	192	13,500	123	1,451	269
1822	10,558	225	12,000	109	1,560	289
1823	7,057	150	13,096	119	1,549	287
1824	4,092	87	11,024	100	1,500	278
1825	2,099	45	8,332	76	1,450	269
1826	3,068	65	6,649	61	1,526	283
1827	2,190	47	7,904	72	1,570	291
1828	4,393	93	8,223	75	1,555	288
1829	4,000	85	6,479	59	1,400	259
1830	3,840	82	7,428	68	980	182
1831	3,762	80	8,999	82	950	176
1832	3,170	67	8,282	75	700	130

Table A1.14: Livestock Reported at Santa Inés Mission, 1804–1834

Year	Cattle	Index (1810=100)	Sheep	Index (1810=100)	Horses	Index (1810=100)
1804	500	16	1017	44	146	35
1805	1330	42	1500	65	170	41
1806	1832	57	1600	70	287	68
1807	2300	72	1701	74	229	55
1808	2500	78	1800	78	269	64
1809	3000	94	2000	87	305	73
1810	3200	100	2300	100	420	100
1811	3300	103	3000	130	500	119
1812	3300	103	5000	217	560	133
1813	3400	106	5200	226	620	148
1814	4000	125	5300	230	660	157
1815	4400	138	5600	244	700	167
1816	5000	156	5000	217	800	191
1817	6000	188	5000	217	770	183
1818	6000	188	5500	239	540	129
1819	6000	188	5500	239	580	138
1820	7000	218	5000	217	600	143
1821	6000	188	6000	261	630	150
1822	6500	203	3500	152	710	169
1823	6000	188	3000	130	740	176
1824	5800	181	2400	104	740	176
1825	6000	188	2800	122	736	175
1826	6400	200	2700	117	218	52
1827	6500	203	3600	157	370	88
1828	7000	218	3000	130	300	71
1829	7100	222	2800	122	270	64
1830	7200	225	2100	91	280	67
1831	7300	228	2200	96	320	76
1832	7200	225	2100	91	390	93
1833	7000	218	2100	91	350	83
1834	7000	218	2000	87	400	95

Appendix 2
Crude Birth and Death Rates per 1,000 Population for Seven Alta California Missions

Appendix 2. Crude Birth and Death Rates per 1,000 population for Seven Alta California Missions

Year	San Carlos		San Antonio		S.Luis Obispo		Santa Cruz		Soledad		S.Juan Bautista		San Miguel	
	BR	DR	BR	DR	BR	DR	BR	DR	BR	DR	BR	DR	BR	DR
1772			0	80										
1773	25	123	56	22										
1774			54	62										
1775	33	87	56	96	42	63								
1776	46	9	46	85										
1777			29	134										
1778			34	53										
1779			58	32										
1780	33	86	65	34	55	35								
1781			42	76										
1782			44	46										
1783	19	58	47	61										
1784	38	72	69	79										
1785	56	107	52	100	70	56								
1786	41	97	55	79	53	33								
1787	45	52	47	34	31	46								
1788	24	27	63	46	51	36								
1789	44	65	62	33	43	40								
1790	42	138	66	56	43	38								
1791	58	86	43	100	35	92	11	56						
1792	66	101	57	47	35	65	25	38	102	85				
1793	45	54	62	38	30	27								

Appendix 2. (continued)

Year	San Carlos		San Antonio		S.Luis Obispo		Santa Cruz		Soledad		S.Juan Bautista		San Miguel	
	BR	DR	BR	DR	BR	DR	BR	DR	BR	DR	BR	DR	BR	DR
1794	58	66	43	36	33	47	47	116	47	108				
1795	59	66	30	41	32	65	48	226	52	62				
1796	22	67	26	44	31	68	28	180	21	71				
1797	33	62	32	43	25	58	25	122	28	93				
1798	48	57	37	71	24	71	32	129	59	127	94	118		
1799	52	85	35	79	42	101	28	139	52	130	68	112	83	154
1800	51	29	59	72	29	98	24	109	41	74	55	43	69	50
1801	31	72	40	63	39	109	21	106	16	98	29	56	46	126
1802	23	119	37	123	33	98	32	138	23	225	36	116	29	133
1803	31	83	43	71	53	102	32	76	18	71	46	113	54	85
1804	27	76	23	83	41	70	28	112	11	96	22	112	36	77
1805	36	75	57	78	35	49	28	115	13	105	59	101	47	51
1806	26	143	36	118	30	107	32	226	7	164	27	179	18	84
1807	35	75	43	93	34	76	26	114	16	94	53	89	50	32
1808	40	91	35	68	43	55	31	100	8	77	23	87	32	55
1809	35	98	59	61	33	70	12	101	6	61	26	80	41	47
1810	32	83	34	53	26	60	25	136	17	87	31	94	37	49
1811	45	92	53	70	44	77	18	111	12	84	39	90	44	75
1812	35	91	48	63	43	65	20	65	14	89	47	89	35	43
1813	42	59	50	67	33	89	18	112	20	55	52	82	39	53
1814	34	74	44	73	41	78	15	65	26	66	32	74	27	50
1815	60	69	43	79	38	78	28	95	21	90	56	102	30	71

Appendix 2. (continued)

Year	San Carlos		San Antonio		S.Luis Obispo		Santa Cruz		Soledad		S.Juan Bautista		San Miguel	
	BR	DR	BR	DR	BR	DR	BR	DR	BR	DR	BR	DR	BR	DR
1816	43	88	57	81	31	62	33	93	20	76	57	95	29	56
1817	62	72	42	65	27	64	39	92	34	64	70	61	41	66
1818	47	75	34	78	46	88	52	76	32	74	40	86	30	61
1819	77	56	51	73	50	68	32	117	19	89	69	119	49	49
1820	42	95	41	68	34	87	50	87	34	77	97	55	38	67
1821	53	68	42	46	26	56	28	67	12	62	76	121	36	63
1822	32	120	42	89	22	73	39	75	24	122	58	129	42	76
1823	59	103	52	72	26	62	32	106	47	55	43	72	42	50
1824	57	107	43	55	24	80	34	101	24	65	45	91	40	58
1825	56	95	52	60	12	101	39	111	25	109	25	83	23	66
1826	64	58	43	104	15	94	28	75	20	82	30	77	30	52
1827	40	47	52	71	11	72	23	68	12	76	28	71	33	54
1828	40	186	30	73	12	58	24	149	16	139	23	205	22	125
1829	56	64	34	44	18	79	8	113	15	54	34	59	42	67
1830	60	64	31	65	13	84	36	87	15	64	29	51	28	62
1831	31	39	31	60	32	95	28	103	15	102	29	84	34	75
1832	53	57	26	58	15	143	24	118	12	77	38	74	16	47
1833	65	50	31	89	22	130	21	56	15	139	47	104	27	126
1834	77	60	28	102	10	94	51	64	26	145	44	68	35	148
1835	67	49	26	62	42	175	13	80			55	75	22	124
1836			32	91										

Appendix 3
The Development of Building Complexes and Social Policy in the Alta California Missions

> I did it [rebuilt California missions] the way they would have done it
> if they'd had a little money. [Harry Downie][1]

For tourists the restored or reconstructed tile-roofed structures at the different mission sites in California evoke images of a romantic Hispanic past. Scholars have analyzed mission buildings as examples of colonial Spanish architecture that contributed to the emergence in the early years of the present century to a new secular architectural style known as "mission revival."[2] Or else mission churches alone are examined as examples of religious architecture.[3] Archaeologists have excavated mission-building complexes in some instances in preparation for the stabilization of existing ruins or to define the dimensions of buildings slated for reconstruction.[4]

Mission-building complexes rarely come under scholarly scrutiny as manifestations of Spanish colonial policy. In other words mission-building complexes reflected the functionalism of the mission as an independent community, but also the ways in which missionaries attempted to enhance social control over Indian converts. This appendix examines the development of the mission-building complexes in the Alta California missions with reference to the types of buildings constructed, the chronology of building construction, and the ways in which mission-building complexes enhanced social control over the Indian converts. Detailed annual reports prepared by Franciscan missionaries stationed in Alta California contained details of building construction, although the completeness of the data varies from year to year and from missionary to missionary. However, there is enough information to reliably reconstruct a general picture of the development of the Alta California mission-building complexes. This is followed by summaries of building construction at each of the twenty-one missions.

The single structure most frequently associated with missions is the church. Moreover since different bodies within the Catholic church control the majority of the mission sites (eighteen out of twenty-one), the religious aspect of mission history is stressed and at times glorified. Even in recent years, reconstruction of churches has enjoyed priority over the reconstruction or restoration of other buildings from the mission complexes, as evidenced by the rebuilding from the foundations up in the mid-1980s of the San Jose Mission church destroyed by an earthquake and the construction at San Juan Capistrano of a replica of the great stone church destroyed by an earthquake in 1812.

Tables A3.1–A3.3 summarize data abstracted from the annual reports on the construction of churches at the Alta California missions. Altogether the Franciscans directed the building of sixty-eight churches, or an average of slightly more than three built at each establishment. Churches were built of a variety of materials. Twenty-one were temporary structures, built at fifteen missions, of wattle and daub (*palizada*) or wood. The most common material was sun-dried adobe bricks, used in forty-four churches (65 percent). Finally three churches (at San Carlos, San Gabriel, and San Juan Capistrano) were built primarily of stone (several other churches were built with some stone, but adobe was still the primary building material).

The Franciscans directed the building of the final church, usually the largest, at each mission, only when the main mission complex had taken shape. Fifteen (75 percent) were built ten years after the establishment of the mission, and eight (38 percent) were built twenty years following the founding of the mission. While important as spiritual centers for the mission communities, the large churches were not major projects that took labor away from other important activities, such as agriculture, ranching, and textile production. The building of thirteen churches (62 percent) took less than five years, while only two (at San Gabriel and San Buenaventura) took more than ten years. The average construction period was 4.8 years. When abundant labor was available, the building of a church could take as little time as one year, but in many cases the construction period was extended because labor was assigned to other activities.

The missions were self-sufficient communities, where a variety of economic activities took place—farming, ranching, and the production of textiles and leather goods. The importance of these activities can be measured by the number of structures built for these activities. The missions produced large quantities of grain for consumption at the missions as well as for distribution to the local military garrisons and settlers. The extant annual reports contain references to the building of 101 granaries, or an average of more than 4 (4.8) per mission (see table A3.4). The Franciscans also organized ranchos (farming stations and livestock ranches) at different locations within the territory assigned to each mission. There are references to the construction of buildings at twenty-one mission ranchos.

Disease claimed the lives of many Indians brought to live at the missions. To deal with the high rates of illness, the Franciscans directed the construction of hospitals to provide care for sick Indians. There are specific references to the building of thirteen medical facilities at the missions (see table A3.4), although similar facilities may have been located at other missions.

Buildings were also designed to control the Indian population, such as dormitories built to house children and/or single women, soldiers' barracks, and permanent adobe housing for Indian families, which in some instances were surrounded by high walls (see table A3.5). There are thirty-two specific references to the construction of Indian dormitories at the missions: fifteen (47 percent) within the first five years of the establishment of the missions and twenty (63 percent) within the first ten years of the establishment of the missions. Most were dormitories for girls and single women, reflecting Franciscan concerns over what they considered to be the promiscuity of Indian women. Soldiers' barracks were built at most missions to house the permanent detachment (*escolta*) stationed at each mission to ensure discipline among the Indian converts. There are twenty-three specific references to the construction of soldiers' barracks, ten (44 percent) within the first ten years of the establishment of missions.

One major multiyear construction project at all of the missions was the building of permanent adobe housing for Indian families, which took the form of small houses, row houses, or long multiple-apartment buildings. The Franciscans had Indian family housing built once the mission complex took shape; in the case of some of the older missions, the building of housing began two to three decades following the establishment of the mission. At six of the missions, the building of Indian housing began twenty-five years or more after the establishment of the missions.

Several European visitors to the California missions left graphic descriptions of Indian housing. In the late 1820s, Beechy described Indian housing in the Alta California missions: "The buildings are variously laid out, and adapted in size to the number of Indians which they contain; some are enclosed by a high wall, as at San Carlos, while others consist merely of a few rows of huts, built with sun-burnt mud bricks. . . . It is only the married persons and officers of the establishment who are allowed these huts, the bachelors and spinsters having large places of their own, where they are separately incarcerated every night."[5]

In early 1792, Menzies described family Indian housing at San Francisco and Santa Clara missions, documenting the transition from housing con structed of traditional native materials to more permanent adobe structures.

> Their Habitations or Wigwams were aptly compared to a crouded
> cluster of Bee-hives each of which was of a hemispherical form about
> nine feet high & nearly the same in diameter & consisted of slender
> sticks or rods stuck in the ground & lashed together with thongs into
> the above form & afterwards closely thatched all round with Bul-
> rushes, excepting a small hole left on one side just sufficient to creep
> in at . . . [At Santa Clara t]hey saw a crowded Indian village close to
> the Mission, composed of mean huts of Wigwams similar in form &
> materials to those we have already described at the Mission of San
> Francisco . . . They were at this time building for themselves . . . a
> long row of Homes similar to those of the Spaniards, with two snug
> apartments in each . . . [6]

More than twenty years later, in 1816, Kotzebue described Indian housing in San Francisco mission in the following terms: "After dinner they
showed us the habitations of the Indians, consisting of long, low houses,
built of bricks, and forming several streets. The uncleanliness in these barracks baffles description, and this is perhaps the cause of the great mortality
. . . The Indian girls, of whom 400 are in the mission, live separate from the
men, likewise in such barracks . . . "[7]

A decade later F.W. Beechey offered a grim appraisal of Indian housing at
San Francisco Mission: "Their hovels afforded scarcely any protection against
the weather, and were black with smoke: some of the Indians were sleeping
on the greasy floor; others were grinding baked acorns to make into cakes,
which constitute a large portion of their food."[8]

Notes

1. Quoted in David Hurst Thomas, "Harvesting Ramona's Garden: Life
in California's Mythical Mission Past," in David Hurst Thomas, ed., *Columbian Consequences: The Spanish Borderlands in Pan-American Perspective*
(Washington, D.C., 1991), pp. 119–57.

2. See, for example, Rexford Newcomb, *Spanish-Colonial Architecture
in the United States* (New York, 1937); Rexford Newcomb, *The Old Mission
Churches and Historic Houses of California* (Philadelphia, 1925); Rexford
Newcomb, *Franciscan Mission Architecture of California*, reprint ed. (New
York, 1988); Frances Rand Smith, *The Architectural History of Mission San
Carlos Borromeo* (Berkeley, 1921). See also Thomas, "Harvesting Ramona's
Garden."

3. See, for example, George Kubler, *The Religious Architecture of New*

Mexico in the Colonial Period and Since the American Occupation (Colorado Springs, 1940).

4. See, for example, Joseph Toulouse, *The Mission of San Gregorio de Abo: A Report on the Excavation and Repair of a Seventeenth-Century New Mexico Mission* (Albuquerque, 1949); and Alden Hayes, *The Four Churches of Pecos* (Albuquerque, 1974).

5. F. W. Beechey, *Narrative of a Voyage to the Pacific* (London, 1831) 1:16.

6. Alice Eastwood, ed., "Menzie's California Journal," *California Historical Society Quarterly* 2(1924):265–340.

7. August Mahr, *The Visit of the "Rurick" to San Francisco in 1816* (Stanford, 1932), p. 325.

8. Beechey, *Narrative,* 1:20.

Table A3.1 Number of Churches Built at the Alta
California Missions

Mission	Wattle & Daub, Wood	Adobe	Stone
San Diego	2	2	0
San Carlos	2	2	1
San Antonio	1	2	0
San Gabriel	1	2	1
S. L. Obispo	1	2	0
San Francisco	2	2	0
S. J. Capistrano	0	2	1
Santa Clara	2	3	0
San Buenaventura	1	2	0
Santa Bárbara	1	2	0
La Purísima	2	3	0
Santa Cruz	2	1	0
Soledad	1	2	0
San José	1	1	0
S. J. Bautista	0	2	0
San Miguel	1	2	0
San Fernando	0	3	0
San Luis Rey	0	2	0
Santa Inés	0	3	0
San Rafael	0	2	0
S. F. Solano	1	2	0
Total	21	44	3

Table A3.2 Number of Years Following
Mission Establishment When
Construction of Last Church Begun

Years	Number of Churches Begun
0–5	3
5–10	3
10–15	5
15–20	2
20–25	3
25–30	1
30–35	1
35–40	2
40–45	0
45–50	1

Table A3.3 Construction Period in Years of Last Church Built

Years	Churches Built
0–1	2
1–5	11
5–10	6
10–15	2

Table A3.4 Number of Granaries, Medical Facilities, and Ranchos Where Building Construction Reported

Mission	Granaries	Medical Facilities	Ranchos
San Diego	7	2	1
San Carlos	4	1	0
San Antonio	5	0	4
San Gabriel	11	2	1
S. L. Obispo	6	1	4
San Francisco	4	1	1
S. J. Capistrano	9	1	0
Santa Clara	6	0	0
San Buenaventura	5	0	1
Santa Bárbara	8	0	1
La Purísima	4	1	1
Santa Cruz	4	2	1
Soledad	2	0	0
San José	3	0	0
S. J. Bautista	3	0	0
San Miguel	1	0	3
San Fernando	8	1	1
San Luis Rey	5	0	2
Santa Inés	3	0	0
San Rafael	1	1	0
S. F. Solano	2	0	0
Total	101	13	21

Table A3.5 References to Construction of Soldiers'
Barracks, Dormitories, and First Construction of
Indian Family Housing

Years Following Mission Establishment	Soldiers' Barracks	Dormitories	Family Housing
0–5	6	15	1
5–10	4	5	4
10–15	3	6	4
15–20	6	1	1
20–25	0	3	2
25–30	1	0	1
30–35	1	1	1
35–40	1	0	2
40–45	0	1	0
45–50	1	0	0

Table A3.6 Building Construction at San Diego Mission

1769–75: The mission located at San Diego presidio, where the Franciscans had two buildings. One was a set of apartments that were the residences of the missionaries, and the second a dormitory for Indian converts. The Franciscans moved the mission in August of 1774.

1775: Several structures reportedly built including quarters for the missionaries and a granary.

1777: The church and other buildings repaired.

1779: Existing buildings reroofed, including the two structures at the presidio which served as offices for the Franciscans to carry out negotiations with ships that arrived in San Diego harbor. A corridor added to the structures at the presidio.

1780: A new church built of adobe.

1782: Two corrals built.

1783: At the end of 1783 a large complex existed at San Diego that included an adobe church and sacristy, cemetery, granary, dormitories for single women and men, and a soldiers' barracks with a guard house. The buildings formed three wings, and a wall enclosed the square, which made the complex easy to defend. Outside of the quadrangle was a tannery and several corrals. In 1783 two rooms in the southern wing completely rebuilt, and adjoining rooms remodeled with their walls being raised. A corridor with eleven pillars added to the wing. A dormitory for *vaqueros* of *palizada* built in the Valle de San Luis.

1784: A portico or vestibule added to the church, a hospital, kitchen, and two new apartments for the Franciscans built, and a new cemetery opened.

1786: A kiln to make tiles built.

1787: A granary and store room built. More than three thousand trees planted to protect the fields. An irrigation ditch opened.

1788: A building with four rooms completed as quarters for the Franciscans, and a storeroom built. An irrigation ditch and orchard prepared.

1789: Several corrals built.

1790: Buildings repaired including a granary, dormitory for girls, weaving room, and hospital.

1791: A corral and patio with brick floor built.

1792: One half of a wall surrounding an orchard built.

1793: The orchard wall completed, and a granary built.

1794: Three buildings enlarged, a wall built to protect the mission, and a vineyard enclosed by a wall.

1795–97: A new irrigation system with a dam built.

1796: Two houses built.

1797: Four store rooms built.

1799: A new soldiers' barracks, storeroom for tools, and several other structures built.

1800: An earthquake on November 22, 1800, damaged buildings at the mission.

1806: New quarters for the missionaries built.

1808–13: A new church built. This is the structure rebuilt in the 1930s at the mission site.

1813–16: A new irrigation system with a dam built.

1815–16: A new hospital built.

1820: New granaries built on the ruins of the old ones.

Sources: Annual reports, Archivo General de la Nación, Mexico City, and Santa Barbara Mission Archive-Library, Santa Barbara, California; Zephyrin Engelhardt, OFM, *San Diego Mission* (San Francisco, 1920), pp. 151–60.

Table A3.7   Building Construction at San Carlos Mission

1775: Five rooms built of adobe including a kitchen and a storeroom.

1778: Four rooms built of adobe and palizada including a storeroom, carpenter's shop, and a dormitory for single women.

1781: An adobe structure and corral built.

1771–84: After being relocated to its present site in 1771, a church and other structures built of palizada surrounded by a thick wall of palizada for defense. Over the next twelve years buildings of adobe and stone built including a church, quarters for the missionaries, two granaries one of which had a loft, an office, reception room and an apartment for visitors to the mission, dormitories for girls and single women, a carpenter's shop, quarters for the family of the blacksmith, a storeroom for wood, a kitchen, hen house, and corrals.

1786: A portal and a room were added to the soldiers' barracks.

1787: A bread bakery with an oven built. Roofs of existing buildings repaired.

1788: Two rooms added to the wing that contained the quarters for the missionaries.

1789: The church reroofed.

1790: A granary built. Roof tiles were manufactured for the first time to protect buildings from fire.

1791: A new church and kitchen built.

1792–97: The present stone church built.

1796: A tannery with stone pillars built.

1798: Four adobe rooms built.

1799: A wing of rooms 107 *varas* long built.

1800: A new cemetery opened.

1801: The walls of the church raised one *vara*.

1806: Fifty-six houses for Indian families built.

1807: Thirty-seven houses for Indian families built, and the soldiers' barracks renovated.

1813: Two rooms built for sick men and women.

1814: The roof on the church rebuilt, and a wing of rooms 22 *varas* long built.

1815: The quadrangle completed with the construction of a wing of rooms 50 *varas* long.

1817: A chapel added to the church.

1822: A passage (*portón*) to the patio closed, and a new passage built leading to the Indian village.

1826: No new construction undertaken because of labor shortages caused by the declining Indian population. Indians worked in the fields and produced textiles.

1829: An adobe house built in the orchard.

1831: Uninhabited Indian houses have collapsed for lack of repair, but enough houses were available for the surviving Indian population.

1840: Mission building deteriorating, and an earthquake in 1840 damaged the roof on the church.

Sources: Annual reports, Archivo General de la Nación, Mexico City, Santa Barbara Mission Archive-Library, Santa Barbara, California.

Table A3.8 Building Construction at San Antonio Mission

1774: A granary and irrigation ditch built.

1775: A dormitory for single girls and women, two kitchens one for preparing *pozole,* a tack room, a hen house, and several other structures built.

1777: A room for storing provisions built.

1778: A wing of four rooms 24 varas long built, the quarters for the missionaries renovated, and a dam and two irrigation ditches built.

1779: Work began on a new adobe church.

1781: Three rooms built.

1784: A room with a tile roof built.

1786: Two walls built to enclose the Indian *ranchería,* and several houses for Indian families erected. A field was prepared for planting wheat.

1787: A new two story quarters for the missionaries with apartments, offices, and a reception room built.

1788: Fields opened for producing wheat.

1791: Eight houses for Indian families built.

1794: Two buildings built. One had a loft, and may have been a granary. The second was a pozole kitchen.

1797: A new entrance to the mission opened.

1799: Three granaries, a guest room, and a store room for clothing built.

1801: A wing 43 *varas* long built.

1802: A new soldiers' barracks built.

1804: A cemetery built away from the main mission complex.

1805: Houses for Indian families built.

1806: A mill and houses for Indian families built.

1808: A storage area for lumber, a tannery with four tanks, and half of a wall surrounding the garden built. An irrigation ditch begun in 1805 extended.

1809: Twenty-five houses for Indian families built. The irrigation ditch begun in 1805 completed.

1810: Thirty-one houses built for Indian families, as well as a mill for wheat.

1810–13: A new church built.

1811: A pozole kitchen built.

1812: A house built in the orchard and the tannery repaired with the addition of a new roof.

1813–14: The old church dismantled down to the foundations, and the materials used to build a wing containing the new quarters for the missionaries.

1814: A granary enlarged and a loft added. A loft added to the tack room. The wing containing the weaving room dismantled, and the materials used to build a hen house.

1815: A wing containing workshops 86 varas long built. The wing also had a loft. The walls of an old granary raised.

1815–16: Corridors added to the four wings surrounding the patio.

1816: The walls of one wing raised. A house with a kitchen built at Rancho San Bartólome de Pleyto. A wall 460 varas long built surrounding the orchard.

1817: Walls damaged by heavy rains repaired. A house built in an orchard.

1818: A corridor added to one wing of Indian houses. A house built in an old orchard. The walls of one wing of Indian houses raised. A wall built surrounding a corn field.

1819: A wing 50 varas long containing a dormitory for single men, a house, and a kitchen built.

1820: A house and kitchen built at Rancho San Benito. An irrigation ditch also built.

1821: A roof added to the portico on the church. Three corrals and a fence surrounding a corn field built.

1822–27: The irrigation system updated, including the construction of a *noria* (well) to irrigate an orchard, and new irrigation ditches. The water supply improved with the addition of several wells.

1822: A corral built at Rancho San Benito.

1823: Two two-story barracks built at Rancho San Antonio de los Ojitos and Rancho San Miguelito, located west of the mission. A grist mill built.

1824: A mill built.

1825: Walls damaged by rain repaired, and two corridors added to the mission complex.

1828: A hen house built, as well as a wall to protect the granary and soldiers' barracks from stream erosion. A loft added to the weaving room. Corridors on buildings at Rancho San Barthólome and Rancho San Benito repaired.

1829: Twenty-nine Indian houses built.

Sources: Annual reports, Archivo General de la Nación, and the Santa Barbara Mission Archive-Library, Santa Barbara, California; and Zephyrin Engelhardt, OFM, *Mission San Antonio de Padua* (Ramona, 1972).

Table A3.9 Building Construction at San Gabriel Mission

1771–75: (first mission site): A chapel, quarters for the missionaries, storeroom, dormitory for young girls, dormitory for young boys, tack room, carpenter shop, and other structures built. These were temporary buildings, many of which were not built of adobe.

1775–83: (second mission site): An adobe church and sacristy, three storerooms, a kitchen, reception room, three apartments for guests to the mission. These buildings formed a single quadrangle. A second quadrangle being completed, and consisted of a two-room hospital, a dormitory for girls, a dormitory for boys, a tannery, hen house, storeroom, and barracks for the mission guard.

1784: A wing in the main quadrangle raised and replaced because it threatened to collapse.

1789: Work of roofing mission buildings with tile completed. Three rooms built.

1790: A storeroom built.

1791–1805: A large church of stone and masonry (the present church) built. Problems with the roof delayed the completion of the church.

1803: A temporary church built.

1804: A wing measuring 125 *varas* [one vara is about .838 meters] with ten rooms built, including a granary, weaving room, carpenter shop, storage rooms, and new quarters for the missionaries.

1805: A wing of nine rooms measuring 155 varas in length built, containing a granary and other rooms.

1806: A wing of six rooms measuring 70 varas in length built, which completed the reconstruction of the main quadrangle replacing the structures built in the 1780s. One other building constructed.

1807: Thirty Indian houses built.

1808: Forty-seven Indian houses built.

1809: A large granary built.

1811: Two granaries built.

1812: Two granaries built. A severe earthquake in December of 1812 damaged mission buildings, including the church. Repair of the church was not completed until 1828.

1813: A granary with a loft built, adjoining another granary built in the previous year. The two granaries served as a temporary church.

1814: A hospital built.

1815: A structure measuring 100 varas in length built. It formed a separate square with the hospital completed in the previous year. A chapel for the hospital built.

1816: A mill and smithy built.

1817: A water basin built for a fountain.

1819: A combination hen house and dovecote built.

1820: Two mills built.

1821: Two rooms built for storing seed reserved for planting.

1823: A forge and room to house a lumber mill built.

1825: A corn mill built, and the lumber mill completed.

1827: Several structures including a chapel built at Rancho San Bernardino.

Sources: Ms. San Gabriel Mission Libro de Padrones, San Gabriel Mission, California; Annual reports, Archivo General de la Nación, Mexico City, Santa Barbara Mission Archive-Library; Maynard Geiger, OFM, "The Building of Mission San Gabriel: 1771–1828," *Southern California Quarterly* 50(1–4) (1968):33–42.

Table A3.10 Building Construction at San Luis Obispo Mission

1774: An adobe structure built, but the roof remained incomplete because of rains and the need to plant wheat. Two granaries built of *palizada* with tule roofs, and a carpenter shop built of the same materials. Wood cut for building, for making furniture, etc.

1779: A granary, quarters for the missionaries, and other structures built.

1781: Two adobe buildings with tule roofs built, as well as two sections of a wall surrounding the Indian village. The roof on the church and granary had

to be replaced after Indians set them on fire.

1786: The church and granary reroofed with tiles.

1787: Buildings damaged by rains repaired.

1788–1790: A new church built.

1788: A tile kiln and two weaving rooms built.

1789: A storeroom built.

1791: A corral and a wall surrounding the orchard built.

1792–94: New quarters for the missionaries built.

1792: A corral built, and a cornfield fenced with stone and live trees.

1793: A portico with a loft added to the church. Fields fenced with stones.

1794: A wing built containing work rooms and a soldiers' barracks.

1800: A granary and weaving room built.

1801: A wing with seven rooms built. A wall twelve *varas* long built closing the quadrangle. Three corrals and six houses for Indian families erected.

1802: Twenty-eight Indian houses built.

1804: A hospital built.

1805: Thirteen Indian houses, a grist mill, and a water reservoir built.

1808: Four Indian houses built, and a granary erected at the Rancho de Playa.

1809: A building erected at Arroyo Grande.

1810: Six houses for Indian families, two granaries, and a kitchen described as a *corralito* built.

1811: Four houses for Indian families built.

1813: Four Indian houses received tile roofs. The mission patio given a brick surface. Two mill stones prepared.

1814: Lofts added to the granaries. Nine Indian houses, the women's dormitory, and other structures repaired.

1816: Pillars added to the corridor in front of the quarters for the missionaries. Two houses built for Indian families. A wing 94 varas long built, and the hospital renovated.

1817: A wing of rooms added to the quadrangle.

1818: A wing of rooms added to the quadrangle.

1819: A second quadrangle (*lienzo doble del cuadro*) completed.

1820: A house built at an unnamed ranch.

1830: Many buildings reportedly in bad condition because of earthquake and other damage, including the hospital, Indian houses, ranch buildings at San Miguelito and Santa Margarita, and other structures. One cause was insufficient labor, because many Indians living at the mission were old or sick.

Sources: Annual reports, Archivo General de la Nación, Mexico City, and Santa Barbara Mission Archive-Library, Santa Barbara, California; and Zephyrin Engelhardt, OFM, *San Luis Obispo in the Valley of the Bears* (Santa Barbara, 1933).

Table A3.11 Building Construction at San Francisco Mission

1778: A building of *palizada* with a granary and offices built. Existing buildings, including a dormitory for girls and single women, reroofed. A cornfield and orchard fenced, and a corral and irrigation ditch built.

1782: Buildings erected included an adobe church with sacristy, quarters for the missionaries with a reception room and three small apartments, a wing built of palizada containing a kitchen, dormitory for girls and single women, and offices, and a pozole kitchen also built of palizada.

1783: The mission relocated to a site 400 *varas* to the west. A temporary church of palizada, an office, and quarters for the missionaries built.

1784: An adobe structure with three rooms including a reception room built adjoining the church. Two orchards laid out.

1786: At San Pedro y San Pablo a chapel, granary, tack room, and three other rooms built. Two thousand adobe bricks prepared for future building projects.

1787: At the main mission a pozole kitchen, tack room, and carpenter shop built. Several workshops rebuilt. At San Pedro y San Pablo a pozole kitchen and quarters for when the Franciscans visited the rancho, built of *palizada*. These two structures formed a third wing of the quadrangle.

1788: Work continued on a new adobe church. A dam and irrigation ditch built. At San Pedro y San Pablo two rooms of adobe were added to existing buildings.

1789: At San Pedro y San Pablo a granary, quarters for the *mayordomo*, and quarters for the missionaries built. A covered passage also built, but temporarily served as a kitchen. At the main mission the addition of two rooms and a covered passageway extended the eastern wing of the quadrangle to the church. When completed the new church would complete the southern wing. The sacristy for the new church has been added to the western wing of the quadrangle, which also contains a storeroom, quarters for visitors to the mission, and a kitchen. The northern wing consists of two granaries, with lofts and an office. Outside of the main quadrangle was a storeroom for supplies for the pozole kitchen, a pozole kitchen, and a dormitory for boys and single men.

1790: A carpenter shop and residence for a California Indian and his family built.

1791: New adobe church completed. Other structures built included a granary 47 varas long, and a wing of rooms 54 varas long west of the main quadrangle, with a weaving room, hen house, storeroom, kitchen, room to store wool, tack room, and dispensary.

1792: Two corrals, a soldiers' barracks, and a wing 59 varas long, divided into six rooms, built.

1793: Nineteen houses for Indian families built, as well as a grist mill and a wall surrounding an orchard.

1794: A granary 53 varas long built. The church and two granaries received roofs of tile.

1795: Other buildings received roofs of tile, including the soldiers' barracks and a wing 90 varas long, containing workshops and quarters for servants.

1796: A pottery kiln and twenty houses for Indian families built.

1797: Houses for Indian families finished.

1799: A bathhouse and pottery kiln built.

1800: Eight houses for Indian families built.

1801: Twelve houses for Indian families built.

1802: Twelve houses for Indian families built.

1811: Nine houses for Indian families built.

Sources: Annual reports, Archivo General de la Nación, Mexico City, Santa Barbara Mission Archive-Library; and Zephyrin Engelhardt, OFM, *San Francisco or Mission Dolores* (Chicago, 1924).

Table A3.12 Building Construction at San Juan Capistrano Mission

Mission established at the end of 1777, but relocated to a new site in October of 1778.

1778–83: Main quadrangle developed at the new site included an adobe church 25 *varas* long, two adobe granaries, four storerooms, quarters for the missionaries, two offices, a kitchen, a dovecote and hen house, and a dormitory for girls and single women. Outside of the main quadrangle was a storeroom for tools, a tack room, a structure 20 varas long that had been the first church built at the new mission site, and two corrals.

1784: A granary 22 varas long built.

1786: A granary 25 varas long and a corral built.

1788: A tile roof added to a granary.

1789: An adobe structure and corral built. Tile roofs and a corridor added to a wing of buildings.

1790: Walls of the church raised, and a tile roof added. A tile roof also added to a granary. Two rooms and two corrals built of adobe.

1791: Buildings erected in 1791 included a granary 36 varas long, a residence for the *mayordomo*, a new soldiers' barracks (the old barracks received a new roof and corridor), a dormitory for girls and single women, and an adobe structure with an unspecified use.

1792: One older wing demolished and rebuilt, with two granaries and weaving room. An old corridor replaced.

1793: Buildings constructed included an adobe structure 30 varas long, an adobe room, a corral, and a fence.

1794: Two granaries and forty houses for Indian families built.

1795: An orchard walled.

1796: A new soldiers' barracks and an adobe structure 16 varas long built.

1797–1806: A stone church 53 varas long built. Ruins of the church destroyed by an earthquake in 1812 can still be seen at the mission.

1798: A reception room, quarters for visitors to the mission, and two offices built.

1801: Two corridors built and the roofs on two granaries and two other structures replaced.

1802: An adobe structure built and a corridor added to an existing building.

1807: Thirty-four houses for Indian families built.

1809: An aqueduct built to bring water to the mission.

1810: An irrigation ditch extended 500 varas, and older buildings repaired.

1812: A soap works, carpenter shop, and wagon shop built. A severe earthquake destroyed the church completed in 1806, killing forty Indians.

1814: A hospital with a small chapel built. A wall separated the hospital from the main square.

1817: A new chapel added to the hospital.

Sources: Annual reports, Archivo General de la Nación, Mexico City; and Zephyrin Engelhardt, OFM, *San Juan Capistrano Mission* (Los Angeles, 1922).

Table A3.13 Building Construction at Santa Clara Mission

1777–79: Two structures of *palizada* built. The first was a chapel, and the second contained ten rooms, including quarters for the missionaries, quarters for the servants, offices, and a granary. An irrigation ditch opened.

1779: A flood on January 23, 1779, destroyed the buildings erected in the previous years, and the Franciscans relocated the mission to a new, higher site. During the winter a new temporary chapel and quarters for the missionaries and some Indians built. Beginning in the spring following the rainy season, an irrigation ditch was opened. New buildings of palizada were built, including a church, residence for

the missionaries, granary, kitchen, office, and three corrals.

1780: An adobe structure with eight rooms built. Its uses included a new residence for the missionaries, offices, and granary.

1781–84: A new adobe church built, 40 1/2 *varas* in length.

1781: A granary and a second structure built, both of adobe.

1783: One of the palizada buildings erected in 1780 burned.

1787: An adobe wing 40 varas long built to complete the mission quadrangle. It contained a reception room, four other rooms, and a *zaguán* (a covered passageway). A storeroom for firewood built, and a new irrigation ditch opened.

1788: Fire destroyed the tule roofs of four buildings, which had to be replaced. An adobe wall built, and a retaining wall of stakes erected along one of the five planting fields.

1789: A two-story adobe structure with an overhanging balcony built near the sacristy. The walls of the residence of the missionaries raised.

1790: Two adobe structures and an adobe corral built. One building served as the residence for the *mayordomo*.

1791: A granary and tile kiln built.

1792: A granary and eight houses for Indian families built.

1793: Fourteen houses for Indian families built. An adobe corral renovated, as well as the quarters of the missionaries.

1794: Nine houses for Indian families built.

1795: Two wings of the quadrangle roofed with tiles. The church enlarged.

A retaining wall built along one of the planting fields.

1796: The other buildings of the mission complex received tile roofs, and a soldiers' barracks built.

1797: Four rows of Indian houses received tile roofs.

1798: One hundred and sixty houses built for Indian families. Each had an enclosed patio.

1799–1809: No annual reports available for these years.

1813: A new soldiers' barracks built.

1815: An adobe corral built for cattle.

1818–19: A new church built to replace the structure completed in 1784.

1822: The quadrangle built in the 1780s abandoned and relocated to a new site a short distance away. Two wings of the new quadrangle were built. However, the Indian houses built in the 1790s continued to be used.

1823: Two adobe wings and a new soldiers' barracks built.

1824–25: A new adobe church built.

Sources: Annual reports, Archivo General de la Nación, Mexico City, and Santa Barbara Mission Archive-Library, Santa Barbara, California.

Table A3.14 Building Construction at San Buenaventura Mission

1782–84: Various structures, including a church of *palizada*, built.

1785: Four rooms rebuilt, including the quarters for the missionaries.

1786: Three rooms and a granary built.

1787–90: Work began on a new larger church, which had to be demolished in 1790. Work on a new church begun in 1793.

1789: Older buildings of palizada, reportedly in bad condition, replaced with adobe structures.

1790: Two granaries added to the quadrangle.

1792: A temporary church and two other structures built. Three sides of the quadrangle now complete.

1793–1809: A new church, the structure that stands today, built.

1793: Rooms added to the northern wing of the quadrangle.

1794: A tack room built.

1795: A tannery and quarters for the *mayordomo* built, outside of the main quadrangle.

1796: A wall built surrounding an orchard.

1799: A granary and a large storeroom built. The sacristy for the new church neared completion.

1800: A granary built, and twenty looms were set up.

1802: A mill built.

1804–6: Sixty-nine adobe houses for Indian families built.

1811: A soap works and storeroom built.

1812: A severe earthquake in December damaged mission buildings.

1813–16: Earthquake damage repaired, and the chapel of San Miguel completely rebuilt.

1818–21: Forty adobe houses built for Indian families.

1819: Walls surrounding the orchard rebuilt.

1832: Floods destroyed the chapel of San Miguel.

Sources: Annual reports, Archivo General de la Nación, Mexico City, and Santa Barbara Mission Archive-Library, Santa Barbara, California; and Zephyrin Engelhardt, OFM, *San Buenaventura: The Mission by the Sea* (Santa Barbara, 1930).

Table A3.15 Building Construction at Santa Bárbara Mission

1786–87: Wattle and daub structures erected included a church, quarters for the missionaries, kitchen, a granary, a dormitory for single women and girls, a dormitory for single men and boys, and quarters for the servants. Four adobe rooms were begun, but could not be completed until 1788.

1788: The church enlarged, and a kitchen and another room built. Roof tiles were added to existing structures. A corral built.

1789: An adobe church, granary, dormitory for single women and girls, a hen house, a storeroom, and a corral built.

1790: Among the buildings erected were new quarters for the missionaries; a wing of eight rooms 60 *varas* long with a kitchen, storerooms, granary, residence for the *mayordomo*, and a pozole kitchen.

1791: Structures built included a soldiers' barracks, carpenter's shop, and storerooms.

1792: Two corrals built.

1793: A church with a portico and a sacristy built.

1794: A granary, two weaving rooms, a cemetery, and a corral built.

1795: Two wings of the quadrangle renovated, with the addition of new roofs. Four rooms added to the wing, containing the quarters of the missionaries.

1796: Roof beams on six rooms replaced with pine roof beams. A corridor added to the weaving rooms and another structure. Two small rooms built.

1797: Structures built included three granaries, a tack room, a storeroom, and a hen house. These buildings formed a second quadrangle.

1798: An orchard and vineyard fenced.

1800: Corridors added to the wings facing the main patio.

1802: A residence built for the mayordomo and tanner, both with colonnades.

1803: A chapel dedicated to San Miguel built at Cieneguitas.

1798–1807: Two hundred and fifty-two houses built for Indian families.

1808: A fountain and laundry basin built.

1809–11: The wing containing the quarters for the missionaries rebuilt with stone walls.

1811: Work on a new facade for the church begun.

1812: Many mission buildings damaged in a severe earthquake in December.

1814: Buildings in the *ranchería* destroyed by the 1812 earthquake rebuilt.

1815–20: A new church built, with one tower.

1817: A wing with a granary, tack room, and several other rooms built.

1831: A second tower added to the church.

1833: One church tower replaced, and a buttress added to the church.

Sources: Annual reports, Archivo General de la Nación, Mexico City, and Santa Barbara Mission Archive-Library, Santa Barbara, California; and Maynard Geiger, OFM, *Mission Santa Barbara, 1782–1965* (Santa Barbara, 1965).

Table A3.16 Building Construction at La Purísima Mission

1788: Temporary structures of *palizada* or adobe, with roofs of packed earth, built, including a chapel, quarters for the missionaries, a granary, two corrals, and two rooms for which a use was not specified.

1789: A church, granary, and common kitchen built of adobe.

1790: A wing with seven rooms of adobe added to the growing complex, and a kiln built to fire roof tiles. After 1790 buildings constructed of adobe with tile roofs.

1791: A granary of adobe built as a part of the main quadrangle, and three buildings erected outside of the quadrangle, including a kitchen, oven, and chicken coop.

1792: The adobe church and a granary renovated.

1793: An adobe wing containing new quarters for the missionaries, apartments for visitors, an office, a storage room for Indian clothing, and a kitchen added to the main quadrangle.

1794: A soldiers' barracks, apartment for the *mayordomo*, a carpenter shop, and tack room built.

1795: A granary and office built.

1796: Three storerooms built.

1797: A new residence built for the missionaries.

1798: A new barracks with nine rooms built for the mission guard. The foundations for a larger church laid.

1799: Two rooms built.

1800: A wing with eight rooms added to the mission complex.

1802: The adobe church begun in 1798 completed. A garden enclosed with an adobe wall.

1804: A new barracks built for the mission guard.

1808: A dam and aqueduct built.

1810: A granary and house built at Rancho San Antonio, north of the mission.

1812: An earthquake and heavy rains in December of 1812 destroyed most of the mission complex. The report prepared at the end of 1812 noted that temporary buildings had been put up and mentioned a hundred housing units for Indian families not previously reported in the annual reports, as well as a dormitory for girls and single women.

1813: In April of 1813, the mission moved to a new site, several miles away. A temporary church, built of palizada with an adobe veneer, and other temporary buildings erected.

1815: A large adobe structure completed that contained quarters for the missionaries, apartments for visitors to the mission, weaving room, and a chapel.

1816: A large adobe structure built with quarters for the mission guard, quarters for the mayordomo, and workrooms. A hospital built.

1817: Foundations laid for a new church, although there is no evidence that the larger church was ever completed. A fountain added to the Indian village.

1818: The temporary church built in 1813 collapsed and was replaced by a new temporary church built of adobe. The church completed in 1818 may have been built on the foundations laid in the previous year.

1821: A bell tower added to the church.

1823: More housing units added to the Indian village.

1835: The chapel in the building constructed in 1815 renovated, because the church completed in 1818 was in poor condition. The renovated chapel served for the reduced Indian population.

Sources: Zephyrin Engelhardt, OFM, *Mission La Purísima Concepción de María Santísima* (Santa Barbara, 1932); La Purisima Mission annual reports, Archivo General de la Nación, Mexico City, and the Santa Barbara Mission Archive-Library, Santa Barbara, California.

Table A3.17 Building Construction at Santa Cruz Mission

1791: Two buildings of *palizada* erected, including a church and a second structure, which contained offices and quarters for the missionaries. Two corrals were also built, and an irrigation ditch opened.

1792: An adobe structure with a corridor 64 *varas* long built, with a reception room, two other rooms, and a granary. A temporary church built of planks in the corridor. A corral of stakes built.

1793–94: An adobe church with a stone facade built.

1793: Several structures built, including an office, a temporary dormitory for unmarried girls, tack room, dispensary, kitchen, *pozole* kitchen, and common area. Cattle corral repaired.

1794: A granary, weaving room, storeroom, and corral for sheep built.

1795: Two wings built of adobe completed the quadrangle, and a mill was built.

1796: The residence of the missionaries damaged and temporary apartments built of planks.

1797: Three wings of the quadrangle roofed with tiles, and a water-powered mill built.

1798: A mill and hen house built.

1806: Forty houses for Indian families completed, and eight still needed to be roofed.

1809: Twenty-five houses for Indian families built.

1810: A dormitory for single women and widows built.

1811: Church roofed with tiles, and four room infirmary built.

1812: Construction projects included a new sacristy with a wooden floor, a portico added to the church, a wooden floor added to the presbyterium, and the addition of corridors and roof tiles to two wings surrounding the inner patio.

1813: A tile roof added to a granary, a wooden floor and three buttresses added to the church, and a tannery built.

1814: A new granary roofed with tiles, a bell wall added to the church, and the corridor in front of the residence of the missionaries paved with tiles.

1815: Soldiers' barracks built between 1799 and 1809, and the dormitory for single women and widows roofed with tiles.

1816: Tiled patio with laundry area added to the dormitory for single women and widows, two houses for Indian families roofed with tiles, and a mill built.

1817: Thirty-six houses for Indian families and a part of the infirmary roofed with tiles, and five rooms added to the infirmary.

1821: Two houses with lofts built in the Villa de Branciforte, one for the use of the community and the second for a former *mayordomo* for services to the mission. Two walls built to form a patio for the dormitory for single women. Stone-lined water ditch ran through the patio of the dormitory.

1822: A building 103 *varas* long with a corridor on both sides built. A granary with a loft occupied one section, and ten houses with half-lofts for recent Indian converts took up the other section.

1822–24: A structure containing seventeen houses for Indian families built.

1823: A common area added to the Indian village.

1825: Buttresses on church and residence of the mayordomo repaired.

1828: All necessary repairs not completed, because of a shortage of labor.

1830: A bell tower added to the church, and a large cross raised in the cemetery.

1832: A large buttress added to the cemetery side of the church.

1833: A stone pillar built on the east side of the church, and an adobe building erected at Rancho Refugio.

1840: Bell tower collapsed.

Sources: Annual reports, Archivo General de la Nación, Mexico City, and Historical Society of Southern California, Los Angeles, California, Santa Barbara Mission Archive-Library, Santa Barbara, California.

Table A3.18 Building Construction at Soledad Mission

1791: Temporary structures built of wattle and daub included a wing that contained the church, granary, and quarters for the missionaries, a second wing containing a kitchen, and a dormitory for girls and single women. Other structures were a pozole kitchen, carpenter's shop, and three corrals.

1792: An adobe wing with three rooms built.

1793: An adobe wing 80 *varas* long built. It contained a church, quarters for the missionaries, and a granary 40 varas long. A new dormitory for single girls

and women and an animal-powered mill built.

1794: Half of the front wing of the mission quadrangle built.

1799: A soldiers' barracks built.

1800–1809: In 1805 the church was enlarged and probably now measured 40 varas. A fourth adobe wing closing the mission quadrangle and houses for Indian families most likely built during this period.

1832: A flood destroyed the church built in 1793, and a small temporary chapel replaced it.

Sources: Annual reports, Archivo General de la Nación, Mexico City; and Zephyrin Engelhardt, OFM, *Mission Nuestra Señora de la Soledad* (Santa Barbara, 1929).

Table A3.19 Building Construction at San José Mission

1797: Temporary buildings described as *jacales* (wattle and daub roofed with tules) built, including quarters for the missionaries, an office, and a chapel. Other projects included corrals for the livestock and a fence around an orchard.

1798: A granary with a loft built. The chapel enlarged. Irrigation ditches built for the cornfields.

1799–1809: No annual reports for this period survive. However, data from other sources, including an 1837 inventory, give an indication of building projects undertaken during the decade. A new church was built

between 1805 and 1809, and completed the main quadrangle. The wing adjoining the church, measuring 100 by 17 *varas* and containing fifteen rooms, was built. It housed the quarters for the missionaries. Two granaries were added to the one built in 1798 and apparently formed one whole wing of the main quadrangle, measuring 100 by 10 varas. Workshops and storage rooms were also built, and construction on adobe apartments for Indian families probably began.

1810: Ten apartments built for as many Indian families, as well as a dovecote and room to house looms.

1811: Twenty-four apartments built for Indian families, and a room added to the soldiers' barracks.

1812: The roof on the church raised by three varas.

1813: One wing of the quadrangle roofed with tiles.

1814: A new soldiers' barracks built, all roofed with tile. The barracks consisted of six apartments for the soldiers and their families, each with a kitchen on

the side, a guard house, and a storage room.

1820: A water powered mill built.

1823: An orchard enclosed with an adobe wall.

1825: Twenty-two houses built for as many Indian families.

1826: Twenty-three houses built for as many Indian families.

1827: A tanning vat, storage room for hides, and a soap works built.

Sources: Annual reports, Archivo General de la Nación, Mexico City, and Santa Barbara Mission Archive-Library, Santa Barbara, California; and Stephen Dietz, et al., "Final Report of Archaeological Investigations at Mission San Jose," unpublished manuscript, 1984, pp. 17–18, 23–24.

Table A3.20 Building Construction at San Juan Bautista Mission

1797: Buildings constructed included a chapel, quarters for the missionaries, soldiers' barracks, kitchen, granary, and dormitory for single girls and women.

1798: A large granary built.

1799–1806: Main quadrangle of the mission built.

1802: A granary and new soldiers' barracks built.

1803–12: A new large church, the present structure, built.

1810: A storeroom, pozole kitchen, and new quarters for the missionaries built.

1813–14: A new soldiers' barracks built.

1815: A dormitory built for single men and widowers and six houses for Indian families.

1817: The walls raised on thirteen Indian houses.

1817–18: A mill built.

1819: Six houses built for Indian families.

1820: Seven houses built for Indian families.

1821: Ten houses built for Indian families.

1823: Corrals built for cattle and sheep.

1824: Twenty-two houses built for Indian families, and a corral built.

1826: A corral and two small buildings built.

1831: A barracks for Indian *vaqueros* built.

1832: A new dormitory with walled patio built for women and single girls.

Sources: Annual reports, Archivo General de la Nación, Mexico City, and Santa Barbara Mission Archive-Library, Santa Barbara, California; and Zephyrin Engelhardt, OFM, *San Juan Bautista Mission* (Santa Barbara, 1931).

Table A3.21 Building Construction at San Miguel Mission

1797: A large *jacal* of wattle and daub with a tule roof covered with packed earth built, as well as an adobe church and a second adobe structure.

1798: An adobe church and dormitory for single girls and women built.

1799: Quarters for the missionaries of adobe and three additional rooms added to the mission complex.

1800: A granary and another structure built.

1801: Work continued on completing the main quadrangle.

1804: New quarters built for the missionaries.

1805: Forty-seven houses built for Indian families, and roof tiles manufactured.

1806: Buildings damaged by a fire repaired.

1808: A carpenters shop, weaving room, and a new dormitory for single girls and women built. More roof tiles manufactured.

1809: Five rooms added to the mission complex, and more roof tiles manufactured.

1810: A corral, adobe house, and granary built at Rancho San Simeón, "en la playa." Adobe bricks prepared for a new church.

1811: A tile kiln, corral, and soap works built. Existing structures received roof tiles.

1812: Tanning vats and a warehouse built. An adobe structure built at Rancho Asunción. Existing structures received roof tiles.

1813: Two adobe structures built at Rancho Asunción. Existing buildings received roof tiles.

1814: Two adobe structures built at Rancho San Simeón. Existing buildings received roof tiles.

1815: An adobe structure with tile roof built at Rancho Aguaje.

1816–19: A new church, the present structure, built.

1830: A large adobe structure built at Rancho San Simeón.

Sources: Annual reports, Archivo General de la Nación, Mexico City, and Santa Barbara Mission Archive-Library, Santa Barbara, California; and Zephyrin Engelhardt, OFM, *San Miguel Arcangel: The Mission on the Highway* (Ramona, 1971).

Table A3.22 Building Construction at San Fernando Mission

1797: An adobe church built.

1798: A granary, office, and weaving room built.

1799: A new adobe church, granary, storeroom, and quarters for the missionaries built.

1801: A wing containing two granaries, a weaving room, and a dormitory for single girls and women added to the mission quadrangle. A barracks built for the mission guard.

1802: A wing containing granaries and a carpenter shop added to the quadrangle.

1804: Seventy housing units built for Indian families. A new larger church begun. A building with a granary and other rooms built at Rancho San Francisco Xavier.

1806: The church begun in 1804 completed. A granary and tack room built.

1808: A masonry dam built.

1810: New quarters built for the missionaries.

1811: A fountain and aqueduct built.

1812: A corridor added to the missionaries quarters.

1813: Buildings damaged in the December 1812 earthquake repaired. A fountain and two houses for the *mayordomo* built. Converts moved to the new *ranchería*.

1818: A soap works and forty houses for Indian families built.

1819–22: The "long building," which contained the quarters for the Franciscans, reception room, and other offices renovated. The walls raised, and a new roof added.

1821: A hospital built.

Sources: Zephyrin Engelhardt, OFM, *San Fernando Rey: The Mission in the Valley* (Chicago, 1927); San Fernando Mission annual reports, Archivo General de la Nación, Mexico City, and Santa Barbara Mission Archive-Library, Santa Barbara, California.

Table A3.23   Building Construction at San Luis Rey Mission

1798: A church, quarters for the missionaries, soldiers' barracks, and a storeroom built of adobe with roofs of beams covered with packed earth. Work began on a dormitory for single girls and women and a second structure, but rains prevented their completion.

1800: A new soldiers' barracks with a roof of beams covered with packed earth built. Two structures begun could not be completed until 1801.

1801: A granary and two other structures added to the quadrangle. The first tile roofs installed.

1804: Four granaries built that completed the quadrangle. Two tanning vats and a soap works built.

1806: A dormitory for single women with a patio that communicated to the main mission square built. A corral and an adobe structure built at an unnamed rancho, possibly San Antonio de Pala.

1808: Walls on two wings of the quadrangle raised. Two corrals built.

1810: A granary built at Rancho San Antonio de Pala, and a vineyard at the main mission complex partially walled.

1811–15: A new church, the present structure, built.

1812: Wall surrounding the vineyard completed.

1813: A row of buildings with a corridor added to the quarters of the missionaries. Corridors added to the buildings that surround the patio.

1819: The chapel at Pala enlarged, and two granaries and a dormitory for single men and women built there.

1823: Granaries and other structures built in the form of a quadrangle at Rancho Los Flores.

Sources: Annual reports, Archivo General de la Nación, Mexico City, and Santa Barbara Mission Archive-Library, Santa Barbara, California; and Zephyrin Engelhardt, OFM, *San Luis Rey Mission* (San Francisco, 1921).

Table A3.24 Building Construction at Santa Inés Mission

1804: Six months prior to the formal establishment of the mission, a wing of rooms built that contained a chapel, residence for the missionaries, and a granary.

1805: A wing of rooms added to the mission complex.

1806: A wing of rooms added to the mission complex.

1807–8: A wing containing a new residence for the missionaries built.

1810: A soldiers' barracks built.

1811: A residence built for the *mayordomo*.

1812: Eighty housing units built for Indian families. December 1812 earthquakes damaged many buildings.

1813: A granary built to serve as a temporary church. Walls of the wing containing the residence of the missionaries lowered.

1814–17: A new church, the current structure, built to replace the church damaged in the 1812 earthquake.

1817: Soldiers' barracks repaired.

1820: A hydraulic flour mill built.

1821: Mill stone installed in the mill.

1823: A tack room built.

1824: Buildings damaged during the Chumash uprising. Over the next five years, damaged buildings repaired.

1832: A granary built.

Sources: Zephyrin Engelhardt, OFM, *Mission Santa Inés and its Ecclesiastical Seminary* (Santa Barbara, 1932); Santa Inés Mission annual reports, Archivo General de la Nación, Mexico City, and the Santa Barbara Mission Archive-Library, Santa Barbara, California.

Table A3.25 Building Construction at San Rafael Mission

1818: An adobe structure with tule roof 29 *varas* long with a corridor built. The structure contained a chapel, quarters for the missionaries, dispensary, dormitory for girls and single women, and rooms for visitors to the mission. In 1819 20 varas of length added to the building.

1819: Buildings constructed in 1819 included a kitchen, another dormitory for single women, carpenter's shop, residence for the *mayordomo*, and a tack room. All had tule roofs.

1820: Tile roofs added to older buildings including the chapel, granaries, weaving room, and quarters for the missionaries.

1821: A granary not previously mentioned in the annual reports enlarged.

1822: An unspecified number of houses built for Indian families.

1823: A new church under construction whitewashed.

1824: New church completed. Other structures built included a soldiers' barracks and a dormitory for recent recruits still receiving religious instruction.

1825: A kitchen and dormitory for boys and single men built.

1826: Six houses for Indian families and another dormitory for recent recruits receiving religious instruction built.

1827: Two houses for Indian families and a tanning vat built.

1828: A granary enlarged.

1829: A residence for the mayordomo built.

1830: A granary renovated, and houses for Indian families built.

1831: Houses for Indian families and a member of the mission guard built.

1832: A kitchen and the quarters for visitors to the mission enlarged.

1840: Church reportedly in bad condition, and the south wall threatened to collapse.

1841: Church continued to deteriorate.

Source: Annual reports, Santa Barbara Mission Archive-Library, Santa Barbara, California.

Table A3.26 Building Construction at San Francisco Solano Mission

1824: An adobe wing with a corridor 40 *varas* long built. The wing contained two rooms and a reception room. A smithy and weaving room built of adobe. A temporary chapel built of planks.

1825: Quarters for the missionaries, a granary, and houses for Indian families built.

1826: The wall of *palizada* surrounding the cemetery replaced by adobe, and a planting field fenced.

1827–28: A wing 50 varas long with a double row of buildings built as new quarters for the missionaries.

1827–32: An adobe church 55 varas long built.

1827–28: A granary 30 varas in length built.

1829: An adobe wing with tile roof and a double row of rooms built. It measured 50 varas in length.

1833: Foundations of the wing containing the quarters of the missionaries and the new church replaced. Twenty thousand adobe bricks prepared for future building projects.

1840: An adobe chapel 40 varas long built to replace the church completed in 1832, which reportedly was in poor condition.

Source: Annual reports, Santa Barbara Mission Archive-Library, Santa Barbara, California, and Bancroft Library, University of California, Berkeley.

Notes

Introduction

1. H. H. Bancroft, *History of California,* 6 vols. (San Francisco: The History Company, 1884–90).

2. First published in 1908 and republished in 1929–30 by J. H. Barry.

3. Republished in 1976 by the University of California Press.

4. Published in 1976 by the University of California Press.

5. Published in 1979 by the University of California Press.

6. The challenges to Cook's findings, specifically the results of his initial research in the late 1930s and 1940s, have taken place at both the popular and professional level. At the professional level see, for example, Francis Guest, OFM, "An Examination of the Thesis of S. F. Cook on the Forced Conversion of Indians in the California Missions," *Southern California Quarterly* 61(1979):1–77. Professional historians who support the Serra canonization campaign have publicized their ideas in the popular history magazine *The Californias.* For example, in 1984, the bicentennial of Serra's death, a series of short articles edited by W. Michael Mathes was published in an issue entitled "God's Conquistador: The Serra Story," *The Californias* 2(5) (1984). And in 1989 Gloria Ricci Lothrop published an article entitled "El Viejo: Serra in Context," *The Californias* 7(1989):16–27. In this article, which is an example of advocacy disguised as objective historical analysis, Lothrop attempts to challenge many of Cook's conclusions about and characterizations of the Alta California missions. In 1986 a publicist working for the Monterey Diocese Chancery office released a series of interviews with carefully selected scholars called "The Serra Report," which challenged Cook's arguments, denigrated California Indian culture, and incorrectly stated that no professional scholars are critical of the Serra canonization campaign and its basic eurocentric assumptions.

7. In the area of ethnography, the most important publication is Robert Heizer, ed., *Handbook of North American Indians: California* (Washington, D.C., 1978); and David H. Thomas, ed., *Columbian Consequences: Historical and Archaeological Perspectives on the Spanish Borderlands West* (Washington, D.C., 1989). Anthropologists and archaeologists have made important contributions to the study of California Indians and the missions. See, for example, John Johnson, "The Chumash and the Missions," in, Thomas, ed., *Columbian Consequences,* pp. 365–75; and Paul Farnsworth, "The Econom-

ics of Acculturation in the Alta California Missions: An Historical and Archaeological Study of Nuestra Señora de la Soledad," Ph.D. diss., University of California, Berkeley, 1987. Edward Castillo, a California Indian, recently published the 1877 oral-historical account of Lorenzo Asisara, an Indian born at Santa Cruz mission in 1820; see his "An Indian Account of the Decline and Collapse of Mexico's Hegemony over the Missionized Indians of California," *American Indian Quarterly* 13(1989): 391–406; and also his "The Assassination of Padre Andrés Quintana by the Indians of Mission Santa Cruz in 1812: The Narrative of Lorenzo Asisara," *California History* 68(1989):116–25, 150–52. Doyce Nunis, editor of the *Southern California Quarterly,* and Harry Kelsey, both supporters of the Serra canonization cause, have attacked the Asisara account, primarily because they are only willing to accept Franciscan sources for the history of the missions. For Nunis's attack and Castillo's reply, see "California Mission Indians: Two Perspectives," *California History* 70(1991):206–15, 236–38.

8. Sabine MacCormack, *Religion in the Andes: Vision and Imagination in Early Colonial Peru* (Princeton, 1991), p. 140.

9. There are several general handbooks on California ethnohistory and ethnography that provide more detailed information and the different Indian groups brought into the missions. The first handbook published, Alfred Kroeber, *Handbook of the Indians of California* (New York, reprint edition 1976), first appeared in print in 1925. A more recent compilation of information on California Indians is Heizer, *Handbook of North American Indians.* General observations made in this section rely primarily on Heizer's work.

10. Campbell Grant, "Eastern Coastal Chumash," in Heizer, *Handbook of North American Indians,* pp. 510–11; Roberta Greenwood, "Obispeño and Purisimeño Chumash," in Heizer, *Handbook,* p. 523.

11. Grant, "Eastern Coastal Chumash," p. 513.

12. Richard Levy, "Costanoan," in Heizer, *Handbook of North American Indians,* 485–95; Thomas Hester, "Salinan," in Heizer, *Handbook of North American Indians,* 500–504.

13. Ibid.

14. Grant, "Eastern Coastal Chumash," in Heizer, *Handbook of North American Indians,* 512–13.

Chapter 1

1. Robert H. Jackson, "La colonización de la Alta California: Un Análisis del desarrollo de dos comunidades misionales," *Historia Mexicana* 45 (1991):83–110.

2. San Luis Rey mission annual reports, Santa Barbara Mission Archive-

Library, Santa Barbara, California (hereinafter cited as SBMA).

3. San Miguel mission annual reports, SBMA.

4. William Hartnell, "Diario, informe, y borradores de correspondencia," Bancroft Library, University of California, Berkeley (hereinafter cited as BLUC).

5. Robert Jackson, Edna Kimbro, and MaryEllen Ryan, "Como la Sombra Huye la Hora: Restoration Research, Santa Cruz Mission Adobe, Santa Cruz Mission State Historic Park," unpublished report on file with the California State Department of Parks and Recreation Cultural Resource Support Unit, Sacramento, California.

6. Robert H. Jackson, "Population and the Economic Dimension of Colonization in Alta California: Four Mission Communities," *Journal of the Southwest* 33(1991):387–439.

7. Robert H. Jackson, "Patterns of Demographic Change in the Missions of Central Alta California," *Journal of California and Great Basin Anthropology* 9(1987):259.

8. San Gabriel mission annual reports, Archivo General de la Nación, Mexico City (hereinafter cited as AGN).

9. San Diego mission annual reports, AGN.

10. San Gabriel mission annual report, 1824, SBMA.

11. Ibid., 1785, 1786, 1787, 1788, 1789.

12. David Hornbeck, "Economic Growth and Change at the Missions of Alta California, 1769–1846," in Thomas, *Columbian Consequences*, pp. 423–31.

13. Julia Costello, "Variability among the Alta California Missions: The Economics of Agricultural Production," in Thomas, *Columbian Consequences*, 435–50.

14. Robert H. Jackson, "Population and the Economic Dimension of Colonization"; Homer Aschmann, *The Central Desert of Baja California: Demography and Ecology* (Berkeley and Los Angeles, 1959), p. 213.

15. Jackson, "Population," 388–90.

16. The classic statement on Mexican grain-price history is Enrique Florescano, *Precios de maíz y crisis agrícolas en México (1500–1821)* (Mexico City, 1969). See also Richard Garner, "Price Trends in Eighteenth Century Mexico," *Hispanic American Historical Review* 65(1985): 279–325. Both Florescano and Garner documented a trend of rising prices at the end of the eighteenth century. Changes in the economy of late eighteenth-century Mexico recently received attention in Arij Ouweneel and Catrien C. J. H. Bijleveld, "The Economic Cycle in Bourbon Central Mexico: A Critique of the *Recaudación del diezmo líquido en pesos*," *Hispanic American Historical Review* 69(1989):479–530, and the comments on the article made by David Brading, John Coatsworth, and Hector Lindo-Fuentes in the same issue.

17. In their response to the 1813 questionnaire, the Franciscans stationed at La Purísima mission described the functioning of the arancel. See Zephyrin Engelhardt, *Mission La Concepción Purísima de María Santísima* (Santa Barbara, 1932), p. 16.

18. Hornbeck, "Economic Growth and Change," p. 425.

19. See among others, Charles Gibson, *The Aztecs under Spanish Rule* (Stanford, 1964); Nancy Farriss, *Maya Society under Colonial Rule: The Collective Enterprise of Survival* (Princeton, N.J., 1984); Karen Spalding, *Huarochiri: An Andean Society under Inca and Spanish Rule* (Stanford, 1984); and Steve Stern, *Peru's Indian Peoples and the Challenge of Spanish Conquest: Huamanga to 1640* (Madison, 1982).

20. Hornbeck, "Economic Growth and Change," pp. 426–27. On population change in the Alta California missions, see Johnson, "The Chumash," pp. 368–73; Robert H. Jackson, "Gentile Recruitment and Population Movements in the San Francisco Bay Area Missions," *Journal of California and Great Basin Anthropology* 6(1984):225–39; Robert H. Jackson, "Patterns of Demographic Change in the Missions of Central Alta California, *Journal of California and Great Basin Anthropology* 9(1987):251–72; Robert H. Jackson, "The Population of the Santa Barbara Channel Missions (Alta California), 1813–1832," *Journal of California and Great Basin Anthropology,* forthcoming; and Robert H. Jackson, "La dinámica del desastre demográfico de la población india en las misiones de la bahia de San Francisco, Alta California, 1776–1840," *Historia Mexicana* 40 (1991):187–215.

21. Sherburne Cook, *The Conflict Between the California Indian and White Civilization.* Reprint; Berkeley and Los Angeles, 1976; and Albert Hurtado, *Indian Survival on the California Frontier* (New Haven), p. 52.

22. In "The Conversion of the Chumash Indians: An Ecological Perspective," *Human Ecology* 5, (1977):309–28, Gary Combs and Fred Ploogh showed that the growth in the Indian population in the Chumash missions prior to 1804 tended to vary with grain production. After 1804 the variance was not as great. The authors argued that mission-produced grain attracted Indian converts. However, the variance between the two variables, Chumash conversion and grain production, does not necessarily establish a causal relationship. Increases in grain production may have been related to growth in the size of the labor force. The variance may also be the result of coincidence. Following the establishment of the missions, the Franciscans recruited the local Indian population and at the same time developed mission agriculture. After the Franciscans recruited the bulk of the local population (which marked the period of most rapid growth in the size of the mission populations, which coincided with the expansion of grain production), the variance between the recruitment of new converts and grain-production levels was weak. This fact casts doubt on the significance of the causal relationship between the two variables.

23. Hornbeck, "Economic Growth and Change," p. 428.

24. The Santa Cruz Mission account book, Historical Society of Southern California (Los Angeles), records the planting of winter wheat in late December or early January and of spring corn following the wheat harvest. Early annual reports from San Gabriel and San Diego missions (1780s), preserved in the Archivo General de la Nación, Mexico City, record a similar agricultural cycle.

25. Costello, "Variability."

26. Julia Costello, "Variability among the Alta California Missions," Paper presented at D-Q University, Davis, California, March 2, 1990.

27. San Gabriel Mission annual report 1824, SBMA.

28. San Gabriel Mission annual report 1824, SBMA.

29. Costello, "Variability," pp. 446–47.

30. Hurtado, *Indian Survival*, p. 52; Sylvia Broadbent, "Conflict at Monterey: Indian Horse Raiding 1820–1850," *Journal of California Anthropology* 1 (Spring 1974):86–101; and George Phillips, *Indians and Intruders in Central California, 1769–1849* (Norman, 1993), especially chapter 6.

31. Costello, "Variability," p. 436, following Hornbeck, argues that most major building projects at the missions were completed by 1805.

32. See the annual reports of the individual missions in the Archivo General de la Nación, Mexico City, and the Santa Barbara Mission Archive-Library, Santa Barbara, California.

33. Max Moorhead, *The Presidio Bastion of the Spanish Borderlands* (Norman, 1975), pp. 73, 219.

34. For a description of the economy of the northernmost Baja California missions, see Peveril Meigs, *The Dominican Mission Frontier of Lower California* (Berkeley, 1935).

35. Maynard Geiger, OFM, *The Life and Times of Junipero Serra* (Washington, D.C., 1959), 1:181.

36. Zephyrin Engelhardt, OFM, *The Missions and Missionaries of California* (Santa Barbara, 1929–30), 2:144–45.

37. Engelhardt, *Missions*, 1:306–7.

38. Engelhardt, *Missions*, 2:140.

39. Jackson, "Population and the Economic Dimension of Colonization."

40. Robert Archibald, *The Economic Aspects of the Alta California Missions* (Washington, D.C., 1978), pp. 11, 64.

41. Santa Cruz Mission account book, Historical Society of Southern California, Los Angeles.

42. Ramón Olbes, OFM, Santa Cruz, November 20, 1819, "Lista de los Neofitos de la Misión de Sta Cruz que no viven congregados en d[ic]ha Misión," Alexander Taylor Collection, Archdiocese of San Francisco Chancery Archive, Colma, California, #2369.

43. Donald Howard, *California's Lost Fortress: The Royal Presidio of Monterey* (Monterey, 1976), p. 30.

44. Santa Cruz Mission account book, Historical Society of Southern California and Saint Mary's College, Moraga, California.

45. See Archibald, *Economic Aspects.*

Chapter 2

1. Paul Farnsworth, "The Economics of Acculturation in the Alta California Missions: A Historical and Archaeological Study of Mission Nuestra Señora de la Soledad," Ph.D. diss., University of California, Los Angeles, 1987, p. 105.

2. Farnsworth, "Economics of Acculturation," p. 77, discusses the potential weakness of the responses to the questionnaire as sources of information on Indian cultural change. However, he does not consider the politics of the liberal Cadiz Cortes. On the background of the Cortes, see Stanley Payne, *A History of Spain and Portugal* (Madison, 1973), vol. 2, chap. 19. For a discussion of the Cortes and its American policies see Mario Rodriguez, *The Cadiz Experiment in Central America, 1808–1826* (Berkeley and Los Angeles, 1978).

3. The exceptions are James Deetz, "Final Summary Report of Investigations at La Purísima Mission State Historical Monument," unpublished manuscript, 1963; Robert Hoover and Julia Costello, eds., "Excavations at Mission San Antonio: The First Three Seasons," unpublished manuscript, 1980; and Farnsworth, "Economics of Acculturation."

4. Farnsworth, "Economics of Acculturation," p. 78.

5. David Huelsbeck, "Wild Animals in the Mission Diet: Luxury or Necessity?" in David Huelsbeck, ed., *Lost and All But Forgotten: Archaeology and History at the Santa Clara Mission Site,* in press.

6. Edward Harrison, *History of Santa Cruz County, California* (San Francisco, 1892), p. 47.

7. Farnsworth, "Economics of Acculturation," pp. 610–11.

8. Robert H. Jackson, "Patterns of Demographic Change in the Missions of Central Alta California," *Journal of California and Great Basin Anthropology* 9(1987):251–72.

9. Farnsworth, "Economics of Acculturation," pp. 616–17.

10. Robert H. Jackson, "Demographic Change in Northwestern New Spain," *The Americas* 41(1985): 44–45.

11. Robert H. Jackson, "La colonización de la Alta California: Un análisis del desarrollo de dos comunidades misionales," *Historia Mexicana* 41 (1991): 107–8.

12. Farnsworth, "Economics of Acculturation," pp. 616–17.

13. See Robert Ricard, *The Spiritual Conquest of Mexico: An Essay on the Apostolate and the Evangelizing Methods of the Mendicant Orders in*

New Spain, 1523–1572, trans. and ed. by Lesley Byrd Simpson (Berkeley and Los Angeles, 1966).

14. Richard Greenleaf, *Zumarraga and the Mexican Inquisition, 1536–1543* (Washington, D.C., 1961), chapters 3–4.

15. The classic study on the world view of the early Mexican missionaries is John Phelan, *The Millennial Kingdom of the Franciscans in the New World,* 2d rev. ed. (Berkeley and Los Angeles, 1970).

16. For example, Nancy Farriss, *Maya Society under Colonial Rule: The Collective Enterprise of Survival* (Princeton, 1984); Inga Clendinnen, *Ambivalent Conquests: Maya and Spaniard in Yucatan, 1517–1570* (Cambridge, 1987); and Sabine MacCormack, *Religion in the Andes: Vision and Imagination in Early Colonial Peru* (Princeton, 1991).

17. Farriss, *Maya Society,* especially chapters 10–11.

18. Ibid., chapter 10; and Clendinnen, *Ambivalent Conquests.*

19. MacCormack, *Religion in the Andes,* pp. 181–204; and Steve Stern, *Peru's Indian Peoples and the Challenge of Spanish Conquest: Huamanga to 1640* (Madison, 1982), pp. 52–71.

20. The most complete biography of Serra, although biased, is Maynard Geiger, OFM, *The Life and Times of Junipero Serra,* 2 vols. (Washington, D.C., 1959).

21. Farnsworth, "Economics of Acculturation," p. 97.

22. Quoted in Erick Langer and Robert H. Jackson, "Colonial and Republican Missions Compared: The Cases of Alta California and Southeastern Bolivia," *Comparative Studies in Society and History* 30(1988):302. A recent study of religious change in the Andean region following the Spanish conquest of the sixteenth century argues that Christian missionaries identified traditional Indian religious practices as artifacts of the devil or demons. The devil or demons spoke to Indians under the guise of their gods, which belief influenced the way missionaries reacted to native religion.

23. Langer and Jackson, "Colonial and Republican Missions," 302–3.

24. Ibid., 301–2.

25. James Sandos, "Levantamiento! The Chumash Uprising Reconsidered," *Southern California Quarterly* 67(1985):109–33.

26. Langer and Jackson, "Colonial and Republican Missions," 301–3.

27. Zephyrin Engelhardt, OFM, *Mission Santa Inés Virgen y Mártir and Its Ecclesiastical Seminary* (Santa Barbara, 1932), pp. 14–15.

28. Sandos, "Levantamiento."

29. Lowell Bean and Sylvia Vane, "Cults and Their Transformations," in Robert Heizer, ed., *Handbook of North American Indians: California* (Washington, D.C., 1978), p. 669.

30. Campbell Grant, "Eastern Coastal Chumash," in Heizer, *Handbook,* p. 313.

31. Lowell Bean and Charles Smith, "Gabrielino," in Heizer, *Handbook,* p. 548; Bean and Vane, "Cults," p. 669.

32. Bean and Vane, "Cults," p. 669.

33. Charles Gibson, *The Aztecs under Spanish Rule: The Indians of the Valley of Mexico, 1519–1810* (Stanford, 1964), chap. 7.

34. Engelhardt, *Mission Santa Inés*, pp. 19–20. See also George Phillips, "The Alcaldes: Indian Leadership in the Spanish Missions of California," *The D'Arcy McNickle Center For the History of the American Indian Occasional Papers in Curriculum Series* 11(1989):83–89.

35. Edward Castillo, trans. and ed., "An Indian Account of the Decline and Collapse of Mexico's Hegemony over the Missionized Indians of California," *American Indian Quarterly* 13(1989):391–408.

36. Zephyrin Engelhardt, OFM, *Mission San Carlos Borromeo: The Father of the Missions* (Ramona, Cal., 1973), p. 131.

37. Zephyrin Engelhardt, OFM, *San Fernando Rey: The Mission of the Valley* (Ramona, Cal., 1973), p. 33.

38. Zephyrin Engelhardt, OFM, *San Antonio de Padua: The Mission in the Sierras* (Ramona, Cal., 1972), pp. 34–35.

39. Zephyrin Engelhardt, OFM, *San Miguel, Arcangel: The Mission on the Highway* (Ramona, Cal., 1971), pp. 17–18.

40. Edith Wallace, "Sexual Status and Role Differences," in Heizer, *Handbook*, pp. 683–89.

41. Ibid.

Chapter 3

1. On the spread of epidemics along trade routes, see Daniel Reff, *Disease, Depopulation, and Culture Change in Northwestern New Spain, 1518–1764* (Salt Lake City, 1991).

2. Fr. Tomás de la Peña, San Francisco, April 28, 1806, BLUC.

3. José Viader, San Francisco, May 29, 1806, BLUC.

4. For examples of studies that document mortality patterns during other epidemic outbreaks in northwestern New Spain, see Robert H. Jackson, "Epidemic Disease and the Population of the Sonora Missions in the 17th, 18th, and Early 19th Centuries," unpublished manuscript, 1990; Robert H. Jackson, "The 1781–1782 Smallpox Epidemic in the Baja California Missions," *Journal of California and Great Basin Anthropology* 3(1981): 138–43; and Robert H. Jackson, "Epidemic Disease and Population Decline in the Baja California Missions, 1697–1834," *Southern California Quarterly* 63(1981):308–46. In most cases the missionaries registering epidemic deaths did not record the specific age of the victims or the amount of time the victim had lived in the mission community. The 1769–70 measles outbreak claimed the lives of young children and recent converts at San Ignacio, Santa María Magdalena, and Caborca in the Pimería Alta, the most susceptible

segment of the population not previously exposed to the disease. In 1781 the majority of smallpox deaths at Tumacacori were of children and young adults under the age of twenty born or brought to the mission since the last major smallpox outbreak in the 1760s.

5. In the 1780s inoculation by variolation, the intentional infection of an individual with smallpox to build up immunity to the disease, was first practiced in northwestern New Spain, where it reduced smallpox mortality. In 1803 the Spanish government sent an expedition to the New World to introduce the Jenner cowpox vaccine, but with limited results. Smallpox still claimed hundreds of lives in Sonora and the Californias until at least the 1830s. Purging and bloodletting, commonly practiced in the eighteenth century, generally proved worse than the disease, while other popular treatments could prove useful. Concern with the spread of Asian cholera in the 1830s prompted the Mexican government to issue instructions for its treatment, including measures to improve sanitation, which generally helped when carried out. For a discussion of some medical practices in northwestern New Spain, see Jackson, "1781–1782 Smallpox Epidemic," and Jackson, "Epidemic Disease." On explanations given by missionaries for high rates of epidemic mortality, see John L. Phelan, *The Millenial Kingdom of the Franciscans in the New World,* 2d rev. ed. (Berkeley and Los Angeles, 1970).

In the late eighteenth and early nineteenth centuries, the Spanish and Mexican governments circulated reports on different forms of disease treatment, such as treatments for smallpox and, when it became a major problem in the 1830s, Asian cholera. These treatments, though not always effective, were at least made available to government officials and missionaries alike in northwestern New Spain.

6. See, for example, E. A. Wrigley and R. S. Schofield, *The Population History of England, 1541–1871: A Reconstruction* (Cambridge, Mass., 1981).

7. A number of the responses to the 1813–15 questionnaires reported the spread of syphilis to the Indian populations living in the missions. The Franciscans stationed at San Gabriel mission reported that "This last named [impurity in sexual relations—syphilis] has permeated them to the very marrow with [the] venereal malady. The consequence is that many children at birth already manifest the only patrimony which their parents give them [congenital syphilis]. Hence it is that of four born, three die in the first and second year of their [life]; and that of the rest who survive, the most reach [only] the age of twenty–five." Quoted in Zephyrin Engelhardt, OFM, *San Gabriel Mission and the Beginnings of Los Angeles* (San Gabriel, 1927), p. 104. The Franciscans stationed at San Buenaventura wrote in 1814 that "The most prevailing diseases are the *gálico* [syphilis], consumption, and dysentery . . . These [maladies] afflict them [the Indians] more forcibly in [the] spring and autumn. The number of births does not correspond with that of deaths; for in some years there are three deaths to two births." Quoted in

Zephyrin Engelhardt, OFM, *San Buenaventura: The Mission by the Sea* (Santa Barbara, 1930), p. 36. The Franciscans at Santa Barbara noted that "The most pernicious [disease], however, and the one from which they [the Indians] suffer most in this region, is the *mal gálico* [syphilis], or French disease. All are infected with it . . . On this account few children are born, and of these many die soon after birth, so that the number of deaths exceeds that of births by three to one." Quoted in Zephyrin Engelhardt, OFM, *Santa Barbara Mission: The Queen of the Missions* (San Francisco, 1923), p. 94.

8. In response to the 1813–15 questionnaire, the missionaries stationed at Santa Clara mission reported that abortion was one of the principal vices of the Indians. See Erick Langer and Robert H. Jackson, "Colonial and Republican Missions Compared: The Cases of Alta California and Southeastern Bolivia," *Comparative Studies in Society and History* 30(1988):302–3. In a recent study, Edward Castillo cited an Indian account of mission life that described how Ramón Olbes, OFM, stationed at Santa Cruz mission, examined the reproductive organs of one Indian women believed to be sterile, had the woman beaten when she resisted the examination, and made her stand in front of the mission church with a small wooden doll, representing a child not born, as a form of public humiliation. Other accounts document similar practices at different missions. Castillo suggests that the missionaries suspected that sterile women practiced abortion, and that the beatings and public humiliation were designed to prevent this behavior. See Edward Castillo, "The Native Responses to the Colonization of Alta California," in David H. Thomas, ed., *Columbian Consequences: Archaeological and Historical Perspectives on the Spanish Borderlands West* (Washington, D.C., 1989), 1:380. Sherburne Cook argued that negative conditions in the missions, including poor diet, social control, and limitations on cultural expression and physical mobility, contributed to the practice of abortion and infanticide. See Sherburne F. Cook, *The Conflict between the California Indian and White Civilization*, reprint ed. (Berkeley and Los Angeles, 1976), p. 112.

9. Diego de Borica, Monterey, June 30, 1797, "Noticias de las misiones que ocupan los religiosos de S. Francisco del colegio de San Fernando de México en dicha provincia," W. B. Stevens Document Collection, #9, University of Texas General Libraries, Austin, Texas. Borica apparently appended his observations on conditions in the missions to a standard biennial report of the type generally prepared by the Father-President of the Alta California missions.

10. On the supply of food to military garrisons, see Robert H. Jackson, "Population and the Economic Dimension of Colonization in Alta California: Four Communities," *Journal of the Southwest* 33(1991):387–439. Between 1810 and 1830, for example, the Franciscans stationed at San Gabriel mission supplied food and clothing to the garrisons at San Diego and Santa Barbara, which according to their own calculations, was worth 56,560 pesos.

See Engelhardt, *San Gabriel Mission,* p. 134. Between 1785 and 1789, the missionaries stationed at San Gabriel mission stored between 50 and 100 percent of the wheat and corn produced at the mission in granaries. See San Gabriel Mission annual reports, AGN.

11. Cook, *Conflict,* pp. 45, 55.

12. Ann Stodder, *Mechanisms and Trends in the Decline of the Costanoan Indian Population of Central California* (Salinas, 1986).

13. Reported in David Huelsbeck, ed., *Lost and All But Forgotten: Archaeology and History at the Santa Clara Mission Site,* in press (Salinas, Cal.).

14. Richard Herr, *Rural Change and Royal Finances in Spain at the End of the Old Regime* (Berkeley and Los Angeles, 1989), pp. 191–93.

15. The Asisara account, an oral history collected in the 1870s from a former resident of Santa Cruz mission, provides additional insights into the use of dormitories at the Alta California missions. The Asisara account is available in translation in two articles edited by Edward Castillo: "The Assassination of Padre Andres Quintana by the Indians of Mission Santa Cruz in 1812: The Narrative of Lorenzo Asisara," *California History* 68(3) (1989):116–25; 150–52; and "An Indian Account of the Decline and Collapse of Mexico's Hegemony over the Missionized Indians of California," *American Indian Quarterly* (fall, 1989):391–408. Sherburne Cook (*Conflict,* pp. 88–90) discussed the use of dormitories at the missions and concluded that women and girls incarcerated in them slept uncomfortably in cramped quarters and faced problems of incomplete, disturbed sleep, poor ventilation, the accumulation of filth, and the emotional strain of forced immobility for a people used to considerable mobility.

16. On the construction of Indian housing at specific missions and the chronology of the development of building complexes see, for example, Robert H. Jackson, "A Chronology of Building Construction at Santa Clara Mission, 1777–1832," in Huelsbeck, *Lost and All But Forgotten.* The missionaries stationed at Santa Clara (established 1777) directed the construction of adobe Indian housing organized in rows in the 1790s. For a second example see Robert H. Jackson, "A Chronology of Building Construction at the First La Purísima Site," *Prelado de los Tesoros* (1988) (this journal is the monthly publication of the La Purísima State Historic Park docents group); Robert H. Jackson, "A Chronology of Building Construction at La Purísima Concepción Mission, 1788–1835," unpublished manuscript, 1988. The Franciscans stationed at La Purísima (established 1787) had Indian housing built between 1798 and 1810. In 1812, following a devastating earthquake, the missionaries reported that a hundred Indian housing units had been rendered unusable because of earthquake damage. The missionaries relocated the mission to a new site and had several large barracks-type housing units built. Both kinds of housing were built at Santa Cruz mission (established 1791); row

houses between 1800 and 1810, large barracks-type housing between 1818 and 1822, to accommodate new recruits brought to the mission from the Central Valley. See Robert Jackson, Edna Kimbro, Randy Miliken, and MaryEllen Ryan, "Como la Sombra Huye la Hora: Restoration Research, Santa Cruz Mission Adobe, Santa Cruz Mission State Historic Park," unpublished report, 1985, State of California Department of Parks and Recreation, Sacramento, California. The Franciscans stationed at San Rafael mission (established 1817) had Indian housing built between 1822 and 1831, although a part of the Indian population probably continued to live in traditional-style housing. There is a reference to Indian housing built at San Francisco Solano (established 1823) in 1825. Again, however, a part of the Indian population probably lived in traditional-style housing. See Robert H. Jackson, "A Chronology of Building Construction at San Rafael and San Francisco Solano Missions," unpublished manuscript, 1986. Although incomplete, the record of building construction at Santa Inés mission (established 1804) indicates that eighty Indian housing units were built in 1812 and probably had to be repaired following the earthquake in December of the same year. Notes on building construction at Santa Inés mission taken from extant annual reports, SBMA. Maps prepared following secularization show that Indian housing at Santa Inés was organized in rows of multiunit buildings.

For other studies that outline the chronology of building construction at California missions and mention Indian housing, see: Maynard Geiger, OFM, "New Data on Mission San Juan Capistrano," *Southern California Quarterly* 49(1967):37–45; Maynard Geiger, OFM, "The Building of Mission San Gabriel: 1771-1828," *Southern California Quarterly* 50(1968): 33–42; and Harry Kelsey, "The Mission Buildings of San Juan Capistrano: A Tentative Chronology," *Southern California Quarterly* 69(1987):1–32. Curiously, although the author of the last article included a series of diagrams showing the development of the main quadrangle of the mission complex of buildings, Kelsey did not indicate the location or spatial organization of the Indian housing. Zephyrin Engelhardt, OFM, included data on building construction at the California missions in his series of individual mission histories published in the 1920s and early 1930s, including references to the construction of Indian housing.

Walls frequently surrounded Indian housing, in order to limit the mobility of converts, and specifically to prevent flight. For example the barracks-like dormitory built at Santa Cruz mission between 1819 and 1822 to house recent Yokuts recruits was partially or completely surrounded by walls. The trail that led to the orchard described in the Asisara account, a possible escape route, may have been closed off by the construction of walls. Several maps of the Santa Bárbara mission building complex, reproduced in Engelhardt, *Santa Barbara Mission,* show a long wall surrounding the Indian housing on three sides, with the fourth side opening to the main complex and the guard house of the soldiers stationed there.

Plat maps were prepared in the mid-1850s for each of the missions, when the properties were returned to the Catholic church, but few record former Indian housing or walls in the building complexes that might have survived in the 1850s. Lack of maintenance and the removal of roofing materials resulted in the rapid physical deterioration of Indian housing between the mid-1830s and mid-1850s. Few examples of Indian housing survive today. The finest example is the 1820s barracks-style family housing unit built at Santa Cruz mission to house Yokuts converts from the Central Valley. The state of California is currently restoring the adobe structure as the central feature of Santa Cruz Mission State Historic Park.

17. On this point see Langer and Jackson, "Colonial and Republican Missions," p. 301. On the psychological disorientation of Indians living in the missions, see George H. Phillips, "Indians and the Breakdown of the Spanish Mission System in California," *Ethnohistory* 21(1974):291–302. In a similar situation the Franciscans stationed in Baja California relocated a group known as the Guaicura, only marginally acculturated, to a mission with well-watered agricultural lands and attempted to force them to work in sustained filed labor for the first time, with negative results. The Indians engaged in active and passive resistance, including flight, work slowdowns, and the destruction of mission property. The Franciscans and civil officials used escalating levels of corporal punishment in an attempt to get the Indians to work, but they eventually had to hire non-Indian agricultural workers to oversee Indian laborers and even to work the land. See Robert H. Jackson, "Patterns of Demographic Change in the Missions of Southern Baja California," *Journal of California and Great Basin Anthropology* 8 (1986):273–79.

18. On fugitivism from Alta California missions, see Robert H. Jackson, "Central Alta California," pp. 258–60. Cook was one of the first scholars to identify the significance of flight from the Alta California missions in *Conflict*, especially p. 426.

A rough estimate can be made of the net flight from selected missions by calculating the difference between the total number of baptisms and burials and the population. The maximum estimate of population loss due to flight would be the difference between the population and baptisms plus burials. However, there are flaws in the methodology. For example Indians could have died or been baptized away from the missions and not have been counted in mission censuses. Moreover non-Indian baptisms were included in the summaries included in the annual reports, thus inflating the estimate of the number of Indians who successfully fled. Nevertheless the figures do indicate the relative magnitude of the problem. Finally in the specific case of the four San Francisco Bay missions of San Francisco, San José, San Rafael, and San Francisco Solano (Santa Clara is excluded), the estimate of the number of fugitives must be combined, since converts were relocated among the four establishments. Data from selected establishments are summarized below for the year 1832.

Estimate of Indians Having Fled from Selected Missions by the Year 1832

Mission	Total Baptisms to 1832	Total Burials to 1832	Pop. in 1832	Estimated No. of Fugitives
San Fernando	2,784	1,983	782	19
San Buenaventura	3,875	3,150	668	57
Santa Inés	1,348	1,227	360	-239[a]
La Purísima	3,256	2,633	372	251[b]
San Luis Obispo	2,644	2,268	231	145
San Miguel	2,475	1,862	658	45
San Antonio	4,419	3,617	640	162
Soledad	2,139	1,705	339	95
Santa Cruz	2,439	1,972	281	186
San Juan Bautista	4,017	2,854	916	247
Four San Francisco Bay Missions	16,098	10,985	3,213	1,900

[a] Indicates that converts were transferred to the mission from another mission.
[b] A part of the difference can be attributed to the transfer of converts to another mission, most likely Santa Inés.

Source: 1832 annual reports, Santa Barbara Mission Archive-Library, Santa Barbara, California.

Several patterns emerge. First and most important, the missions located in central and northern Alta California experienced more of a problem with fugitivism. This can be attributed to the fact that the contact populations there were smaller than those in the southern part of the province, and the missionaries resettled recruits from a greater distance, throwing together a large number of converts from distinct politico-cultural groups. The recruitment of Indians from the Central Valley initiated a phase of increased resistance to the mission regime, especially in the form of large-scale flight. Second, the problem appears to have been greatest in the San Francisco Bay missions, which were relatively close to the Sacramento–San Joaquin River delta, which provided an ideal refuge. Flight was less of a problem in culturally homogeneous areas, such as in the Chumash missions located on the Santa Barbara Channel, until the 1824 revolt and revitalization movement, which led hundreds of former converts to a new life in an isolated part of the Central Valley.

19. The annual reports record a general increase in production levels, both in grains and livestock. The Franciscans engaged in trade with foreign merchants, selling cattle hides and tallow in exchange for manufactured goods not produced in California. Goods supplied to the military also increased in volume. See, for example, Jackson, "Economic Dimension." A major theme in the works of Zephyrin Engelhardt is the way the military exploited and abused the Indians, contributing to increased resistance by converts. However, Engelhardt ignores the fact that the missionaries generally worked in close concert with the military and political leadership of the province, especially after 1810. This connection is evident through a reading of correspondence between missionaries and garrison commanders and the accounts of supplies provided to the military.

20. See Langer and Jackson, "Colonial and Republican Missions," pp. 301–3. The answers to the 1813–15 questionnaire reveal what different missionaries knew about traditional Indian religious practices. The Franciscans stationed at San Gabriel noted that "According to our observations it seems that the Indians have some superstitions, or rather some vain practices peculiar to recent converts . . ." (quoted in Engelhardt, *San Gabriel Mission*, p. 100). A missionary at San Luis Obispo wrote, "I have not observed that they adore the sun and the moon. What I did learn is that the pagans have a sort of oratory, but I have not been able to verify the report, nor to whom they direct their supplications" (quoted in Zephyrin Engelhardt, OFM, *Mission San Luis Obispo* (Santa Barbara, 1933), p. 50). Finally the missionaries at Santa Barbara wrote that, "Though we tried hard, we have not been able to ascertain whether in their pagan state they practiced any formal idolatry or vain observations" (quoted in Engelhardt, *Santa Barbara Mission*, p. 93).

21. Nancy Farriss, *Maya Society under Colonial Rule: The Collective Enterprise of Survival* (Princeton, 1984), pp. 286–354. Farriss argues that the Yucatec Maya incorporated the Christian god and saints into their own religion at different levels of worship. For example specific saints became transformed into the fertility god of a village, and the adoration of the saint became the primary act of communal religious practice. The evidence from the Alta California missions suggests that some missionaries did not believe that the California Indians could have a complex religion and world view.

22. Langer and Jackson, "Colonial and Republican Missions," pp. 302–3.

23. Ibid., p. 302.

24. See Robert H. Jackson, "Demographic Change in Northwestern New Spain," *The Americas* 41(1985):462–79.

25. Phillips develops this interpretation in "Breakdown of the Spanish Mission System."

26. Robert H. Jackson, "La dinámica del desastre demográfico de la población india en las misiones de la bahia de San Francisco, Alta California, 1776–1840," *Historia Mexicana* 40(1991):204–5.

27. Maynard Geiger, OFM, *Franciscan Missionaries in Hispanic California, 1769–1848* (San Marino, 1969), pp. xi, 282–93.

Chapter 4

1. Zephyrin Engelhardt, OFM, *Missions and Missionaries of California,* 2d ed. (Santa Barbara, 1930), 2:47; H. H. Bancroft, *History of California* (San Francisco, 1886–90), 1:138–39. The Cabrillo expedition, the first Spanish expedition to California (1542–43), also met hostility from California Indians. During the winter of 1542–43, the Spaniards established a camp on Catalina Island. There were many Indian attacks on the camp, which eventually cost Cabrillo his life. See Henry Wagner, *Spanish Voyages to the Northwest Coast of America in the Sixteenth Century* (San Francisco, 1929); and Harry Kelsey, *Juan Rodriguez Cabrillo* (San Marino, 1986).

2. Engelhardt, *Missions and Missionaries* 2:116; and Edward Castillo, "Neophyte Resistance and Accommodation in the Missions of California," in *The Spanish Missionary Heritage of the United States* (San Antonio, 1993).

3. For a useful overview of revitalization movements, see Michael Adas, *Prophets of Rebellion: Millenarian Protest Movements against the European Colonial Order* (Chapel Hill, 1979). Other Indian revitalization movements include the 1680 Pueblo Revolt in New Mexico and the Ghost Dance movement among the Great Plains tribes, during the late nineteenth century. The most detailed ethnographic studies of any North American revitalization movement are James Mooney, *The Ghost Dance Religion and Wounded Knee,* reprint ed. (New York, 1973); and Alice Kehoe, *The Ghost Dance Ethnohistory and Revitalization* (New York, 1989).

4. William Taylor, *Drinking, Homicide, and Rebellion in Colonial Mexican Villages* (Stanford, 1979).

5. Michael Craton, *Testing the Chains: Resistance to Slavery in the British West Indies* (Ithaca, 1982), p. 53, states that noncooperation was the most common form of slave resistance, and that the theft of plantation property was perceived as a challenge to the slave system. On passive resistance in the missions, see Castillo, "Neophyte Resistance and Accommodation."

6. Rafael Verger, OFM, Mexico City, October 22, 1771, W. B. Stevens Collection, General Libraries of the University of Texas, Austin, Document no. 72 (hereinafter cited as Verger, WBS).

7. Florence Shipek, "California Indian Reactions to the Franciscans," *The Americas* 41(April 1985):53–66.

8. Quoted in Edward Castillo, "The Native Response to the Colonization of Alta California," in David. H. Thomas, ed., *Columbian Consequences* (Washington, D.C., 1989) 1:377–94; and Antonine Tibesar, OFM, trans. and

ed., *Writings of Junipero Serra* (Washington, D.C., 1955) 1:362–63.

9. Zephyrin Engelhardt, OFM, *Missions and Missionaries* 2:116; and Edward Castillo, "California Indian Women and the Missions of Alta California," paper presented at symposium on "Spanish Beginnings in California, 1542–1822," Santa Barbara, California, July 16, 1991.

10. Edward Castillo, "Neophyte Resistance and Accommodation."

11. Engelhardt, *Missions and Missionaries,* 2:230–31.

12. Ibid., 2:192.

13. Castillo, "California Indian Women."

14. Verger, WBS.

15. Ibid.

16. On the 1781 Yuma revolt, see Jack Forbes, *Warriors of the Colorado: The Yumans of the Quechan Nation and Their Neighbors* (Norman, 1965); and Castillo, "Native Responses," p. 386.

17. Castillo, "California Indian Women."

18. The trial record is found in the AGN Provincias Internas 120, expediente 34.

19. Ibid.

20. For a description of the 1824 Chumash revolt, see James Sandos, "Levantamiento," pp. 109–33; Maynard Geiger, OFM, trans. and ed., "Fray Antonio Ripoli's Description of the Chumash Revolt at Santa Barbara in 1824," *Southern California Quarterly* 52(1970):345–64.

21. Quoted in Castillo, "Neophyte Resistance,", p. 69.

22. Nancy Farriss, *Maya Society under Colonial Rule,* pp. 67–79.

23. Sylvia Broadbent, "Conflict at Monterey: Indian Horse Raiding 1820–1850," *Journal of California Anthropology* 1(1974):86–101; Albert Hurtado, *Indian Survival on the California Frontier* (New Haven, 1988), chap. 2; Castillo, "Native Responses"; and George Phillips, *Indians And Intruders in Central California, 1769–1849* (Norman, 1993).

24. Jack Holterman, "The Revolt of Estanislao," *The Indian Historian* 3(1970):43–54. Not all alcaldes turned resistance leaders led their followers to the Central Valley. Pomponio, a Coast Miwok baptized at San Francisco mission in 1803 as a young child, who may have been an alcalde at San Rafael, led a band of fugitives from the missions that raided settlements in 1823 in the San Francisco Bay area and as far south as Soledad mission. Soldiers caught Pomponio at a hideout near modern Novato, and he was sent to Monterey Presidio and was executed on February 6, 1824. Pomponio's band established hideouts at different sites in what is today Marin County, north of San Francisco, and in the mountains on the San Mateo Peninsula. See Alan Brown, "Pomponio's World," *Argonaut* (publication of the San Francisco Corral of Westerners) 6(1975):1–20.

25. Cook, *Conflict,* p. 60; see also Castillo, "Responses," pp. 381–83.

26. Cook, *Conflict,* pp. 116–21. Franciscan concerns over fugitivism and

the depletion of the mission labor force can be seen in several letters written
to local military officials by the Santa Cruz missionary Manuel Fernandez,
reporting the flight of 138 Indian converts and the return several months
later of a number of the fugitives: "I tell you that the Neophytes that are
presently fugitives are 46 adult males, 34 adult [females], 27 boy children 8
years [of age and] below, and 35 girl children, that together are 138 [people].
Those that daily unite for the labors are something more than 30 to 40 men.
Joaquin Mesa arrived with 52 of the recent fugitive Neophytes: 30 are 15
years [of age] and above, and so above [of advanced age] *that only 14 of
them half serve for work* and 22 are *parvulos* [young children]" (emphasis
added; quoted in Jackson, "Central Alta California," p. 259).

27. Ibid., pp. 198–207, 245–51; Sherburne Cook, "Colonial Expeditions to
the Interior of California: Central Valley, 1800–1820," *University of California Anthropological Papers* 16(1960):239–92; and Sherburne Cook, "Colonial Expeditions to the Interior of California: Central Valley, 1820–1840,"
University of California Anthropological Papers 20(1962):151–214.

28. Edward Castillo, "The Assassination of Padre Andrés Quintana by the
Indians of Mission Santa Cruz in 1812: The Narrative of Lorenzo Asisara,"
California History 68(1989):116–25, 150–52.

29. Zephyrin Engelhardt, OFM, *San Antonio de Padua: The Mission in
the Sierras,* reprint ed. (Ramona, 1972), pp. 104–7.

30. Edward Castillo and Doyce Nunis, "California Mission Indians: Two
Perspectives," *California History* 70(1991):206–15, 236–38.

31. Ibid., p. 207.

32. Ibid., pp. 213–14.

33. Shipek, "California Indian Responses," p. 59.

34. Verger, WBS.

35. This conclusion is based upon an analysis of extant annual reports
from the AGN and SBMA.

36. Quoted in Edward Castillo, trans. and ed., "An Indian Account of the
Decline and Collapse of Mexico's Hegemony over the Missionized Indians
of California," *American Indian Quarterly* 13(1989):396.

37. Quoted in Zephyrin Engelhardt, OFM, *San Francisco or Mission Dolores* (Chicago, 1924), p. 141.

38. Quoted in Castillo, "California Indian Women."

39 Robert Heizer, ed., *The Indians of Los Angeles County: Hugo Reid's
Letters of 1852* (Los Angeles, 1968), pp. 75–76.

40. Castillo, "Responses," p. 379.

41. Quoted in ibid., p. 379.

42. Quoted in Langer and Jackson, "Colonial and Republican Missions,"
pp. 286–311.

43. Quoted in Castillo, "An Indian Account," p. 398.

44. Heizer, *Indians of Los Angeles County,* p. 87.

45. Langer and Jackson, "Colonial and Republican Missions," p. 301.

46. The description of corporal punishment at San Carlos mission is taken from the journals of Jean François de la Perouse, recently republished by Heydey Books (Berkeley, 1989), as *Monterey in 1786: The Journals of Jean François de La Perouse*, pp. 82, 89.

47. Quoted in Engelhardt, *San Francisco or Mission Dolores*, p. 140.

48. Pablo Vicente de Sola, "Manifiesto del Sr. Gob[ernado]r dirigido al Vireinato en Vindicación de la fama del Dif[unt]o P. Quintana contra lo alegado por los reos de su muerte con carta circular que le acompana en 1 dia de 1816," SBMA.

49. Travis Hudson, ed., *Breath of the Sun: Life in Early California as Told by a Chumash Indian, Fernando Librado to John P. Harrington* (Banning, Cal., 1979), p. 17.

50. Minna and Gordon Hewes, trans. and ed., "Indian Life and Customs at Mission San Luis Rey: A Record of California Mission Life Written by Pablo Tac, an Indian Neophyte (Rome ca. 1835)," *The Americas* 9(1952): 87–106.

51. Nellie Van der Grift Sanchez, ed., "Recollections of My Youth at San Luis Rey Mission: The Memoirs of a full-blooded Indian, of affairs and events witnessed at one of California's most famous "cathedrals of the sun," *Touring Topics* 22(1878):42–43.

52. Heizer, *Indians of Los Angeles County*, p. 76. The historian George Phillips, in "Indians and the Breakdown of the Spanish Mission System in California," *Ethnohistory* 21(1974):291–302, discusses what he identifies as the "psychological dislocation" of converts living in the regimented and paternalistic mission regime. In another article Phillips further develops the theme of Indian social disintegration, but in this case outside of the missions. The author focuses on former mission Indians who settled at Los Angeles following the secularization of the missions. See his "Indians in Los Angeles, 1781–1875: Economic Integration, Social Disintegration," *Pacific Historical Review* 43(1980):427–51.

53. Quoted in Langer and Jackson, "Colonial and Republican Missions," p. 301.

54. "Interview With Dr. Harry Kelsey," in Edward Castillo, ed., *Native American Perspectives on the Hispanic Colonization of Alta California* (New York, 1991), p. 452.

55. "Interview with Doyce Nunis," in Castillo, *Native American Perspectives*, p. 445.

Chapter 5

1. The standard history of politics in Mexico in the 1820s and 1830s is Michael P. Costeloe, *La primera república federal de México (1824–1835): Un estudio de los partidos políticos en el México independiente* (Mexico

City, 1975). For a study of one of the violent episodes in Mexican political life during this period, see Silvia Arrom, "Popular Politics in Mexico City: The Parian Riot, 1828," *Hispanic American Historical Review* 68(1988): 245–68.

2. On the content of Mexican liberalism, see Charles Hale, *Mexican Liberalism in the Age of Mora, 1821–1853* (New Haven, 1968); on politics during the 1820s and 1830s, see Costeloe, *La primera república;* Daniel Cosío Villegas, ed., *Historia general de México* (Mexico City, 1976), pp. 737–1016; and Jan Bazant, *Alienation of Church Wealth in Mexico: Social and Economic Aspects of the Liberal Revolution, 1856–1875,* ed. and trans. by Michael Costeloe (Cambridge, 1971).

3. For the background to secularization, the concern for the sparse population of the northern frontier region, and Mexican colonization policy, see David Weber, *The Mexican Frontier 1821–1846 The American Southwest under Mexico* (Albuquerque, 1982). Recent examinations of the legal background of secularization include Manuel Servin, "The Secularization of the California Missions: A Reappraisal," *Southern California Quarterly* 47(1965):133–49; and C. Alan Hutchinson, "The Mexican Government and the Mission Indians of Upper California, 1821–1835," *The Americas* 21(1965): 335–62.

4. Hale, *Mexican Liberalism,* pp. 220–21. The arguments against the missions were a variant on the general liberal analysis of the changes necessary in the legal status of Indians so that they could be fully integrated into Mexican society.

5. On liberal views on corporate wealth and privilege, see Hale, *Mexican Liberalism,* chapters 4 and 8; and Bazant, *Alienation,* chap. 1.

6. On the administration of the Pious Fund in early republican Mexico, see Bazant, *Alienation,* pp. 22–29.

7. On the decrees of expulsion of the Spanish-born from Mexico, see Romeo Flores Caballero, *La contrarrevolución en la independencia: Los españoles en la vida política, social y económica de México (1804–1838)* (Mexico City, 1973), chapters 6 and 7.

8. Local government officials in northern Sonora expelled Spanish-born Franciscans stationed in the Pimería Alta missions in 1828. See John Kessell, *Friars, Soldiers, and Reformers: Hispanic Arizona and the Sonora Mission Frontier, 1767–1856* (Tucson, 1976), pp. 269–74. Under the federalist political system that existed in Mexico between 1824 and 1835, the national government could enact nationwide policies, but the individual state and territorial governments were responsible for passing enabling legislation to enforce the policies. The civil government in Alta California did not pass such legislation to enforce the expulsion of Spanish-born Franciscans from the missions.

9. Hale, *Mexican Liberalism,* pp. 221–22.

10. Stanley G. Payne, *A History Of Spain and Portugal* (Madison, 1973), 2:428–29.

11. On the 1820 restoration of the liberal Cortes in Spain and Mexican independence, see Payne, *Spain and Portugal* 2:429–35; and Brian Hamnett, *Revolución y contrarrevolución en México y el Perú (liberalismo, realeza y separatismo 1800–1824)* (Mexico City, 1978), chap. 9.

12. On the politics of the period 1832–34, see Costeloe, *La primera república*, chapters 12–15.

13. Ibid., p. 396.

14. Ibid., chap. 15.

15. Zephyrin Engelhardt, OFM, *Missions and Missionaries of California* (Santa Barbara, 1929–30) 3:239–41.

16. San Carlos Mission annual reports, 1827–32, SBMA.

17. "Mission Statistics," BLUC. For a detailed discussion of the formation of the Los Angeles Indian community, see George Phillips, "Indians in Los Angeles," 427–51.

18. Ibid.

19. Zephyrin Engelhardt, OFM, *San Juan Capistrano Mission* (Los Angeles, 1922), pp. 112–15, 121–23, 125, and 140–42.

20. Engelhardt, *Missions and Missionaries*, 3:466–82.

21. Kimbro, Jackson, and Ryan, *"Como la Sombra,"* pp. 64–69.

22. Engelhardt, *Missions and Missionaries*, 4:17.

23. William Hartnell, "Diario, Informe, y Borradores de Correspondencia" (hereinafter cited as DIB), BLUC.

24. Jose Anzar, OFM, and Andrés Pico, "Ynventario de los muebles raices semovientes en la Mision de S[an]ta Cruz por la comisión nombrada p[o]r el Exc[elentísi]mo S[eñ]or Gobernador," BLUC.

25. San Rafael Mission annual report, 1840, SBMA.

26. San José Mission annual report, 1840, SBMA.

27. San Antonio Mission annual report, 1840, SBMA.

28. San Rafael Mission annual report, 1840, SBMA.

29. "Quaderno en donde consta las familias casadas, y sus hijos e hijas, los solteros y solteras, los huérfanos y huérfanas de esta Mis[ío]n de S[a]n Ant[oni]o de Padua," BLUC.

30. José Estrada, "Padrón general que manifiesta el número de havitantes que ecsisten en la municipalidad de Monterey 1836," BLUC. In 1846 John Sutter employed a labor force of former mission Indians. There were 395 "tame/neophyte" Indians and 2,373 "wild/gentile" Indians in the lands of New Helvetia, and Sutter employed 103 "tame/neophyte" Indians in his different economic operations. See Hurtado, *Indian Survival*, pp. 66–67.

31. Ibid.

32. Hartnell, DIB, BLUC.

33. San Rafael Mission annual reports, 1818–32, SBMA; and San Rafael

Mission baptismal register, San Francisco Archdiocese Chancery Archive, Colma, California.

34. Reported in Hartnell, DIB, BLUC. Hartnell reported that he had been told at San Rafael "that in the Russian fields there are many Mission Indians whom they [the mission administrators?] claim."

35. Kimbro, Jackson, and Ryan, "*Como la Sombra*," discusses long-term demographic trends at Santa Cruz mission and the postsecularization Indian populations in the Santa Cruz area.

36. San Juan Bautista Mission annual report, 1840, SBMA.

37. San José Mission annual report, 1840, SBMA.

38. Robert H. Jackson, "The Post-Secularization Dispersion of the Population of the Alta California Missions, 1834–1846," paper presented at the annual meeting of the Rocky Mountain Council of Latin American Studies, Flagstaff, Arizona, February 26–28, 1991.

39. Hartnell, DIB, BLUC. In a letter dated November 8, 1839, Hartnell scolded the administrator of San Miguel mission for having given one Indian a hundred lashes, when the mission administrators were authorized to apply no more than twenty-five lashes to converts.

40. William Hartnell recorded such complaints during his 1839 and 1840 inspection tours. Indians living at San Fernando, San Buenaventura, San Luis Obispo, San Miguel, Santa Cruz, San Francisco, and San Rafael registered complaints about the granting of mission lands to prominent Mexican settlers. Moreover the Indians at San Juan Capistrano, Santa Cruz, and San Rafael requested the distribution of mission property and the conversion of the former missions into pueblos. Finally the Indians living at San Juan Capistrano objected to the plan of the Pico brothers to lease the mission rather than distribute mission goods to the Indians. Hartnell attributed the petition of the San Juan Capistrano Indians to bad advice from settlers trying to manipulate them, but as noted in a letter sent to Andrés Pico on July 24, 1840, the inspector general was confident that the Indians' request would be granted.

41. Kimbro, Jackson, and Ryan, "*Como la Sombra*," p. 68.

42. Ibid., p. 68.

43. Ibid., pp. 64–69, 104, 112–13, and 137–56.

44. William Hartnell to Manuel Jimeno Casarín, San José, August 21, 1839, DIB, BLUC.

45. For example see Hartnell's discussion of the slaughter of livestock in the diary entry for San Miguel mission. Hartnell stated his intention to write to the mission administrator to inquire about licenses given to individuals to slaughter cattle for hides. DIB, BLUC.

46. The following drafts of letters in the Hartnell document collection discuss the slaughter or sale of mission livestock for different reasons related to mission administration: William Hartnell to the Administrator of San Luis Rey Mission, May 31, 1839; William Hartnell to the Secretary of

the California Department Government, San Fernando, June 20, 1839; William Hartnell to the Administrator of San Buenaventura Mission, San Buenaventura, June 30, 1839; William Hartnell to the Administrator of San Antonio Mission, La Purísima, July 24, 1839; William Hartnell to the Administrator of La Purísima Mission, La Purísima, July 24, 1839; and William Hartnell to Manuel Jimeno, San Luis Rey, July 16, 1840. DIB, BLUC.

47. William Hartnell to Pio Pico, San Luis Rey, July 13, 1839. DIB, BLUC.

48. William Hartnell to the Administrator of San Luis Rey Mission, San Juan Capistrano, June 1, 1839. DIB, BLUC.

49. Zephyrin Engelhardt, OFM, *Mission Nuestra Señora de la Soledad* (Santa Barbara, 1929), pp. 33–34.

50. Thomas Savage, "Records in the Parish (ex-Mission) Church of Santa Cruz Cal. Copies and Extracts by Thomas Savage for the Bancroft Library 1877," BLUC.

51. Robert H. Jackson, "La colonización de la Alta California: un análisis de desarrollo de dos comunidades misionales," *Historia Mexicana* 41 (1991): 83–110.

52. The record of building construction at San Miguel mission between 1810 and 1832 includes references to construction projects at the ranches. San Miguel Mission annual reports, various years, SBMA. The Franciscans directed the construction of buildings at San Simeón, near the coast, in 1810, 1814, and 1830, including a granary built in 1810. Buildings were raised at Asunción in 1812 and 1813, and at Aguaje in 1815.

53. Hartnell, DIB, BLUC.

54. See the chapter on the history of the Villa de Branciforte in Kimbro, Jackson, and Ryan, *"Como la Sombra."*

55. For a useful overview of the granting of ranches in Alta California, see David Hornbeck, *California Patterns: A Geographical and Historical Atlas* (Palo Alto, 1983), pp. 58–61.

56. See, for example, William Hartnell to Juan Temple, San Fernando, August 21, 1840; DIB, BLUC.

57. "Inventario general y avalúo de los bienes muebles, raices semoventes pertenecentes a la ecspresada [Mision de Santa Cruz] que forman los que suscriben con arreglo al artículo 13 y presención 2a del reglamento provisional de secularización de 9 de agosto de 1834," transcription of original document, BLUC.

Conclusions

1. Robert H. Jackson, "Epidemic Disease and Population Decline in the Baja California Missions, 1697–1834," *Southern California Quarterly* 63:4 (1981), 321–23.

2. John Phelan, *The Millennial Kingdom of the Franciscans in the New*

World (Berkeley and Los Angeles, 1970), pp. 92–96.

3. Sherburne F. Cook, *The Conflict Between the California Indian And White Civilization* (Berkeley and Los Angeles, 1976), pp. 205–361; Sherburne F. Cook, *The Population of the California Indians 1769–1970* (Berkeley and Los Angeles, 1976), p. 56; Edward Castillo, "The Impact of Euro-American Exploration and Settlement," in Robert Heizer, editor, *Handbook of North American Indians: California* (Washington, D.C., 1978), pp. 99–127; Albert Hurtado, *Indian Survival On The California Frontier* (New Haven, 1988).

4. Robert H. Jackson, "Demographic Change In Northwestern New Spain," *The Americas* 41:1 (1985), 35–52.

5. On the population of one California region in 1845 on the eve of the American conquest of the province see Robert H. Jackson, "The 1845 Villa de Branciforte Census," *Antepasados* 4 (1980–1981), 45–57.

6. Robert H. Jackson, "Population and the Economic Dimension of Colonization in Alta California: Four Mission Communities," *Journal of the Southwest* 33:3 (1991), 387–439.

7. Robert H. Jackson, et al, "Como La Sombra Huye La Hora: Restoration Research Santa Cruz Adobe, Santa Cruz Mission State Historic Park," unpublished manuscript, Part 1, pp. 51–54.

8. Ibid., Part 1, pp. 52–53.

9. Ibid., Part 1, p. 62.

10. Ibid., Part 1, p. 62.

11. Ibid., Part 1, p. 59.

12. Ibid., Part 1, pp. 56–57.

Bibliography

Archival Sources

Archivo General de la Nación, Mexico City (AGN): This archive contains copies of reports, letters, judicial actions, and other documents sent to Mexico City from California. In the *Documentos para la Historia de México* collection and *Ramo de Californias* is a set of annual and biennial reports written by the Franciscans stationed at each mission in the 1770s, 1780s, and 1790s. The annual reports contain information on the population of the missions, agricultural production, the numbers of livestock, and building construction, as well as church equipment and vessels.

The Bancroft Library, University of California, Berkeley (BLUC): The Bancroft Library contains a number of document collections used in the preparation of this study. In the 1870s H. H. Bancroft sent paid researchers out to interview different individuals about aspects of California history. In addition Bancroft had access to a large document collection subsequently destroyed in the fire that followed the 1906 earthquake. Bancroft's assistants summarized, in a series of tables, data on population, agricultural production, and numbers of livestock; in another set of documents they copied verbatim or abstracted most of the documents contained in the archive.

In addition to these resources, the Bancroft Library houses many original documents related to the history of Spanish and Mexican California. Included are documents presented to Bancroft by ex-officials in the Mexican-era government of California, such as Mariano Vallejo, a large set of mission documents cataloged as "Archivos de las Misiones," documents collected by Bancroft's researchers, documents purchased in recent years by the library, as well as microfilm copies of large sections of the Archivo General de la Nación (Mexico City), Archivo General de las Indias (Sevilla, Spain), and the San Francisco Archdiocese Chancery Archive.

Monterey Diocese Chancery Archive: The archive maintained by Monterey diocese office in Monterey, California, preserves original sacramental registers for the missions from Santa Cruz in the north to San Luis Obispo in the south. The registers include baptisms, burials, marriages, *libros de patentes,* and *libros de padrones.*

Santa Barbara Mission Archive-Library (SBMA): At the end of the Mexican period, the head of the chain of Franciscan missions in California resided in Santa Barbara mission. The document holdings of the Santa Barbara Mission Archive-Library include the archive maintained by the father-presidents of the California missions, which consists of annual and biennial reports primarily for the years 1810–32, as well as copies of the responses written to a questionnaire sent to California in 1812 by the liberal Spanish Cortes. The archive-library also houses the sacramental registers of Santa Barbara, San Buenaventura, La Purísima, and Santa Inés missions.

San Francisco Archdiocese Chancery Archive: This archive, located in Colma, California, south of San Francisco, preserves the sacramental registers of four San Francisco Bay–area missions, excluding Santa Clara. In addition the archive also houses the Taylor collection, a set of more than four thousand letters and reports written by missionaries in Baja and Alta California.

W. B. Stevens Collection, University of Texas, Austin: This large document collection contains a variety of sources relevant to the history of the Spanish borderlands, including some on Spanish California.

Reports, Dissertations, and Published Sources

Adas, Michael. *Prophets of Rebellion: Millenarian Protest Movements Against the European Colonial Order.* Chapel Hill: University of North Carolina Press, 1979.

Archibald, Robert. *The Economic Aspect of the Alta California Missions.* Washington, D.C.: Academy of American Franciscan History, 1978.

Arrom, Sylvia. "Popular Politics in Mexico City: The Parian Riot, 1828." *Hispanic American Historical Review* 68(1988):245–68.

Aschmann, Homer. *The Central Desert of Baja California: Demography and Ecology.* Berkeley and Los Angeles: University of California Press, 1959.

Bancroft, H. H. *History of California.* 7 vols. San Francisco: The History Company, 1884–90.

Bazant, Jan. *Alienation of Church Wealth in Mexico: Social and Economic Aspects of the Liberal Revolution, 1856–1875.* Trans. and ed. Michael Costeloe. Cambridge: Cambridge University Press, 1971.

Bean, Lowell, and Charles Smith. "Gabrielino." In Heizer, ed., *Handbook of North American Indians,* pp. 538–49.

Bean, Lowell, and Sylvia Vane. "Cults and Their Transformations." In Heizer, *Handbook of North American Indians,* pp. 662–72.

Beechey, F. W. *Narrative of a Voyage to the Pacific.* London, 1831.

Broadbent, Sylvia. "Conflict at Monterey: Indian Horse Raiding 1820–1850." *Journal of California Anthropology* 1(1974):86–101.

Brown, Alan. "Pomponio's World." *Argonaut* 6(1975):1–20.

Castillo, Edward. The Impact of Euro-American Exploration and Settlement." In Heizer, *Handbook of North American Indians: California.* Washington, D.C., 1978, pp. 99–127.

———, trans. and ed. "An Indian Account of the Decline and Collapse of Mexico's Hegemony over the Missionized Indians of California." *American Indian Quarterly* 13(1989):391–406.

———. "The Native Responses to the Colonization of Alta California." In Thomas, *Columbian Consequences,* pp. 377–94.

———, trans. and ed. "The Assassination of Padre Andres Quintana by the Indians of Mission Santa Cruz in 1812: The Narrative of Lorenzo Asisara." *California History* 68(1989):116–25, 150–52.

———. "Neophyte Resistance and Accommodation in the Missions of California." *The Spanish Missionary Heritage of the United States.* San Antonio: National Parks Service, 1993, pp. 60–75.

———. "California Indian Women and the Missions of Alta California." Paper presented at symposium on "Spanish Beginnings in California, 1542–1822," Santa Barbara, California, July 16, 1991.

———, ed. *Native American Perspectives on the Hispanic Colonization of Alta California.* New York: Garland Publishing, 1991.

Castillo, Edward, and Doyce Nunis. "California Mission Indians: Two Perspectives." *California History* 70(1991):206–15, 236–38.

Clendinnen, Inga. *Ambivalent Conquests: Maya and Spaniard in Yucatan, 1517–1570.* Cambridge: Cambridge University Press, 1987.

Combs, Gary, and Fred Ploogh. "The Conversion of the Chumash Indians: An Ecological Perspective." *Human Ecology* 5(1977):309–28.

Cook, Sherburne F. "Colonial Expeditions to the Interior of California: Central Valley, 1800–1820." *University of California Anthropological Papers* 16(1960):239–92.

———. *The Conflict between the California Indian and White Civilization.* Reprint ed. Berkeley and Los Angeles: University of California Press, 1976.

———. *The Population of the California Indians, 1769–1970.* Berkeley and Los Angeles, 1976.

Cosío Villegas, Daniel, ed. *Historia General de México.* 2 vols. Mexico City: El Colegio de México, 1976.

Costeloe, Michael. *La primera república federal de México (1824–1835): Un estudio de los partidos políticos en el México independiente.* Mexico City: Fondo de Cultura Económica, 1975.

Costello, Julia. "Variability among the Alta California Missions: The Economics of Agricultural Production." In Thomas, *Columbian Consequences,* pp. 435–50.

Craton, Michael. *Testing the Chains: Resistance to Slavery in the British West Indies.* Ithaca: Cornell University Press, 1982.

Deetz, James. "Final Summary Report of Investigation at La Purisima Mission State Historical Park." Unpublished manuscript. Sacramento: California State Department of Parks and Recreation, 1963.

Dietz, Stephen et al. "Final Report of Archaeological Investigations at Mission San Jose." Sacramento: California State Department of Parks and Recreation, 1984.

Eastwood, Alice. "Menzie's California Journal." *California Historical Society Quarterly* 2(1924):265–340.

Engelhardt, Zephyrin, OFM. *Missions and Missionaries of California.* 4 vols. Santa Barbara: Mission Santa Barbara, 1908–1915 (2d ed., 1930).

———. *San Juan Capistrano Mission.* Los Angeles, 1922.

———. *Santa Barbara Mission: The Queen of the Missions.* San Francisco: James H. Barry Co., 1923.

———. *San Francisco or Mission Dolores.* Chicago: Franciscan Herald Press, 1924.

———. *San Gabriel Mission and the Beginnings of Los Angeles.* San Gabriel: Mission San Gabriel, 1927.

———. *San Buenaventura: The Mission by the Sea.* Santa Barbara: Mission Santa Barbara, 1930.

———. *San Juan Bautista: A School of Church Musie.* Santa Barbara, 1931.

———. *Mission La Concepción Purísima de María Santísima.* Santa Barbara: Mission Santa Barbara, 1932.

———. *Mission Santa Inés Virgen y Mártir and Its Ecclesiastical Seminary.* Santa Barbara: Mission Santa Barbara, 1932.

———. *Mission San Luis Obispo.* Santa Barbara: Mission Santa Barbara, 1933.

———. *San Miguel, Arcangel: The Mission on the Highway.* Reprint ed. Ramona, Cal.: Acoma Books, 1971.

———. *San Antonio de Padua: The Mission in the Sierras.* Reprint ed. Ramona, Cal.: Ballena Press, 1972.

———. *Mission San Carlos Borromeo: The Father of the Missions.* Reprint ed. Ramona, Cal.: Ballena Press, 1973.

———. *San Fernando Rey: The Mission of the Valley.* Reprint ed. Ramona, Cal.: Ballena Press, 1973.

Farnsworth, Paul. "The Economics of Acculturation in the Alta California Missions: A Historical and Archaeological Study of Nuestra Señora de la

Soledad." Ph.D. diss., University of California, Los Angeles, 1987.

Farriss, Nancy. *Maya Society under Colonial Rule: The Collective Enterprise of Survival.* Princeton: Princeton University Press, 1984.

Flores Caballero, Romeo. *La contrarrevolución en la independencia: Los españoles en la vida política, social y económica de México (1804–1838).* Mexico City: El Colegio de México, 1973.

Florescano, Enrique. *Precios de maiz y crisis agricolas en México (1500–1821).* Mexico City: El Colegio de México, 1969.

Garner, Richard, "Price Trends in Eighteenth-Century Mexico. *Hispanic American Historical Review* 65(1985):279–325.

Geiger, OFM, Maynard. *The Life and Times of Junipero Serra.* 2 vols. Washington, D.C.: Academy of American Franciscan History, 1959.

———. "New Data on Mission San Juan Capistrano." *Southern California Quarterly* 49(1967):37–45.

———. "The Building of Mission San Gabriel: 1771–1828." *Southern California Quarterly* 50(1968):33–42.

———. *Franciscan Missionaries in Hispanic California, 1769–1848.* San Marino: Huntington Library, 1969.

———, trans. and ed. "Fray Antonio Ripoli's Description of the Chumash Revolt at Santa Barbara in 1824." *Southern California Quarterly* 52(1970):345–64.

Gibson, Charles. *The Aztecs under Spanish Rule: The Indians of the Valley of Mexico, 1519–1810.* Stanford: Stanford University Press, 1964.

Grant, Campbell. "Eastern Coastal Chumash." In Heizer, *Handbook of North America,* pp. 509–19.

Greenleaf, Richard. *Zumarraga and the Mexican Inquisition, 1536–1543.* Washington, D.C.: Academy of American Franciscan History, 1961.

Guest, OFM, Francis. "An Examination of the Thesis of S. F. Cook on the Forced Conversion of Indians in the California Missions." *Southern California Quarterly* 61(1979):1–77.

Hale, Charles. *Mexican Liberalism in the Age of Mora, 1821–1853.* New Haven: Yale University Press, 1968.

Hamnett, Brian. *Revolución y contrarrevolución en México y el Perú (liberalismo, realeza y separatismo 1800–1824).* Mexico City: Fondo de Cultura Económica, 1978.

Harrison, Edward. *History of Santa Cruz County, California.* San Francisco: Pacific Press Co., 1892.

Hayes, Alden. *The Four Churches of Pecos.* Albuquerque, 1974.

Heizer, Robert, ed. *The Indians of Los Angeles County: Hugo Reid's Letters of 1852.* Los Angeles: Southwest Museum, 1968.

———, ed. *Handbook of North American Indians: California.* Washington, D.C.: Smithsonian Institution Press, 1978.

Herr, Richard. *Rural Change and Royal Finances in Spain at the End of the*

Old Regime. Berkeley and Los Angeles: University of California Press, 1989.

Hester, Thomas. "Salinan," in Heizer, *Handbook of North American Indians,* pp. 500–504.

Hewes, Minna, and Gordon Hewes, trans. and eds. "Indian Life and Customs at Mission San Luis Rey: A Record of California Mission Life Written by Pablo Tac, an Indian Neophyte (Rome ca. 1835)," *The Americas* 9(1952):87–106.

Holterman, Jack. "The Revolt of Estanislao." *Indian Historian* 3(1970): 43–54.

Hoover, Robert and Julia Costello, eds. "Excavations at Mission San Antonio: The First Three Seasons." Unpublished manuscript, UCLA, 1980.

Hornbeck, David. *California Patterns: A Geographical and Historical Atlas.* Palo Alto: Mayfield, 1983.

———. "Economic Growth and Change at the Missions of Alta California." In Thomas, *Columbian Consequences,* pp. 423–31.

Howard, Donald. *California's Lost Fortress: The Royal Presidio of Monterey.* Monterey: Privately published, 1976.

Hudson, Travis, ed. *Breath of the Sun: Life in Early California as Told by a Chumash Indian, Fernando Librado to John P. Harrington.* Banning, Cal.: Maliki Museum Press, 1979.

Huelsbeck, David. "Wild Animals in the Mission Diet: Luxury or Necessity?" In David Huelsbeck, ed., *Lost and All But Forgotten: Archaeology and History at the Santa Clara Mission Site.* In press. Salinas, Cal.: Coyote Press.

Hurtado, Albert. *Indian Survival on the California Frontier.* New Haven: Yale University Press, 1988.

Hutchinson, C. Alan. "The Mexican Government and the Mission Indians of Upper California, 1821–1835." *The Americas* 21(1965):335–62.

Jackson, Robert H. "The 1781–1782 Smallpox Epidemic in the Baja California Missions." *Journal of California and Great Basin Anthropology* 3(1981):138–43.

———. "Epidemic Disease and Population Decline in the Baja California Missions, 1697–1834." *Southern California Quarterly* 63(1981): 308–46.

———. "Gentile Recruitment and Population Movements in the San Francisco Bay Area Missions." *Journal of California and Great Basin Anthropology* 6(1984):225–39.

———. "Demographic Change in Northwestern New Spain." *The Americas* 41(1985):462–79.

———. "Patterns of Demographic Change in the Missions of Southern Baja California." *Journal of California and Great Basin Anthropology* 8(1986):273–79.

———. "Patterns of Demographic Change in the Missions of Central Alta California." *Journal of California and Great Basin Anthropology* 9(1987):251–72.

———. "The Post-Secularization Dispersion of the Population of the Alta California Missions, 1834—1846." Paper presented at the Rocky Mountain Council of Latin American Studies, Flagstaff, Ariz., February 1991.

———. "La colonización de la Alta California: Un análisis del desarrollo de dos comunidades misionales." *Historia Mexicana* 41(1991):83–110.

———. "Population and the Economic Dimension of Colonization in Alta California: Four Mission Communities." *Journal of the Southwest* 33(1991):387–439.

———. "La dinámica del desastre demográfico de la población india en las misiones de la bahia de San Francisco, Alta California, 1776–1840." *Historia Mexicana* 40(1991):187–215.

Jackson, Robert H., Edna Kimbro, and MaryEllen Ryan. "Como La Sombra Huye la Hora: Restoration Research, Santa Cruz Mission Adobe, Santa Cruz Mission State Historic Park." Unpublished manuscript. Sacramento: California Department of Parks and Recreation, 1985.

Johnson, John. "The Chumash and the Missions." In Thomas, *Columbian Consequences*, pp. 365–75.

Kehoe, Alice. *The Ghost Dance Ethnohistory and Revitalization.* New York, 1989.

Kelsey, Harry. "The Mission Buildings of San Juan Capistrano: A Tentative Chronology." *Southern California Quarterly* 69(1987):1–32.

———. *Juan Rodríguez Cabrillo.* San Marino: Huntington Library, 1986.

Kessell, John. *Friars, Soldiers, and Reformers: Hispanic Arizona and the Sonora Mission Frontier, 1767–1856.* Tucson: University of Arizona Press, 1976.

Kroeber, Alfred. *Handbook of the Indians of California.* Reprint ed. New York: Dover, 1976.

Kubler, George. *The Religious Architecture of New Mexico in the Colonial Period and Since the American Occupation.* 5th ed. Albuquerque, 1990.

La Perouse, Jean François de. *Monterey in 1786: The Journals of Jean François de la Perouse.* Berkeley: Heydey Books, 1989.

Langer, Erick, and Robert H. Jackson. "Colonial and Republican Missions Compared: The Cases of Alta California and Southeastern Bolivia." *Comparative Studies in Society and History* 30(1988):286–311.

Levy, Richard. "Costanoan," in Heizer, *Handbook of North American Indians,* pp 485–95.

Lothrop, Gloria Ricci. "El Viejo: Serra in Context." *The Californians* 7(1989):16–27.

MacCormack, Sabine. *Religion in the Andes: Vision and Imagination in Early Colonial Peru.* Princeton: Princeton University Press, 1991.

Mahr, August. *The Visit of the "Rurick" to San Francisco in 1816.* Stanford, 1932.

Meigs, Peveril. *The Dominican Mission Frontier of Lower California.* Berkeley: University of California Press, 1935.

Mooney, James. *The Ghost Dance Religion and Wounded Knee.* Reprint ed. New York: Dover, 1973.

Moorhead, Max. *The Presidio Bastion of the Borderlands.* Norman: University of Oklahoma Press, 1975.

Newcomb, Rexford. *The Old Mission Churches and Historic Houses of California.* Philadelphia, 1925.

————. *Spanish-Colonial Architecture in the United States.* New York, 1937.

————. *Franciscan Mission Architecture of California.* Reprint ed. New York, 1988.

Ouweneel, Arij, and Catrien Bijeveld. "The Economic Cycle in Bourbon Central Mexico: A Critique of the *Recaudación del diezmo líquido en pesos.*" *Hispanic American Historical Review* 69(1989):479–530.

Payne, Stanley. *A History of Spain and Portugal.* 2 vols. Madison: University of Wisconsin Press, 1973.

Phelan, John. *The Millenial Kingdom of the Franciscans in the New World.* 2d rev. ed. Berkeley and Los Angeles: University of California Press, 1970.

Phillips, George. "Indians and the Breakdown of the Spanish Mission System in California." *Ethnohistory* 21(1974):291–302.

————. "Indians in Los Angeles, 1781–1875: Economic Integration, Social Disintegration." *Pacific Historical Review* 49(1980):427–51.

————. "The Alcaldes: Indian Leadership in the Spanish Missions of California." *The Struggle for Political Autonomy: Papers and Comments from the Second Newberry Library Conference on Themes in American History.* Chicago: Occasional Papers in Curriculum Series, no. 11(1989):83–87.

————. *Indians and Intruders in Central California, 1769–1849.* Norman: University of Oklahoma Press, 1993.

Reff, Daniel. *Disease, Depopulation, and Culture Change in Northwestern New Spain, 1518–1764.* Salt Lake City: University of Utah Press, 1991.

Ricard, Robert. *The Spiritual Conquest of Mexico: An Essay on the Apostolate and the Evangelizing Methods of the Mendicant Orders in New Spain, 1523–1572.* Trans. and ed. by Lesley Byrd Simpson. Berkeley and Los Angeles: University of California Press, 1966.

Rodriguez, Mario. *The Cadiz Experiment in Central America, 1808–1826.* Berkeley and Los Angeles: University of California Press, 1978.

Sandos, James. "Levantamiento! The Chumash Uprising Reconsidered." *Southern California Quarterly* 67(1985):109–33.

Servin, Manuel. "The Secularization of the California Missions: A Reappraisal." *Southern California Quarterly* 47(1965):133–49.

Shipek, Florence. "California Indian Reactions to the Franciscans." *The Americas* 41(April 1985):53–66.

Smith, Frances Rand. *The Architectural History of Mission San Carlos Borromeo.* Berkeley, 1921.

Spalding, Karen. *Huarochiri: An Andean Society under Inca and Spanish Rule.* Stanford: Stanford University Press, 1984.

Stern, Steve. *Peru's Indian Peoples and the Challenge of Spanish Conquest: Huamanga to 1640.* Madison: University of Wisconsin Press, 1982.

Stodder, Ann, *Mechanisms and Trends in the Decline of the Costanoan Indian Population of Central California.* Salinas: Coyote Press, 1986.

Taylor, William. *Drinking, Homicide, and Rebellion in Colonial Mexican Villages.* Stanford: Stanford University Press, 1979.

Thomas, David H., ed. *Columbian Consequences: Historical and Archaeological Perspectives on the Spanish Borderlands West.* Washington, D.C.: Smithsonian Institution Press, 1989.

————. *Columbian Consequences: The Spanish Borderlands in Pan-American Perspective.* Washington, D.C., 1991.

Tibesar, Antonine, OFM, trans. and ed. *Writings of Junipero Serra.* 4 vols. Washington, D.C.: Academy of American Franciscan History, 1955.

Toulouse, Joseph. *The Mission of San Gregorio de Abo: A Report of the Excavation and Repair of a Seventeenth-Century New Mexico Mission.* Albuquerque, 1949.

Van der Grift Sanchez, Nellie, ed. "Recollections of My Youth at San Luis Rey Mission: The Memoirs of a full-blooded Indian, of affairs and events witnessed at one of California's most famous 'cathedrals of the sun.'" *Touring Topics* 22(1878):42–43.

Wagner, Henry. *Spanish Voyages to the Northwest Coast of America in the Sixteenth Century.* San Francisco: California Historical Society, 1929.

Wallace, Edith. "Sexual Status and Role Difference." In Heizer, *Handbook of North American Indians*, pp. 683–89.

Weber, David. *The Mexican Frontier 1821–1846: The American Southwest under Mexico.* Albuquerque: University of New Mexico Press, 1982.

Wrigley, E.A., and Robert Schofield. *The Population History of England, 1541–1871: A Reconstruction.* Cambridge: Harvard University Press, 1981.

Index

Abortion, 44, 82–83
Acculturation, measuring intensity of, 33
Acculturation, patterns of, 33
Acculturation program of Franciscan missions, 7, 8, 9, 108; deemphasized, 15,17; described, 19; as focus of study, 4; impact of, 36, 107; intensity of, 33, objectives of, 31, 51–53; origins of, 6; and social control, 92
Agricultural cycle, 20
Agricultural goods, price movements of, 16
Agriculture: decline of mission, 20–21; European-style, 36; on missions, 13–14; self-sufficiency in, 27
Alta California as frontier region, 6
Alvarado, Governor Juan Bautista (1836–42), 93, 100
Andean region, 34
Anticlericalism, 87
Anti-idolatry trials, 34
Apostolic College of San Fernando, 3–4
Apostolic College of Santa Cruz de Querétaro, 76
La Asunción, 103
Attacks by Indians. See Indian attacks, Indian raids

Bancroft, H.H., 4, 114
"Black Legend," 108
Borah, Woodrow, 5
de Borica, Diego report of 1797, 44–51, 109,
Bouchard, Hypolite, 29, 77
Bourbon Reforms, 26
Branciforte, pueblo de, 103, 110; rental of Indian labor to, 29; supplies from missions, 28; Villa de, 12, 110–11
de Bucareli, Viceroy Antonio, 27

Cadiz Cortes questionnaire on Indians, 31–32, 35, 38
Cahuilla, 8
Catholic church: 19th century reforms to, 8–9; role of, 8–9; conversion to, 33–34
Catholic ritual attractive to Indians, 52
Central Mexico: agreement to supply missions, 11; anticlericalism, 87; anti-idolatry trials, 34; Bourbon Reforms, 15; and California frontier, 110; civil war, 51; civil war of 1810, 26, 28; colonial order of, 6; colonization laws of 1822 and 1824, 100; conversion of Indians, 33–34; goods from, 16, 28, 35; indig-

About the Book and the Authors

Indians, Franciscans, and Spanish Colonization
The Impact of the Mission System on California Indians
ROBERT H. JACKSON AND EDWARD CASTILLO

This ethnohistory examines Indian life in the twenty-one missions Franciscans established in Alta California. In describing how the missions functioned between 1769 and 1848, the authors draw on previously unused sources to analyze change and continuity in Indian material culture and religious practices. The twin goals of Franciscans were to mold Indians into a work force that would produce surplus grain for military garrisons and to regulate their moral conduct and religious practices.

The authors use production records to show the missions were quite effective in serving the economic goals of Spanish colonialism on the Alta California frontier. Even after Mexican independence when the Church's role diminished, Indian labor continued as a mainstay of much local, seasonal work.

The special concern of this study is to assess efforts to transform the culture and world view of Indians. Acculturation to mission life by California's native peoples is carefully assessed to delineate how they coped, their history of disease and death, and their efforts at resistance and cultural survival, especially following decrees issued in 1833 that secularized missions.

"A publication of major significance."—George H. Phillips, author of *Indians and Intruders in Central California*

Robert J. Jackson and Edward Castillo are borderlands scholars teaching, respectively, at Texas Southern University and Sonoma State University.